T0317708

Coins, Trade, and the State

Economic Growth
in Early Medieval Japan

Harvard East Asian Monographs 334

Coins, Trade, and the State

Economic Growth
in Early Medieval Japan

Ethan Isaac Segal

Published by the Harvard University Asia Center
and distributed by Harvard University Press
Cambridge (Massachusetts) and London, 2011

Printed in the United States of America

The Harvard University Asia Center publishes a monograph series and, in coordina-
tion with the Fairbank Center for Chinese Studies, the Korea Institute, the Reischauer
Institute of Japanese Studies, and other faculties and institutes, administers research
projects designed to further scholarly understanding of China, Japan, Vietnam, Korea,
and other Asian countries. The Center also sponsors projects addressing multidisci-
plinary and regional issues in Asia.

Library of Congress Cataloging-in-Publication Data

Segal, Ethan Isaac.
    Coins, trade, and the state : economic growth in early medieval Japan / Ethan
Isaac Segal.
        p. cm.
    Includes bibliographical references and index.
    ISBN 978-0-674-06068-5 (hardcover : alk. paper)
        1. Japan--Commerce--History--To 1500. 2. Japan--Commerce--History--16th century.
3. Japan--Economic conditions--To 1868. 4. Coinage--Japan--History. 5. Money--Japan--
History. I. Title.
    HF3825.S45 2011
    330.952'02--dc22

                                                                            2011005774

Index by the author, with the assistance of William Londo

♾ Printed on acid-free paper

Last figure below indicates year of this printing

21 20 19 18 17 16 15 14 13 12 11

In memory of my father, Eliezer,
with gratitude to my mother, Joyce,
and with special thanks to Miho and Naomi

Acknowledgments

Writing a book is a long journey and many people helped along the way. My interest in Japan brought me to the University of Washington in the 1990s, where Kozo Yamamura and Susan Hanley encouraged me to study premodern economic history. I then moved to Stanford University, where I was fortunate to train with Jeffrey Mass before his untimely passing in 2001. Jeff was an outstanding scholar, teacher, mentor, and friend, whose dedication to his research was matched only by his concern for his graduate students. Peter Duus, Philippe Buc, and Robert Borgen demanded just as much of me as Jeff would have, and I am grateful for their time and support. Peter and Philippe provided thoughtful comments and asked difficult questions that forced me to rethink my work. Bob graciously joined my committee after Jeff's passing and has been an extremely supportive mentor and friend ever since. Others at Stanford who provided valuable assistance over the years include Naomi Kotake, Richard Roberts, Matt Sommer, Carolyn Lougee, Paula Findlen, Gordon Chang, Zephyr Frank, and Avner Greif.

My thanks also to Joan Piggott, who organized summer intensive *kanbun* workshops that made it possible for graduate students like myself to learn the language of medieval documents. It was during those summers that I first became acquainted with the amazing scholars of the University of Tokyo Historiographical Institute, where I conducted much of the research for this book. I am indebted to faculty Ishigami Ei-ichi, Kondō Shigekazu, Kurushima Noriko, Murai Shōsuke, Inoue Satoshi, Hongō Kazuto, and Kikuchi Hiroki, as well as (then) graduate students Hashimoto Yu, Masuyama Hideki, and Mieda Akiko. I am particularly indebted to Mr. Kondō, my advisor, and Mr. Inoue, who aided me in interpreting medieval documents. In addition, I gained tremendously from my frequent visits to the National Museum of Japanese History in Chiba. My thanks to Kurushima Hiroshi for many long, insightful conversations about Japanese history, and Takahashi Kazuki for help in obtaining image permissions. The National Museum of Japanese History, the Bank of Japan Currency Museum, Shōjōkō Temple, and the Kitamori City Board of Education generously provided the images. Bruce Batten graciously offered his map of medieval Japan, and Jackie Hawthorne customized it for inclusion in this book. William Londo assisted with the index.

The History Department at Michigan State University has been an outstanding place to teach and work. Stimulating conversations with colleagues and students have helped make this book better than it would have been otherwise. I thank all of the members of the department for their support, especially Linda Cooke Johnson, Aminda Smith, Charles Keith, Lisa Fine, Kirsten Fermaglich, Susan Sleeper-Smith, Walter Hawthorne, and Liam Brockey. I was also fortunate to be invited to serve as a visiting assistant professor at Harvard University for the 2008–2009 academic year. Andrew Gordon, Shigehisa Kuriyama, Ryūichi Abé, Sun Joo Kim, Wes Jacobsen, Edwin Cranston, Kuniko McVey, and many others helped make it an interesting and productive year. My thanks also to Stacie Matsumoto and everyone at the Reischauer Institute of Japanese Studies for their kindness to my family and me during our time in Cambridge.

Many scholars and friends provided feedback that helped shape the direction of my work. They include Drake Langford, Vyjayanthi Selinger, Karl Friday, Bruce Batten, Wayne Farris, Michael Dylan Foster, Robert Tierney, Elizabeth Oyler, Ron

Toby, Laura Nenzi, Bettina Gramlich-Oka, Mark Ravina, Mikael Adolphson, Hans Thomsen, Judith Fröhlich, Noell Wilson, Catherine Ryu, John Davis Jr., William Londo, Stephen Miller, Greg Matza, Jen Wakefield, and Andrew Gemrich, among others. I especially thank Michael Lewis, Roderick Wilson, and Thomas Conlan for reading and critiquing earlier versions of the manuscript. In addition, Bina Arch, Elizabeth Dutridge-Corp, Chelsea Gagnon, Sejong Hong, Mitcheka Jalali, Martin Kroher, Di Yin Lu, Grace Ruch, Kendra Slayton, John Somerville, and Tim Weber were students in my graduate seminars at Harvard and Michigan State who read sections of the manuscript. Their questions and comments were extremely helpful as I revised for final submission.

William Hammell has been a constant source of support as my editor. I am grateful for his calm encouragement, patience, and attention to detail as he guided my book through the publication process. Two anonymous readers and one copy editor for the Harvard University Asia Center read the manuscript very thoroughly and made valuable suggestions for improvement. After having worked on this project for so long, it was a pleasure to receive such expert questions (even the ones that I could not answer). I tried to follow their advice when possible, and hope that they will agree that the final product is better for it. Any errors remain the sole responsibility of the author.

Many institutions and organizations funded aspects of this project. With gratitude I acknowledge the generous support of the Fulbright Foundation, the Japan-U.S. Educational Commission, the Stanford Humanities Center and the Geballe family, the Mellon Foundation, the Japan Fund of the Institute for International Studies at Stanford University, and the Michigan State University Department of History. The MSU History Department Sesquicentennial Fund helped defray the costs of summer research trips to East Asia, and an IRGP award from the MSU Office of the Vice President for Research provided one semester of leave time to work on my manuscript. My thanks to the staff and selection committees of these organizations.

Parts of the research contained in this book have been presented at meetings of the Association for Asian Studies, the Midwest Japan Seminar, the Reischauer Institute of Japanese Studies at Harvard University, the University of Michigan, Cornell University, Columbia University, the University of Tokyo, Tübingen University, Bowdoin College, and the University of Western Ontario. I am indebted to the many participants in those meetings who provided feedback, suggestions, and criticisms, and apologize that I could not always follow their recommendations. Some of the material in this volume was published as "Awash in Coins: The Spread of Money in Early Medieval Japan," in *Currents in Medieval Japanese History: Essays in Honor of Jeffrey P. Mass*, ed. Gordon M. Berger, Andrew Edmund Goble, Lorraine F. Harrington, and G. Cameron Hurst III, 331–61 (Los Angeles, CA: Figueroa Press, 2009). Other material appears in the chapter "Money and the State: Medieval Precursors of the Early Modern Economy," in *Economic Thought in Early Modern Japan*, ed. Bettina Gramlich-Oka and Gregory Smits, 21–46 (Leiden: Brill, 2010). My thanks to the editors and presses for allowing me to include the material in this book.

Last but not least, there are not words enough to express my gratitude to my family. My parents taught me to be intellectually curious as well as how to read and write at an early age—little did they know where that would lead. I have always appreciated their pride in my achievements. My wife Miho has been a source of strength, comfort, and encouragement throughout our years together in California, Tokyo, Michigan, and Massachusetts. Having finished this project, my only regret is that the slowness of my work kept me away from her and our daughter Naomi for so long. My thanks to them for their patience and understanding. Now, Naomi, we can play!

Ethan Isaac Segal
Okemos, Michigan
November 2010

Contents

List of Figures

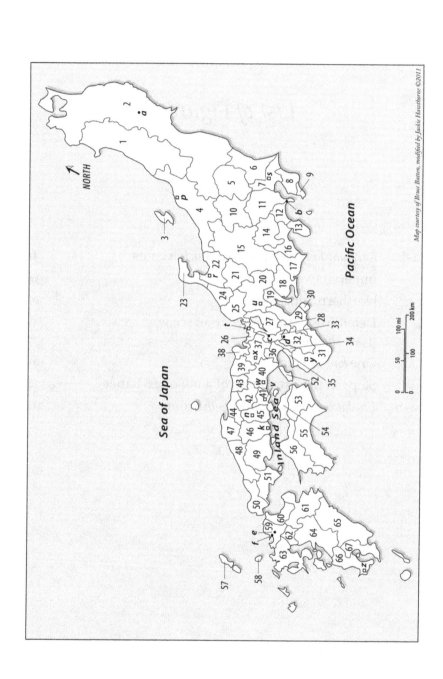

NORTH

Sea of Japan

Pacific Ocean

Inland Sea

100 km

0   50   100

0   100   200 km

Map courtesy of Bruce Batten, modified by Jackie Haczebourne ©2011

Provinces of medieval Japan (by numerical marker)

1 Dewa	10 Kōzuke	19 Owari	28 Iga	37 Tanba	46 Bingo
2 Mutsu	11 Musashi	20 Mino	29 Ise	38 Tango	47 Izumo
3 Sado	12 Sagami	21 Hida	30 Shima	39 Tajima	48 Iwami
4 Echigo	13 Izu	22 Etchū	31 Kii	40 Harima	49 Aki
5 Shimotsuke	14 Kai	23 Noto	32 Yamato*	41 Bizen	50 Nagato
6 Hitachi	15 Shinano	24 Kaga	33 Yamashiro*	42 Mimasaka	51 Suo
7 Shimōsa	16 Suruga	25 Echizen	34 Kawachi*	43 Inaba	52 Awaji
8 Kazusa	17 Tōtōmi	26 Wakasa	35 Izumi*	44 Hōki	53 Awa
9 Awa (Kantō)	18 Mikawa	27 Ōmi	36 Settsu*	45 Bitchū	(Shikoku)

54 Sanuki	63 Hizen
55 Tosa	64 Higo
56 Iyo	65 Hyūga
57 Tsushima	66 Satsuma
58 Iki	67 Ōsumi
59 Chikuzen	
60 Buzen	* denotes Kinai
61 Bungo	provinces
62 Chikugo	

Provinces of medieval Japan (in alphabetical order)

Aki 49	Buzen 60	Higo 64	Iwami 48
Awa (Kantō) 9	Chikugo 62	Hitachi 6	Iyo 56
Awa (Shikoku) 53	Chikuzen 59	Hizen 63	Izu 13
Awaji 52	Dewa 1	Hōki 44	Izumi 35
Bingo 46	Echigo 4	Hyūga 65	Izumo 47
Bitchū 45	Echizen 25	Iga 28	Kaga 24
Bizen 41	Etchū 22	Iki 58	Kai 14
Bungo 61	Harima 40	Inaba 43	Kawachi 34
	Hida 21	Ise 29	Kazusa 8

Kii 31	Ōmi 27	Shimōsa 7
Kōzuke 10	Ōsumi 67	Shimotsuke 5
Mikawa 18	Owari 19	Shinano 15
Mimasaka 42	Sado 3	Suo 51
Mino 20	Sagami 12	Suruga 16
Musashi 11	Sanuki 54	Tajima 39
Mutsu 2	Satsuma 66	Tanba 37
Nagato 50	Settsu 36	Tango 38
Noto 23	Shima 30	Tosa 55

Tōtōmi 17
Tsushima 57
Wakasa 26
Yamashiro 33
Yamato 32

Cities

a Hiraizumi
b Kamakura
c Kyoto (Heian)
d Nara (Heijō)
e Dazaifu
f Hakata

Some estates and markets mentioned in the text (followed by province)

k Kusado sengen market (Bingo)
n Niimi estate (Bitchū)
p Okuyama estate (Echigo)
r Ishiguro estate (Etchū)
s Sōma mikuriya (Shimōsa)
t Tara estate (Wakasa)

u Akanabe estate (Mino)
v Fukuoka market (Bizen)
w Yano estate (Harima)
x Ōyama estate (Tanba)
y Ategawa estate (Kii)
z Shimazu estate (Satsuma)

Coins, Trade, and the State

Economic Growth
in Early Medieval Japan

INTRODUCTION

Medieval Money

In the spring of 1334, less than a year after his dramatic reentry into the capital following escape from exile, Emperor Go-Daigo (1288–1339) proclaimed that his administration would begin minting copper coins and printing paper bills. This might seem an unusual priority for the new government, which arguably had other, more pressing concerns to occupy its attention, such as restoring calm and order after the violence that led to its creation. Just months earlier, as Go-Daigo languished in exile on a remote island, loyal supporters had fought on his behalf against Japan's warrior government, the Kamakura *bakufu*. Their victory enabled the emperor's return to power, an event known as the Kenmu Restoration. Conditions across the country, however, remained unsettled as the government attempted to assert its authority over warriors. Given that the Japanese imperial court had not produced its own official currency in almost four hundred years, minting coins might not appear to have been an urgent need. Nonetheless, Go-Daigo made it a priority, ordering the creation of a mint and appointing its officials. Regrettably for the emperor, his short-lived regime (1333–36) ended before the mint actually produced any money.[1]

---

1. Go-Daigo's decree, dated Kenmu 1 (1334) 3rd month 28th day, can be found in *Chūsei seiji shakai shisō*, vol. 2, 75–76. It is presumed that his mint

Go-Daigo's decision may seem even more puzzling given the abundance of money already in circulation. Medieval Japanese did not lack for copper currency. From the twelfth to the sixteenth centuries, imported Chinese coins became an increasingly important medium of exchange in Japan. Merchants plied the seas to bring money to the islands from the Asian mainland, risking the wrath of angry storms and hostile government officials. Foreign visitors commented with surprise on the widespread Japanese use of coins. Korean Sin Suk-chu, a scholar and official of the Yi dynasty who traveled to Japan in the early 1440s, wrote in his memoirs that the Japanese used copper cash to purchase everything from a cup of tea to the services of prostitutes. Francesco Carletti, a native of Florence who visited Japan in the late sixteenth century, also made mention of the Japanese use of metal currency. He described Japanese money as "minted out of copper into coins about the size of a penny with a hole in the middle. These they call cash and for convenience of handling they carry them threaded on a string."[2] With so much currency already available in Japan, why was minting coins of such concern to Emperor Go-Daigo when his administration was not yet stable? How did the gradual monetization of the Japanese economy affect its social and political institutions? And, in the broadest sense, what did money *mean* to the people of medieval Japan?

Coins, Trade, and the State attempts to answer these and other questions through an analysis of money, trade, and the economy in pre-1600 Japan. Although the book focuses in particular on the spread and use of copper cash during the first half of Japan's medieval period, it also addresses the use of

---

never produced any *Kenkon tsūhō* coins since no examples have ever been found.

2. Sin Suk-chu wrote in 1471 of his travels to Japan and the Ryukyus; Tanaka Takeo's modern Japanese translation is available as *Kaitō shokokuki*. Francesco Carletti traveled to Japan in the 1590s; excerpts of his account can be found in Cooper, *They Came to Japan*, 236–37.

precious metals and paper bills at various times in premodern Japan. The people of the Japanese islands had been using money in one form or another since at least the seventh century, if not earlier. Depending upon conditions, they employed many different kinds of goods as means of payment, including some types of commodity money that modern readers might not readily identify as currency at all. Provincial estates, for example, often paid part of their taxes in agricultural products ranging from grains, such as rice or barley, to foodstuffs like fish or nuts. In other cases, estates met their obligations by providing lacquer, iron ore, paper, and/or human labor. Around the country, domestically produced materials—including gold, silver, rice, silk, and cloth—served as money at different points in Japanese history, usually with the approval or endorsement of top state authorities. The twelfth through fourteenth centuries are particularly interesting, however, for three reasons: first, the country began a shift from using various forms of commodity money to metal currency; second, the initial shift took place in defiance of government control; and third, the sweeping changes of this period allowed provincial figures greater economic agency than they experienced in earlier times.

Distinct from the earlier Nara (710–84) and Heian (794–1185) periods, political authority was diffuse during Japan's medieval age (1185–1600). This limited the ability of any one central authority to regulate the economy or back a domestic currency. Yet the lack of a unified central government did not inhibit economic growth. Instead, it created opportunities for a wider spectrum of society to participate in trade, markets, and monetization. Some of the most active were elite institutions of long pedigree, including major temples and shrines. The most progressive among them became leaders in the shift to a more monetized economy. But others were provincial figures such as merchants, warriors, and rural estate managers. Individuals from both elite and non-elite groups traded in local and regional markets, developed effective systems of long-distance money remittance, and actively imported Chinese currency. Together they devised new ways to circumvent older forms of exchange that were managed by central government.

The Use of Money in Premodern Japan

For much of Japan's history, money and economic development were closely tied to the state. Under the Japanese *ritsu-ryō* state of the late seventh, eighth, and ninth centuries, the imperial court claimed the paramount role in matters that modern people would label "economic." The court asserted ownership of all land, distributing it to individual households on the basis of census figures and lending out seed rice and other agricultural aids. In return, the government demanded taxes in the form of tribute (*chō*) from the people. It stipulated the types of goods to be paid, from rice and fish to silk and metal ore. In addition, the court minted its own currency, using coins to pay the salaries of imperial officials and accepting the same money in payment from those who sought promotion. Among their duties, officials supervised transactions in land, stipulating that individuals could not alienate rights to land (*shiki*) without the approval of local government representatives.[3] Finally, the court established official markets in the capital. These markets were the primary means for redistributing the wealth that was collected as taxes from the countryside. Through these and other means, central elites dominated the economy and were the key players in all types of economic exchange during the Nara and early Heian periods.[4] Money, in the form of coins, rice, or other goods, primarily served as a means of fulfilling obligations to the state.

––––

3. During the Nara period, the sale of public paddy land (*kōden*) was forbidden, but newly reclaimed land and residential land could be legally sold. An agreement of sale had to meet with the approval of government officials at several levels. If approved at every stage, the original document would receive seals certifying the legitimacy of the transaction.

4. References to other, non-governmental forms of exchange are quite limited. See Farris, "Trade, Money, and Merchants," 309–12.

This situation underwent two dramatic changes in the late Heian and early medieval periods. First, in the tenth and eleventh centuries, the court began to back away from its active involvement in the economic affairs of the countryside. Instead, it delegated much of its authority to provincial officials, especially the governors (*zuryō*).[5] In exchange for delivering taxes to the central government and maintaining the peace, these governors were given a free hand to administer their provinces as they saw fit.[6] Attempts at land redistribution based on census figures had long since been abandoned and individuals no longer sought government approval when selling property. Most significantly, increasing tracts of arable land left the public tax rolls and were incorporated into new private estates known as *shōen*. Yet even the *shōen* still paid part of their agricultural output to proprietors (*ryōke*) and patrons (*honke*): members of the imperial family, the Fujiwara, or the major religious institutions. They could insist that the estates pay specific combinations of goods, leaving those in the provinces with little economic autonomy.

The second major change dates to the late twelfth century, when Minamoto no Yoritomo (1147–99), whose forces won the Genpei civil war (1180–85), established an independent warrior administration known as the Kamakura *bakufu* (1185–1333). Yoritomo and his successors created some new institutions and some that paralleled existing offices, but they did not destroy the older imperial government in Kyoto. The result was a diarchy, with Kamakura handling its vassals' affairs and the imperial court in Kyoto managing other matters. It was an uneasy coexistence. One particularly contentious issue was the *bakufu*'s right to place its own appointees as estate land stewards (*jitō*) and military governors (*shugo*) around the coun-

---

5. Kiley, "Provincial Administration and Land Tenure," 271, 283. On the *zuryō* and their relationship to central government, see Hurst, "*Kugyō* and *Zuryō*," 83–94.

6. *Zuryō* reportedly abused this power with some frequency; see von Verschauer, "Life of Commoners in the Provinces," 305, 322–25.

try. Although nominally sent to maintain order, many *jitō* and *shugo* encroached on the authority of the *zuryō* and estate proprietors. Perhaps the most heated conflicts occurred in the economic realm, as these Kamakura appointees interfered with the collection of taxes, claimed larger portions of private estate produce than those to which they were entitled, and disrupted the flow of tribute from the provinces to centrally-based nobles and temples.

With so many alterations to the political structure, it is not surprising that there was also a change in the nature of money. During Japan's early medieval period, a wide range of people came to use imported copper cash that had little connection to domestic state authorities. In fact, this money first entered Japan in spite of government opposition rather than with its support. It was used by traveling merchants to facilitate exchange with the countryside and by shoppers to purchase items in the marketplace. Religious figures collected alms in coin and accepted cash from individuals who wished to have prayers chanted for their salvation. Warriors appointed to estates taxed agricultural communities to cover the costs of travel to the capital and used coins to pay the periodic levies demanded of them by the shogun. Peasants sold agricultural surplus for cash and, in some instances, pushed estate proprietors to accept payments in coin, allowing them more flexibility to grow the combination of goods they found most profitable.

Of course, change did not come exclusively from the provinces. Elite authorities came to favor cash as well. *Shōen* proprietors found that receiving tribute in cash rather than in kind could be advantageous. The Kamakura *bakufu* promoted the use of coins rather than cloth in the early thirteenth century, and Japan's second warrior government, the Muromachi *bakufu* (1336–1573), relied on commercial taxes levied in coin to help cover its operating expenses. In addition, the Ashikaga shogun and some of the leading temples and warlords engaged in diplomacy with the Ming (1368–1644) in part to secure a steady supply of Chinese copper coins. The Muromachi *bakufu* was probably the largest importer of cash in the late medieval period. But by the early fifteenth century, economic conditions had changed. Central elite institutions were still powerful, but they were unable to dominate medieval trade and dictate terms to those in the provinces as they had in the Nara and Heian periods. Instead, center and periphery worked together to create a more market-centered economy during Japan's medieval age. Particularly from the late thirteenth century onward, their use of money and involvement in expanding trade led to broad social changes and the beginnings of economic growth.

Money and Economic Growth

Money is remarkably difficult to define. Economists often speak about money in terms of its functions, which include serving as a medium of exchange, a measure of value, and a store of wealth. As a medium of exchange, money eliminates the problem of "double wants" inherent in barter—that is, finding someone who is willing to trade the good you have for the good you want. If you want to sell eggs and acquire rice, it is much more convenient to convert your eggs into cash than to find someone selling rice who happens to need eggs. As a measure of value, money is the standard against which all other commodities can be evaluated. You can conveniently compare the relative worth of any two objects if you know their prices in a common form of money. Finally, as a store of wealth, money allows individuals to hold onto the value of goods (such as livestock or agricultural produce) that would otherwise rot or spoil. Some scholars assign money a fourth function: serving as the means of state payments. This refers to a certain good demanded by central government to satisfy tax obligations that takes on value in other transactions and thereby comes to circulate as money. From among these four functions, serving as a medium of exchange seems to be particularly critical, yet there is no scholarly consensus as to which function came first. Different scholars posit that the origins of money lie in one or more of these uses, or even in religious rituals.[7]

Only certain types of goods can serve as money. If we consider modern currencies, we can easily identify special characteristics that items should ideally possess in order to earn acceptance as money. For example, American pennies are sufficiently similar to each other in size, shape, and metal content that they are used interchangeably—in other words, they are fungible. If this were not the case, business transactions would be slowed as people inspected pennies to determine their quality. In addition, legal and technological constraints prevent just anyone from easily producing pennies. If they were readily manufactured by individuals outside of the government (or if money grew on trees), then the market would be flooded and pennies would lose their value. Finally, pennies are durable, frequently lasting for decades without significant wear. Unlike modern societies with their pennies, however, premodern societies did not have the same ability to easily find or produce goods that possessed these basic characteristics of fungibility, limited availability, and durability.

As a result, many premodern economies used forms of commodity money as their currencies. Commodity monies are goods that come to be used as a store of value or medium of exchange because they have recognized value of their own. Common examples include shells, livestock, and silk; more seemingly exotic examples that have been used by certain societies include brass rods, feathers, and peppercorns. Nature limits the supply of the commodity circulating as money. These differ from modern fiat currencies, which consist of materials that have little or no intrinsic value but are assigned value by the minting authority (usually the government). The most common type of fiat currency is the paper bill, which is worth virtually nothing aside from the value printed on it.

---

7. Pryor, "The Origins of Money," 292–93; Kiyotaki and Wright, "On Money as a Medium of Exchange," 927–54; Vilar, *A History of Gold and Money*, 19–22.

Governments determine the supply of fiat money available.[8] Because fiat money is associated with strong, modern state governments, the existence of commodity money is often regarded as an indication of a premodern or less developed economy. As these brief descriptions suggest, analyzing the use and form of money in a particular society can reveal a great deal about the development of the state and economy.

Rice and silk, widely used in Japan from the tenth to the thirteenth centuries, are obvious examples of commodity money. Their value originated in their use as food and clothing, and their production was determined by growing conditions and the environment. Copper coins, which came to replace rice and silk as a medium of exchange, are more difficult to classify. They were produced by the state, but their availability was limited by the supply of copper ore, particularly in the Heian period. The copper contained within the coins had a commodity value of its own which, in a few instances, led Japanese to melt coins for their metal content, proving that the coins could be worth less than the metal from which they were made.[9] But unlike the commodities rice and silk, copper never circulated in an unminted form. The molding and stamp of the Chinese state appears to have been important for coins' acceptance in Japan. Thus, classification can be a tricky business; medieval Japanese coinage seems to have been a form of commodity money that in some ways resembled a fiat currency.

Money was, if not a powerful agent of, then certainly a catalyst for significant social change. In societies such as mid-Heian Japan, where money was used only infrequently, high nobles, major temples, and other proprietors relied on political and religious power to secure wealth from the provinces. Their underdeveloped economy had few local markets and lit-

---

8. Kiyotaki and Wright, "On Money as a Medium of Exchange," 929; Redish, "Anchors Aweigh," 778.

9. For example, coins were melted to make a bell for a Buddhist temple during a copper shortage in the 1230s. See the entries in the *Azuma kagami* (hereafter *AK*), Katei 1 (1235) 6th month 19th day and same month 29th day.

tle agricultural surplus to sell or trade, so whether public lands or private estates, government officials and elite landowners could monopolize agricultural production and demand certain mixes of goods as tax payments. Monetization and the spread of markets throughout the countryside, however, opened up new possibilities to both elite landowners and provincial communities alike. Markets offered new venues for transactions outside of the system of government-controlled payments and allowed agricultural estates the freedom to grow the mix of goods that realized the largest return. At the same time, merchants and estate managers found copper coins easier to handle than other goods used as money. An increasing number of elite landowners also embraced these changes as they found it convenient to receive payments in cash or, in some cases, to lend money at interest. Money and markets helped reduce transaction costs, and partly as a result of these developments, the medieval Japanese economy grew.[10]

In order to fully appreciate the ways in which monetization contributed to prosperity, we must place it in the broader context of social and economic trends. As is well known, improvements in agricultural technology during Japan's medieval period led to surplus production in the countryside. Central elites, who were absentee landlords, had limited success in capturing that increased output. Around the same time, the spread of markets and growing use of imported Chinese currency led to changing consumption habits and the availability of a wider range of goods. Elites had varied reactions to these

---

10. "Economic growth" is generally measured by an increase in gross domestic product, growth in labor productivity, or growth in total factor productivity. Other potential sources of growth include technological advances and the implementation of economies of scale. It is very difficult to apply the term "economic growth" to a premodern society such as medieval Japan, for the sources do not allow the modern scholar to calculate gross domestic product or other numbers that one might expect in an economist's analysis of growth. Nonetheless, it is reasonable to conclude that the factors cited above contributed to a growing economy, and considerable circumstantial evidence supports such conclusions.

developments. Some appreciated being able to acquire more than what was produced by their estates and actively sought ways to increase their cash income. Others, particularly members of the imperial government, resisted the use of foreign coins because they viewed Chinese cash as an affront to their political authority. For those based in the provinces, however, surplus production that could be sold for money in local markets held the potential for greater independence from the demands of their proprietors. Many peasant communities prospered as a result of their involvement in the expanding market economy. By the fourteenth and fifteenth centuries, those living in such communities utilized their newfound economic power to secure greater freedoms for themselves and force changes in traditional structures of elite land management, taxation, and rule.

Reconsidering Medieval Money

Despite the prominent role that coins played in medieval Japan's economy, few Western historians have analyzed monetization and its impact on social and political structures. Instead, money and commercialization are terms more frequently associated with Japan's early modern Edo period (1600–1868). At least one early-twentieth-century historian failed to even acknowledge the presence of money in pre-1600 Japan.[11] Other scholars have emphasized the key role that commercialization played in transforming Edo society without discussing the earlier history of money in Japan. Consider Thomas Smith's description of the origins of Japan's modern economic growth:

There were scattered islands of commercial farming in Japan from very early times, but as late as 1600 peasants still typically produced to feed and clothe themselves, to pay taxes in kind, and to store whatever surplus there might be in good years against the certain

---

11. Matsuyo Takizawa attempted to correct a misperception that money only entered Japan in the nineteenth century by (incorrectly) dating its appearance to the early Edo period; see Takizawa, *Penetration of Money Economy in Japan*.

crop failures of the future. But rural life changed after the Tokugawa conquest. . . . The islands of commercial farming expanded, ran together, and began to fill in the surrounding sea of self-sufficient economy.[12]

Smith's description of the fourteenth and fifteenth centuries as a "sea of self-sufficient economy" is inaccurate, yet the notion that monetization dates to the seventeenth century persists in scholarly publications.[13] To be fair, those works primarily focus on the Edo period, and there is no doubt that merchants prospered under the Tokugawa or that the expansion of commerce led to important social changes that warrant scholarly attention. But is there not also a risk of overemphasizing the sudden nature of those changes by focusing only on the post-1600 use of money?

Even among medievalists, most research published in English has dealt with land rather than coins when addressing the economy.[14] Certainly land was a major concern in the Kamakura period, as reflected in primary sources that speak of judicial battles over land rights. But we must recognize that documents addressing large, disputable properties such as land were likely to be better maintained and therefore overrepresented. There was less need to preserve the receipts from cash transactions once they were completed. Even so, enough survive to show that on occasions the *bakufu* made payments in precious metals, and parents provided monetary legacies for

---

12. Smith, "Growth of the Market," 67.

13. More recent scholarship, though not focused primarily on money, also refers to Edo as the period of monetization. See Najita, *Visions of Virtue in Tokugawa Japan*; Yokota, "Imagining Working Women in Early Modern Japan," 167; and Sone, "Prostitution and Public Authority," 183. These publications are correct in assuming a major shift in the level and degree of monetization during the early modern period, but we should not forget that money began appearing in rural communities centuries earlier.

14. For example, both Hall and Mass, *Medieval Japan,* and Mass, *Origins of Japan's Medieval World,* contain chapters that deal with land, but neither contains a chapter on money and coinage.

their children.[15] Legal disputes over cash income were bitterly contested, and proprietors kept careful records of how much they received from their provincial estates as well as how much remained outstanding. Substituting money (*daisennō*) for rice or cloth in tax payments during the late thirteenth century went hand-in-hand with the spread of provincial markets where cash was the primary medium of exchange. Coins had penetrated rural society sufficiently by those years that, on some estates, peasants pooled their money to create special cash reserve funds.[16] Currency came to play an integral role in medieval Japanese society.

One of the few Western scholars to specifically address medieval coinage was Delmer Brown, whose monograph *Money Economy in Medieval Japan* covers much of what was known circa 1950 about the use of coins in pre-1600 Japan, particularly during the fifteenth and sixteenth centuries. His study presents a wealth of information about mining and metal production, topics that *Coins, Trade, and the State* will not address. Brown's work also differs pointedly from this book in its assumptions regarding the relationship between political stability and economic growth. According to Brown, political stability was a precondition for economic prosperity. He saw the period from the founding of the Kamakura *bakufu* in 1185 to the second Mongol invasion of 1281 as a century of great

---

15. Officials of the early *bakufu* presented gold to the imperial court and paid workers with precious metals; *AK* entries for Kenkyū 5 (1194) 3rd month 22nd day; 5th month 10th day; and Kenkyū 6 (1195) 3rd month 13th day. An example of a father leaving money rather than land to his children is Fujiwara Tametoki's 1265 bequeathment, published in the *Okayama kenshi*, vol. 19, doc. 1138, pp. 535–36.

16. For an example of a legal decision handed down concerning the rate for converting tax payments from goods to cash, see the *Kamakura ibun* (hereafter *KI*), doc. 3649, Karoku 3 (1227) 8th month 16th day. For a legal settlement concerning arrears on cash payments, see Mass, *Kamakura Bakufu*, doc. 125, pp. 147–48. English translations of documents concerning the household tax can also be found in the same volume: see docs. 176–77, pp. 185–86. Finally, for a *jitō* appropriating cash from the peasants' collective fund (*tanomoshi*), see *KI*, doc. 12184, Kenji 1 (1275) 12th month.

political unity that led to extraordinary economic activity, including dynamic foreign and domestic trade and "the development of such modern financial institutions as bills of exchange."[17] After the Mongol attacks, however, he claimed to see 250 years of civil war, uprisings, and piracy that inhibited continued growth. Brown did not observe renewed economic prosperity until the sixteenth-century daimyo efforts at unification, which produced strong central governments.

In contrast with Brown's position, I contend that medieval Japanese enjoyed economic growth during periods of political instability. Instability is commonly thought of as the bane of economic growth, for a stable state is seen as key to ensuring property rights, enforcing contracts, issuing currency, and preventing warfare.[18] But as I prove in the chapters that follow, the medieval Japanese economy grew without a state actively performing any of those functions. The political turmoil of the 1180s, when significant parts of the country were embroiled in the Genpei civil war, did not deter the spread of money and markets (Chapters 1 and 2). Appointing warriors as *jitō* and *shugo* led to confusion and conflict in *shōen* management, but it also created opportunities for people in the provinces to foster new economic relationships outside of the traditional center-mediated tribute economy (Chapters 2 and 3). Later, innovative instruments of conveyance such as bills of exchange emerged independently of central authorities. In fact, it was in part the failure of state authorities to provide safe transportation routes that led to the necessity for bills of exchange (Chapter 4). Only in the fifteenth and sixteenth centuries were *sengoku* daimyo able to craft new institutions and ideologies that enabled them to reassert firm control of economic affairs

---

17. Brown, *Money Economy in Medieval Japan*, 1. Elsewhere Brown specifically ties the demand for coins in Japan to political stability, describing "a growing demand in Japan for coins which in turn was related to the current reemergence of political unity under the military and to the general expansion of industry and commerce," 10.

18. Only recently has this notion begun to be challenged; see, for example, Haber, Armando, and Maurer, *The Politics of Property Rights*.

(Chapter 5). For most of the medieval period, however, political stability appears to have had little to do with medieval economic prosperity.

Other scholars have also commented on the curious relationship in medieval Japan between political decay and economic growth, but they have tended to see the power vacuum created by political fighting among elites as allowing non-elites to prosper. For example, Toyoda Takeshi and Sugiyama Hiroshi wrote that "as the military class became increasingly removed from actual involvement in local production, merchants and artisans were given new opportunities for commercial activity."[19] For these historians, political chaos was the explanation for economic growth: provincial non-elites prospered only because traditional political elites were so preoccupied that they could not deal with changes in the provinces. In their conception of the medieval period, economic growth was merely a by-product of political fragmentation.

Only within the last fifteen years have scholars begun to question that interpretation. Kristina Troost charges that earlier scholarship looked at how warriors gained power and controlled peasants without examining the ways in which peasant initiative led to change. Suzanne Gay proposes that wealthy commoners in the late medieval period were able to "flex their muscles" and use economic leverage to secure their own aims.[20] My findings concur with the critique presented by Troost and Gay. In this book, I attempt to show how early medieval commoners took steps to build the muscles that later medieval Japanese would flex. The new medieval economy provided opportunities for provincials to sell their surplus produce, determine the medium of tax payments, and engage in trade that did not center on the capital. Although we must

---

19. Toyoda and Sugiyama with Morris, "The Growth of Commerce and the Trades," 129. See also Hall's discussion of how the conflict between civil and military authorities kept wealth in the countryside in *Government and Local Power*, 179–83, 191–92.

20. Troost, *Common Property and Community*, 12; Gay, *Moneylenders of Late Medieval Kyoto*, 1, 6.

be careful not to overstate the case, these practices empowered provincial figures and disrupted traditional center-periphery relations. Seen in this light, economic growth was not simply the result of political instability. It also contributed to it.

Japanese researchers have led the way in analyzing the premodern economy, usually in much greater detail. Miura Hiroyuki, Sasaki Gin'ya, Toyoda Takeshi, Kobata Atsushi, and Nagahara Keiji are just a few of the important figures whose publications have shaped the field.[21] Their research provided the starting points for many of the topics addressed in this book, though for some, academic interest in the premodern economy was merely a means to explore the nature of class relations and pinpoint Marxist stages of development.[22] Perhaps due to changing intellectual frameworks, or perhaps simply due to the thoroughness of earlier scholarship, interest in the history of money waned in the 1980s, so much so that historian Ihara Kesao wrote in 1993 that research on the circulation of money (*ryūtsū*) has "completely disappeared."[23] But since the early 1990s several new approaches have greatly added to our understanding of the pre-1600 economy. One trend, inspired by social history, has been to focus on medieval Japanese who engaged in trade and other non-agricultural occupations. Amino Yoshihiko was at the forefront of this new approach to understanding the medieval economy, criticizing older scholarship that portrayed all medieval commoners as rice farmers. Drawing upon anthropological models, he examined the social uses of money and proposed that Chinese

---

21. Representative works include Miura, *Hōseishi no kenkyū;* Toyoda, *Chūsei Nihon shōgyōshi no kenkyū;* Sasaki, *Shōen no shōgyō;* Kobata, *Nihon kahei ryūtsūshi;* and Nagahara, *Nihon chūsei shakai kōzō no kenkyū.* Also, Ōyama, *Nihon chūsei nōsonshi no kenkyū.*

22. Kozo Yamamura addresses the Marxist influence on medieval Japanese scholarship in his introduction to the medieval volume of the *Cambridge History of Japan*, 6–12. However, this Marxist scholarship should not be dismissed lightly, for many of the authors cited above continue to have relevance to today's research.

23. Ihara, "Bakufu, Kamakura-fu no ryūtsū keizai seisaku," 151.

coins worked for medieval Japanese precisely because they were not connected to any indigenous authority.[24]

Another interesting line of inquiry has been to re-examine the relationship between Chinese fiscal policy and the medieval Japanese economy. Adachi Keiji, a historian of middle-period China, started a heated debate by demonstrating the close relationship between fifteenth-century Chinese and Japanese coin laws and proposing that Japan belonged to a zone of Chinese economic control. Although critical of his theory, the response produced insightful new research into when and where coins gained acceptance and how East Asian foreign relations contributed to economic growth.[25] Finally, a third trend has emerged from a heightened Japanese interest in local and regional history, as well as a renewed focus on monetary institutions as a primary object of research rather than as a way to understand agricultural productivity or class relations. These concerns have led scholars to conduct new research on topics such as the trading communities of the Japan Sea coast and the regional circulation of bills of exchange, using some of the insights of neo-classical economic theory to re-explore old problems.[26]

Scope of the Study

The economic history of medieval Japan, like the economic histories of most other places, is a study of trends and processes rather than events. It therefore lacks some of the easily identifiable key dates and names that are frequently used in constructing more straightforward political narratives. None-

24. Amino published prolifically, and this view is put forward repeatedly in his works. Examples include "Kyōkai ryōiki to kokka" and *Nihon shakai saikō.*

25. Adachi, "Chugoku kara mita Nihon kaheishi no ni, san no mondai." Important critical works include Ōta, "12–15 seiki shotō higashi Ajia ni okeru dōsen no rufu," and Sakurai, "Nihon chūsei in okeru kahei to shin'yō ni tsuite."

26. Sakurai, *Nihon chūsei no keizai kōzō;* Usami, *Nihon chūsei no ryūtsū to shōgyō;* Ike, *Senka: zenkindai Nihon no kahei to kokka.*

theless, every project needs a beginning and an end. *Coins, Trade, and the State* focuses primarily on the period from the years 1150 to 1400. I have chosen to refer to this period as "early medieval," though the second half of the fourteenth century is rather late to bear that appellation. As is frequently the case for historians, the object of study has led me to this non-standard periodization. The starting date of 1150 corresponds with the first documentary reference to copper-coin use in the late Heian period. The heart of the study ends in the late fourteenth century as elite institutions such as the Muromachi *bakufu* reasserted the role of government as a major player in the monetary world, though in fact Chapters 4 and 5 carry the book into the sixteenth century and beyond.

These dates are quite similar to those commonly given for Japan's medieval period, though for different reasons. For most of the twentieth century, the term "medieval Japan" was most often used to indicate the years between the Heian and Edo periods (from the late twelfth to the late sixteenth centuries). These were the years of the first two warrior governments, the Kamakura and Muromachi *bakufu*. According to this usage, the creation of the Kamakura *bakufu* marked the "triumph" of the samurai and hence the shift into medieval times.[27] Recently, however, some Western scholars have claimed to see more continuity than change between the Heian and Kamakura periods, leading them to date the start of the medieval period to the fourteenth century. In contrast, some Japanese scholars hold that medieval Japan began much earlier, with the rise of retired emperors in the eleventh century.[28] For a monetary history such as this study, though, the economic changes that began in the twelfth century are too important to ignore and make necessary an "early medieval" period classification.

––––

27. Hane, *Premodern Japan*, 61, 64.

28. For the fourteenth century view, see Mass, *Origins of Japan's Medieval World*, and Adolphson, *Gates of Power*. For Japanese scholars' perspective, see Kuroda, "Chūsei josetsu"; Gomi, *Inseiki shakai no kenkyū*; Ishii, "12, 13 seiki no Nihon: kodai kara chūsei e."

The term "elite" is likewise difficult to define. Kristina Troost writes of the eleventh-century Japanese elite as a narrow, urban, hereditary group of important religious institutions and nobles of high rank who monopolized proprietary interests in land.[29] For medieval Japan, one must also include the leading samurai of the Kamakura and Muromachi *bakufu* as well as the most powerful *sengoku* daimyo. In this book, I use the term "elite" to refer to the highest nobles and members of the imperial family, the leading temple complexes, and the top officials of the warrior government—in other words, those individuals and institutions that held sufficient political power to pass legislation that favored their interests, serve as estate proprietors, and/or tax local estates and peasant communities. These are the same groups that made up the *kenmon* of Kuroda Toshio's famous theory of medieval rulership.[30] Some tried to control the economy by fixing prices or dictating the types of currency that could be used. Their contributions to medieval Japan's growing economy were important, but their stories have been told by others.[31] This study turns instead to the periphery in order to highlight the ways in which non-elite figures became involved in trade, helped spread the use of coins, and came to garner sufficient economic power to challenge more traditional elite authorities.

It is not easy to tell the story of non-elites, for almost all of the surviving primary source materials were prepared by elites. Incomplete document collections offer tantalizing glimpses into the state of the medieval economy but do not contain enough information to allow analysis using the statistical techniques of the economist. The lack of even a single complete set of merchant's records for the Kamakura period led one

---

29. Troost, *Common Property and Community*, 7.

30. Kuroda, *Nihon chūsei no kokka to shūkyō*. In English, see Adolphson, *Gates of Power*, 10–18.

31. Tonomura, *Community and Commerce*; Berry, *Culture of Civil War*; Gay, *Moneylenders of Late Medieval Kyoto*. These authors have primarily focused on the late medieval period, whereas the current study gives greater attention to the early medieval.

scholar to write of pre-1600 commercial history as the "un-retellable history of non-agriculturalists."[32] This study employs a wide range of medieval materials, including diaries, tax records, legal decrees, and judicial decisions, to help compensate for such problems. Examples are drawn from estates in a variety of locations in an effort to avoid any regional bias, though inevitably the large number of records that survive from certain temples, such as Tōji of Kyoto and Tōdaiji of Nara, appear more frequently than records from other proprietors. As Tōji and Tōdaiji both had estate holdings scattered around the country, their documents are able to provide information on conditions beyond the central Kinai provinces. The story that they tell is valuable, for it is a central contention of this book that an understanding of medieval Japan's economic history, while important in its own right, is essential to a complete understanding of the social and political history of this period.

Following this introduction, Chapters 1 through 5 look at specific medieval economic institutions, with each chapter carrying the argument slightly forward in time. Chapter 1 looks at the history of coinage in Japan from the Nara period through the end of the twelfth century. It explores the strong relationship between the *ritsuryō* state and domestically produced coins of the eighth, ninth, and tenth centuries, and explains why those coins fell into disfavor in the second half of the Heian period. The chapter also examines the influx of Chinese coins in the twelfth century and the elite response to this new currency. Although we know little about who actually brought the coins to Japan, it is clear that they succeeded, despite efforts by the nobles to prevent Chinese cash from becoming an important medium of exchange in early medieval Japan.

———

32. Nakai, *Shōnin*, 16. Perhaps the best set of merchant records is the collection of the Ōmi merchants, who were active in the fourteenth, fifteenth, and sixteenth centuries. Hitomi Tonomura analyzes those records in her *Community and Commerce*. The documents offer valuable information on late medieval domestic trade, but no records have yet come to light from the merchants who imported Chinese coins in the late Heian and Kamakura periods.

Chapter 2 moves from the Kyoto-based nobility to the provinces, tracing the spread of markets and monetization in the thirteenth century. After exploring the history of the market in Japan, the chapter looks at the roles played by different provincial groups—merchants, estate-based warriors, religious figures, and agricultural communities—in promoting the use of cash outside of the capital. Chapter 3 analyzes ideas of "virtue" in medieval Japan, as well as the impact of money on the *bakufu* retainer system. It explains how, with many samurai retainers falling into debt and losing their landholdings to money lenders, the *bakufu* chose to appropriate the court notion of virtue and issue "virtuous government edicts" (*tokuseirei*) that declared all retainer debts to be forgiven. The chapter addresses questions such as to what degree did the cost of the Mongol invasions contribute to the *bakufu*'s decision to issue *tokuseirei*? And what can we learn about the nature of thirteenth-century economic and social change from the *bakufu*'s response?

Chapter 4 treats the commutation of taxes from payments in goods to payments in cash. It demonstrates that non-elites—those based in the provinces, such as estate managers and even the agricultural communities themselves—played an important role in pushing for the switch to use cash in paying taxes. This chapter also explores the emergence of one of medieval Japan's most innovative economic instruments, the bill of exchange (*kawase* or *saifu*). These certificates, used to convey money over long distances, circulated in a manner similar to paper currency. But they present intriguing puzzles to the modern scholar, for transactions conducted using these bills were carried out in the absence of a strong state government willing to enforce agreements. How could the various parties that used bills of exchange in the fourteenth century trust that the paper certificates would be honored?

Chapter 5 looks ahead to the later medieval and early modern periods, addressing the new ways in which elites became involved with the growing economy of the fourteenth, fifteenth, and sixteenth centuries. As noted above, the Muromachi *bakufu* was much more commercially savvy than its

Kamakura predecessor, taxing urban businesses and importing massive amounts of cash from China. *Sengoku* daimyo
also came to recognize the importance of trade to their survival, promoting commerce in their own domains and trying
to hinder it in those of their rivals. They also attempted to
control currency by issuing laws (*erizenirei*) that dictated the
types of coins that could be used in various transactions. Although communities and individuals in the provinces retained
greater freedom of action than they had in earlier times, the
sixteenth century is the story of the gradual reassertion of central government authority.

Together, these chapters illustrate how widespread the use
of money was during these centuries. They also highlight the
ways in which the economy grew and contributed to changes
in the relationship between center and periphery in medieval
Japan. As we read of increasing involvement in local markets,
new means of paying taxes, and evolving ideas of good governance, it will hopefully become clear that understanding the
gradual monetization of the economy is tremendously important: money and trade played key roles in the transformation
from a classical society to an early modern one.

ONE

"Cash Fever" and
the Late Heian Response

During the summer of 1179, Heian nobles watched with alarm as an epidemic swept through their realm. They were surely concerned by the rapid spread of the disease and by the fact that it had no known medical cure. The nobles named this epidemic *zeni no yamai*, a term that might be rendered into English as "the money disease" or perhaps "cash fever."[1] It appears to have been their metaphor for the sudden increase in the use of copper coins during the second half of the twelfth century. As was the case with many real medical diseases that plagued premodern Japan, the outbreak had its origins on the Asian mainland. Whether or not its victims were truly suffering, however, is open to debate.[2]

---

1. *Hyakurenshō*, Jijō 3 (1179), 6th month.

2. It is my contention that *zeni no yamai* was not an actual disease but rather a rhetorical flourish by the writers to indicate that they considered this new use of money to be a serious problem. In this interpretation, I differ from Amino Yoshihiko, who argues that the *zeni no yamai* referred to real medical epidemics, "popularly called 'the coin pestilence' because of rumors that it was the use of coins that caused their outbreaks." Amino, *Rethinking Japanese History*.

Equating the use of money with an epidemic might seem extreme, but it reflected both the nobles' high level of concern and their ideas of the foreign. Although Chinese books, medicines, art objects, and other items from abroad were highly prized and therefore sought after, some overseas imports were also seen as a source of contagion and danger. For example, a parrot presented to the imperial court in 1082 by a Song merchant was blamed for an epidemic of *gaibyō* (which caused sore throats and coughing). Other rare animals from China were deemed responsible for the fire that destroyed the Tsuchimikado Palace in 1148.[3] As Allan Grapard has noted, there was a belief in Heian Japan "that disease came from afar along various paths, and that visitors from foreign countries were apt to bring it."[4] The coins that so distressed the nobles in 1179 were neither animals nor people, of course, but the fact that they came from the Asian mainland may have led the nobles to associate them with "fevers" from abroad.

Currency in and of itself should not have upset Heian aristocrats, for money already had a long history in Japan by 1179. The imperial court had minted its own Chinese-style coins during the eighth, ninth, and tenth centuries that were physically quite similar to the (mostly) Song dynasty coins entering Japan in the twelfth century: round with square holes, made of copper alloys, bearing a four-character inscription on one face. Even after people stopped using domestic coins in the mid-Heian period, rice, silk, and cloth continued to function as units of exchange and stores of wealth — two of the essential qualities of money — into the twelfth century and beyond.[5]

---

3. For the parrot, see *Hyakurenshō*, Eihō 2 (1082) 8th month and Ōtoku 1 (1084) 9th month. The fire appears in *Honchōseiki*, Kyūan 4 (1148) 6th month 26th day.

4. Grapard, "Religious Practices," 550. We should note that these examples all involve animals. I have not come across any instances of inanimate objects (such as coins) being blamed for diseases.

5. Carole Cavanaugh presents an interesting discussion of the gendered roles involved in the production and circulation of cloth among Heian elites; see her "Text and Textile."

But in the minds of the nobles, imported Chinese cash was something quite different. The special terms they used reveal that the nobles were very aware of the currency's foreign origins. References in contemporary documents included *kinsen* (money of the times), *Sōchō no zeni* (coins of the Song court), and *Tōdo yori wataruru no zeni* (coins that have come from the land of the Tang).[6] This imported currency started to become a significant medium for exchange in the twelfth century, despite efforts by the nobility to ban its use.

Who brought Chinese coins to the Japanese islands, and how did people come to value them? Why did the nobles try to stop people from using them, and why did they fail? This chapter explores these and other questions surrounding the massive influx of Chinese coins to early medieval Japan. Its story begins much earlier, in the Nara and Heian periods, examining elite policy decisions and demonstrating the strident efforts of the imperial government to impose and monopolize authority over economic matters. Those efforts included government production of Chinese-style copper coins. By the tenth century, however, it was clear that such efforts had failed, and metallic currency fell out of favor. Only an unusual combination of circumstances led to the resumption of coin use in the late twelfth century. Because this new money was imported from the Asian mainland, it presented problems for Japan's ruling nobles. Their response reflected political rather than economic concerns that were based on an outdated view of imperial prerogative. Unlike earlier periods in which money was a creature of the state, during the twelfth century people began using Chinese cash in defiance of government control—an early sign of the breakdown in central authority that characterized Japan's medieval age.

---

6. Other terms for coins included *dōsen* (copper coins) and *yōto* (lit., "that which is used").

Money and Economic Policies in Nara and Early Heian

The use of money in the Japanese archipelago predates the introduction of writing, so there is very little documentary evidence for scholars seeking to understand the economy prior to the seventh century. Chinese written records, as well as archaeological evidence, offer clues that are tantalizing, though not always clear or verifiable. Iron may have been one of the earliest forms of commodity money used in the Japanese archipelago. Wei dynasty chronicles make mention of Koreans and Japanese employing Chinese iron in trade, and excavations of fifth-century Japanese burial mounds confirm the Wei accounts, revealing ingots that are quite similar to those found in Korea.[7] Silver also may have circulated, for one of Japan's earliest official histories, the *Nihon shoki*, mentions silver coins in an entry for the late fifth century.[8] However, since the *Nihon shoki* was not completed until the early eighth century, we must be cautious in trusting its accuracy in describing events from more than two hundred years earlier. In addition, the lack of any corroborating archaeological evidence makes the fifth-century use of silver coins difficult to confirm. Instead, we must turn to the late seventh century for more reliable clues to the first production of coins in Japan.

Even after examining evidence from that period, when Japanese written records such as the *Nihon shoki* are considered far more reliable, scholars were puzzled for many years. On the one hand, the first coins listed as being produced by the imperial government were the *Wadō kaichin* coins of 708. These coins, issued in both silver and copper, were named for their four-character inscription and were the first in a series of twelve different castings that modern scholars refer to as the "imperial twelve coins" (*kōchō jūnisen*). On the other hand, *Nihon shoki* entries refer to the use of copper and silver coins

---

7. Farris, *Sacred Texts and Buried Treasures*, 72–73; von Verschauer, *Across the Perilous Sea*, 8.

8. Hisamitsu, *Nihon kahei monogatari*, 17.

prior to 708. For example, in an entry from 683, the court decreed that "from this time forward, copper coins must be used, and silver ones shall not." Silver coins were banned again in another *Nihon shoki* entry from 694. Since there were no documents that make mention of the minting of coins prior to 708, these earlier entries presented anomalies to monetary historians, who could only speculate on the source of these earlier castings.[9]

The mystery was only recently solved when archaeologists were able to successfully date coins known as *fuhonsen*. Unlike the *Wadō kaichin* and subsequent imperial coins that contain four-character inscriptions, *fuhonsen* bear only two characters: *tomi* (also read *fu*), meaning "wealth," and *moto* (also read *hon*), meaning "basis" or "foundation."[10] The existence of these coins had been known for some time but there had been no way to reliably date them until the discovery of *fuhonsen* coins buried together with a wooden tablet dated to 687. This combination of artifacts, unearthed at an archaeological dig in Nara prefecture in August 1998, established *fuhonsen* as the oldest native coins known in the Japanese islands.[11] It has not yet been determined whether these coins circulated as money or had some other function, such as religious talismans or good luck tokens. Nonetheless, these recent archaeological finds have led scholars, including Sakaehara Towao, to conclude that *fuhonsen* had an economic function and that the

---

9. *Nihon shoki*, Tenmu 11 (683) 4th month 15th day; Jitō 8 (694) 3rd month 2nd day. Delmer Brown proposed that early Japanese may have used coins from the continent (*Money Economy in Medieval Japan*, 3), but there is not sufficient archaeological evidence to support such a view.

10. It is from these two characters that the *fuhonsen* earned their name. However, close examination of the coins shows that the second character is not 本 (*moto, hon*), but rather 夲 (*tō*). This character may have been a variant of *moto, hon*, but some scholars believe it to have been a distinct character, and so they call the coins *futōsen*. For proponents of the second reading, see Takizawa and Nishiwaki, eds., *Kahei*, 173–74.

11. The Nara National Research Institute of Cultural Properties did not announce the discovery until the following year. In English, see "Ancient Coins Alter Japan's Cash History," *Japan Times*, January 20, 1999.

Nihon shoki entries reflect active efforts by the imperial court to switch from silver to copper currency.[12] To date, only copper-alloy *fuhonsen* have been uncovered, but if these are the same coins that are referred to in the *Nihon shoki* entries of 683 and 694, then archaeologists may one day find silver *fuhonsen* in as-yet unexcavated locations. Even without the silver *fuhonsen*, the evidence is strong enough to push Japan's monetary history back at least to the seventh century.

As was true for most premodern societies, the availability of precious metals played a major part in coin production throughout Japan's early monetary history. Government leaders considered the discovery in 674 of silver on Tsushima an important find. Similarly, reports of gold on Tsushima in 701 and of copper in Musashi province in 708 were each considered so auspicious that the era names were changed to Taihō, "great treasure," and Wadō, "native copper," respectively. All three metals were coined during the Nara period, but silver and gold issues were extremely limited and probably did not circulate. When the government first produced its *Wadō kaichin* coins of 708, it made them in both silver and copper. By 709, however, the government was trying to limit the use of silver coins to large transactions only. The following year it prohibited the use of silver coinage altogether.[13] The court briefly reversed this policy in 721 and produced gold (the *Kaiki shōhō*) and silver (the *Taihei genpō*) coins in 760, but those coins were made in very small numbers and were likely given as gifts rather than used for ordinary purchases.[14]

There were several reasons why the court favored copper as its monetary metal of choice. One reason was that the Japanese seemed to have a bountiful supply of copper in the early

---

12. Sakaehara, "Nihon kodai kokka no senka hakkō," 44–48, 54–60.

13. *Shoku Nihongi*, entries for Wadō 1 (708) 5th month 11th day and 8th month 10th day, Wadō 2 (709) 3rd month 27th day, and Wadō 3 (710) 9th month 18th day.

14. As of the year 1999, a mere thirty-two *Kaiki shōhō* have been unearthed (all in the environs of Saidaiji Temple). No examples of *Taihei genpō* have as yet been discovered.

eighth century. A second reason was that gold and silver were valuable for use in trade with the continent. Hence the nobles surely preferred to save those precious metals for transactions with foreign merchants and promote the use of copper coins domestically. But the most important reason for favoring copper-alloy coinage was that Chinese coins were made of that material.

The Japanese were thoroughly enamored with Chinese civilization in the late seventh century. Students, Buddhist priests, diplomats, and other Japanese who visited China found the Tang dynasty at the peak of its glory. They were awed by the flourishing cosmopolitan society that they encountered. The Japanese brought back objects, including religious texts and medicines, as well as knowledge of astronomy, astrology, the calendar, and Chinese notions of law and government. Starting in the mid-seventh century, political factions at the Japanese court pushed through a series of reforms designed to help foster a Chinese-style imperial bureaucratic state in Japan. Their efforts succeeded in fits and starts over a period of six decades and included everything from the construction of a capital city modeled on the Tang capital of Chang'an to the commission of a Chinese-style official history, which eventually became the *Nihon shoki*. The Japanese also chose to follow Chinese practice by instituting their own version of the equal fields system and by adapting the Tang *lü-ling* legal code to form the new Japanese *ritsuryō* legal system. So much of our understanding of Japanese governance in the seventh, eighth, and ninth centuries comes from reading the *ritsuryō* penal and administrative codes that these years are sometimes referred to as the *ritsuryō* period.

Currency was part of this trend of Sinification. Japanese who traveled to China discovered that the Tang economy was partially monetized: cash and cloth were the primary forms of currency, and cash was an important medium for the payment of taxes as well as a significant component of state salaries. Other items such as grain and salt functioned as forms of money in certain instances, but coins were more common and circulated widely in the Tang.[15] Eagerly embracing things Chinese in the late seventh century, the Japanese decided to produce their own copper currency as part of the series of reforms that they were implementing. The court created a mint and appointed a chief minter in the 690s to produce its first Chinese-style coins in the early eighth century—the aforementioned *Wadō kaichin*. These coins bear a striking resemblance to the primary Tang dynasty coin, the *Kaiyuan tongbao*. Both types are approximately the same size (between 2.4 and 2.5 millimeters in diameter) and weight (3.5 grams). Not only do they share a four-character inscription on the obverse face, but the characters are written in a similar calligraphic style (see Figs. 1a and 1b).[16] Following the issuance of the *Wadō kaichin* in 708, the Japanese court went on to issue eleven more named coin varieties, each with its own inscription, over a 250-year period.

The eighth-century court took active steps to promote the circulation of its coins and maintain their value. On the positive side, it paid its officials in cash and offered lower-rank officials the opportunity to use copper money to purchase higher rank.[17] It also touted the convenience of coins for travelers in hopes of stimulating interest in government-issued currency.[18] On the negative side, the court forbade the domestic use of other types of metal currency and issued strict regulations against counterfeiters. The punishment for coun-

---

15. Peng, *A Monetary History of China*, 246–47. For more on the importance of minting coins as an expression of state power, see von Glahn, *Fountain of Fortune*.

16. The coins share one common character, 開 *kai*. On both coins, the bottom middle part of that character is written with the two downward strokes extending above the topmost horizontal line, resembling a miniature version of the character 井 *i*.

17. This law allowed those below the fifth rank to incrementally increase their status for a minimum of five *kan* (5,000 coins). *Shoku Nihongi*, Wadō 4 (711), 10th month.

18. Farris, "Trade, Money, and Merchants," 314–15. Also Sakaehara, "Coinage in the Nara and Heian Periods," 2–6.

Figs. 1a and 1b *Kaiyuan tongbao* (*left*) and *Wadō kaichin* (*right*) coins.
Used by permission of the National Museum of Japanese History (1a)
and the Bank of Japan Currency Museum (1b).

terfeiting was severe: offenders faced 200 lashes with a cane
and the prospect of having all of their assets confiscated and
given to the informants who reported on them. Of course, the
need for skilled coin producers sometimes prevented the government from carrying out its threatened punishment. In one
such case from the year 765, a group of counterfeiters were
arrested but then put to work in the minting bureau.[19] Nevertheless, the fact that counterfeiters risked punishment to produce coins shows that metallic currency had recognized value
in eighth-century Japan.

To what degree did coins penetrate the economy? Were
they used, and if so by whom and as part of what types of
transactions? Historians have long debated whether or not the
imperial twelve coins enjoyed much circulation. Sakudō Yōtarō
held that the imperial twelve were not widely used in Japan because the economy, far less developed than China's, produced
no natural demand for copper currency. Kobata Atsushi, how-

---

19. The punishment for counterfeiters is delineated in *Shoku Nihongi*,
Wadō 2 (709) 3rd month 27th day. In spite of this seemingly harsh treatment,
Shoku Nihongi notes that counterfeiting was widespread; see the entry for
Tenpyō hōji 4 (760) 3rd month 16th day. The case of the counterfeiters of 765
is discussed in Tōno, *Kahei no Nihonshi*, 70.

ever, argued that the coins circulated well in the more economically developed Kinai region but found little acceptance
in outlying provinces. Kozo Yamamura and Tetsuo Kamiki
were convinced that there was a significant degree of monetization during the *ritsuryō* period.[20] Their points of contention
suggest that the debate is part of a larger discussion about
Japan's "suitability" to adopt Chinese institutions. In other
words, was seventh- and eighth-century Japan sufficiently developed to implement the Tang institutions described in the
Japanese *ritsuryō* codes, or did the Japanese merely copy the
codes without creating the institutions?[21]

Textual evidence suggests that people valued the government's coinage, at least in the eighth century. An entry dated
798 in the legal compendium *Ruiju sandai kyaku*, for example,
condemned people in the peripheral provinces for hoarding
coins.[22] Recent archaeological evidence also indicates that the
imperial twelve circulated more widely than was once believed. Excavations over the last 30 years have unearthed *Wadō
kaichin* in all but 10 of Japan's 47 prefectures. Even in the prefectures where *Wadō kaichin* have not been located, other coins of
the imperial twelve series have been found. Of course, we must
be careful in interpreting these archaeological finds. Geographic range does not necessarily equate with volume of
use. The largest numbers of coins have been unearthed in
the centrally located Kinai provinces, giving some credence
to Kobata's contention that the coins primarily circulated in

---

20. Kobata, *Nihon kahei ryūtsūshi*. Sakudō Yōtarō also contends that the
imperial twelve were not used in Japan because there was no natural demand for copper currency; Sakudō, *Nihon kaheishi gairon*, 78. For an opposing
view, see Yamamura and Kamiki, "Silver Mines and Sung Coins," 338.

21. Sir George Sansom held that the reforms failed, citing their unsuitabil-
ity for more primitive Japanese society. Joan Piggott and others, however,
use archaeological evidence to reject this view. Piggott concludes that the
court created a "reasonably centered command structure" that successfully
kept local elites responsive to it. Sansom, *A History of Japan to 1334*, 84–85;
Piggott, *Emergence of Japanese Kingship*, 167–69.

22. *Ruiju sandai kyaku*, Enryaku 17 (798), 9th month, 23rd day, as discussed
in Farris, "Trade, Money, and Merchants," 315.

the region around the capital. Furthermore, some coins may have been moved to remote locations at a later date. That must have been the case for coin finds discovered on Hokkaido, since the island was not yet incorporated into the Japanese economic sphere in the Nara and Heian periods. Nonetheless, repeated discoveries of imperial coins throughout the country suggest that the currency had some value beyond the capital. Coin finds in southern Kyushu and the northeastern regions in particular suggest that the *kōchō jūnisen* circulated to some degree throughout the archipelago.[23]

Problems with Heian Coins and Currency

Even as the imperial twelve coins gained some acceptance in the Nara and early Heian periods, rice, silk, and other forms of cloth remained in use as forms of money. By the middle of the Heian period, the government was encountering difficulty in maintaining the value of its coins. One reason for this difficulty may have been that overproduction led to inflation. Government officials found that issuing coins could be quite profitable and attempted to put increasing numbers of coins into circulation to compensate for declining tax revenues in the mid-eighth century.[24] Another related problem was that the government's dwindling supply of copper led the mints to begin debasing coins. Figure 2 is a photograph of the imperial twelve coins. A simple physical comparison of the different issues shows that their weight, size, and copper content steadily declined over the course of the Heian period. More detailed examination confirms such findings: X-ray fluorescence (XRF) analysis performed by the Nara Cultural Properties Research Institute reveals that the *Wadō kaichin* were made of an almost pure alloy of copper and tin. The *Mannen tsūhō*

---

23. For a detailed breakdown of where coins of the imperial twelve have been unearthed, see the appendix to Sakaehara, *Nihon kodai senka ryūtsūshi*, 1–210.

24. Farris, "Trade, Money, and Merchants," 314–18.

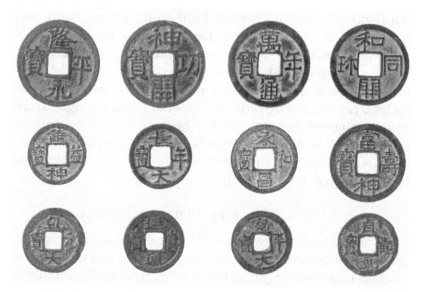

Fig. 2   Imperial twelve coins, starting with the *Wadō kaichin* (top right).
Used by permission of the National Museum of Japanese History.

(first issued in 760) and the *Jingū kaihō* (765) both maintained the same level of copper as the earlier coin but also included significant amounts of lead. Over the course of the ninth and tenth centuries, however, the rate of debasement increased as copper supplies dwindled. Lead came to replace copper and tin as the coins' primary component metal.[25] It should come as no surprise that these coins could not support the values that the government declared them to be worth.

Why did the Japanese court attempt to circulate coins that were obviously smaller and contained less copper than earlier castings? Debasement might reflect government hopes of capturing more income by using less copper to produce coins. This was frequently the case in late antique and medieval Europe, where rulers tried to shore up their finances by circulating coins with reduced precious metal content.[26] But in the Japa-

---

25. Nara kokuritsu bunkazai kenkyūjo, *Heijō no miya hakkutsu chōsa*, 102.

26. Jones, *The Later Roman Empire*, 26–28, 108, 438–39; Allmand, ed., *The New Cambridge Medieval History*, vol. 7, 60.

nese case, debasement appears to have been the result of a
dwindling supply of copper. The problem was already apparent in the ninth century, when a shortage of copper affected
not only the quality of coins but also limited the quantity that
could be produced. Although official figures listed in the mid-
Heian legal compendium *Ruiju sandai kyaku* claim that over
113 million coins were produced between the years 818 and 835,
this number probably reflected a goal rather than an actual
production figure. A letter dated 821 from one of the mints to
the capital confirms this hypothesis, indicating that little more
than half of its four-year coin production quota could be met
due to the lack of copper.[27] The problem of a poor supply of
metal ore was compounded by increased demand for copper
as a key ingredient in bronze Buddhist statues and religious
objects. The Great Buddha at Tōdaiji, for example, stands 50
feet high and is made of bronze. The figure itself required over
250 tons of copper and tin, and the lotus pedestal on which
it sits necessitated another 130 tons.[28] The construction of Tōdaiji alone placed a tremendous strain on the state's supply of
copper! Although the court received varying amounts of the
metal from Musashi, Inaba, Suō, Nagato, Buzen, Bitchū, and
Bingo provinces, supply could not keep up with demand.[29]

Faced with an inadequate supply of copper, the court had
little choice but to debase its currency and reduce output.
Nakajima Keiichi has suggested that the Japanese could have
imported metals for new coin castings; in support of his position, he cites a medieval example wherein the Japanese imported pig iron from the continent. However, even if such a
proposal had been considered, it would not have worked due
to the shortage of copper in China at this time as well. During
much of the Tang and Song dynasties, the Chinese mints were
in such dire need of copper that the government forbade its

---

27. Kobata, *Nihon no kahei*, 20. See also Kobata's *Kōzan no rekishi*.
28. Horiike, *Tōdaiji shi e no izanai*, 17.
29. Piggott, *Emergence of Japanese Kingship*, 266.

use for other purposes.[30] In Japan, the imperial court resorted to collecting and melting old coins in order to supplement the insufficient supply of copper. The Heian court's inability to maintain high levels of coin production surely made it difficult to stabilize the value of its currency.

The court attempted to compensate for its inadequate supply of coins by declaring newly issued coins to be worth ten times the value of older issues. According to the chronicle *Nihon kiryaku*, the court issued the following proclamation to accompany the minting of the new *Engi tsūhō* coin in 907: "We decree that the *Kanpyō taihō* currency is to be changed. The new coin shall be called the *Engi tsūhō*; one shall be worth ten old coins. This new coin shall circulate together with the older coins."[31] This was an attempt to create a higher value for the new coin based on fiat power alone, for as the XRF analysis described above has shown, the metal content of the new coin was not superior to previous issues. Although similar decrees do not survive for all of the ninth- and tenth-century coins, there is every reason to believe that such attempts to dictate value by decree were a common practice.[32] These policies may have met with limited short-term success, for there are some ninth- and tenth-century documents that mention "new" and "old" coins, indicating an awareness of such distinctions.[33]

———

30. Nakajima, "Nihon no chūsei senka," 112. Even with all of China's copper going to the mints, the metal supply was not sufficient to meet the cash needs of the Chinese economy, and so the Northern Song reformer Wang Anshi temporarily repealed the ban on non-monetary uses of copper in hopes of stimulating mine production. This policy led to a massive increase in mint output, but it still did not satisfy demand. Von Glahn, *Fountain of Fortune*, 40–41, 48–51.

31. *Nihon kiryaku*, Engi 7 (907) 11th month 3rd day.

32. See Tōno's discussion of this point in *Kahei no Nihonshi*, 70–71. In English, see Farris, "Trade, Money, and Merchants," 316–18.

33. There are some documents that specify "new coins" (*shinsen*) or "old coins" (*kyūsen* or *kosen*), but they do not indicate that these coins were worth more or less than others in circulation. Other documents list specific coin types by mentioning the reign name (*nengō*) of the period during which the coins were minted. For examples, see *Heian ibun*, doc. 39 (Kōnin 6 [815] 10th

However, surviving documents do not indicate that people followed the 1:10 new-to-old coin rate and, over the long term, all coins appear to have circulated with the same value. Without any true basis (such as increased copper content) for the higher value, government policies only contributed to a further drop in the value of its currency.

In response to these problems, the Heian court tried on numerous occasions to stop the depreciation of its money. One approach was to insist that the Office of Imperial Police (Kebiishichō) enforce regulations mandating coin use. At other times, the government ordered temples to pray for the use of coins by the populace.[34] In spite of these and other efforts, though, coin use appears to have diminished over the course of the tenth century. As the *Nihon kiryaku* noted in 984, "In recent years people have an extreme dislike for coins."[35] The court's inability to return to the higher copper content of its earliest coins may have been a major factor behind the people's rejection of metal currency. Many examples of the last of the imperial twelve, the *Kengen taihō*, issued in 958, have been found to contain over 90 percent lead.[36] People turned away from cash, and no Japanese government would officially mint a coin again until the sixteenth century.

Modern scholars still disagree on whether or not coin use ceased altogether. Kobata Atsushi concluded from an examination of land-sale documents (*baiken*) that coins were no longer in use by the year 1000. He found eighteen documents attesting to the sale of land for cash from mid-Nara through mid-Heian, but no such documents for the second half of the Heian period. Instead, people purchased land with rice, wheat, silk, or other goods.[37] Takizawa Takeo contested Kobata's findings, arguing

---

month 30th day), doc. 4422 (Kōnin 11 [820] 10th month 3rd day), doc. 4393 (Kōnin 5 [814] 6th month 17th day).

34. *Nihon kiryaku*, Eikan 2 (984) 11th month 27th day; Ei'en 1 (987) 11th month 2nd day and 27th day.

35. *Nihon kiryaku*, Eikan 2 (984) 11th month 6th day.

36. Saitō et al., "Kodai senka ni kan suru rikagakuteki kenkyū."

37. Kobata, *Nihon no kahei*, 29–31.

that the number of surviving land-sale documents is too small to draw any firm conclusions. Instead, he turned to sources such as the travel diary *Tosa nikki* to argue that coin use persisted among the people and that this continued use accounts for why imported coins were so easily accepted by the Japanese in the twelfth century. Takizawa's position is interesting, but *Tosa nikki* is not the best source for establishing late Heian coin use, as it is attributed to the 930s, years in which the Japanese government was still minting coins. The late tenth-century romantic tale *Utsuho monogatari* makes mention of coins, but such references are quite rare in mid-Heian fiction and suggest that, if metallic currency was employed at all, it was used sporadically at best.[38]

Turning to documents such as land sales, tax receipts, temple records, and judicial pronouncements, we see that whatever coin use continued during the eleventh century must have been minimal to have so thoroughly escaped the written record. The *Heian ibun*, a chronological compendium of such documents spanning the years from 794 to 1185, includes 99 documents that mention coins (*zeni*) and confirms that coin use in the early Heian period (ninth and tenth centuries) was far more prevalent than coin use in late Heian (eleventh and twelfth), at least prior to 1150. In contrast with Kobata's *baiken* (cited above), the *Heian ibun* coin documents include a much wider range of written materials than just land-sale deeds. Sixty percent of the documents that mention coins were composed during the first half of the Heian period. While this is a majority, it might not seem very significant unless one considers that more documents survive from the latter half of the Heian period.[39] A mere

---

38. Takizawa, "Heian kōki no kahei ni tsuite," 8–11. Tōno has also explored a variety of sources, including the *Utsuho monogatari*, in an effort to clarify the matter of coin use in the late Heian period. His overall conclusion is that eleventh-century coin use was extremely limited—and perhaps nonexistent. Tōno, *Kahei no Nihonshi*, 73.

39. Of course, my conclusion rests on the assumption that the documents included in the *Heian ibun* collection are representative of the larger body of

321 documents survive from the first two centuries of Heian (from 784 to 985), and 58 (18 percent) of those mention coins. By contrast, almost 4,000 documents survive from the next 200 years (from 986 to 1185), but only 41 (1 percent) of those refer to coins. These numbers suggest that coins were much rarer in the eleventh and early twelfth centuries.[40]

Why did government economic policies fail to stimulate coin use in late Heian? Did the court give up on its own currency? To answer these questions, let us turn to one of the policy tools employed by the nobles but not discussed in the paragraphs above: that of declaring "price laws" (*kokahō*). These price laws were imperial edicts that mandated the value of various commodities in terms of coin.[41] In the Nara and early Heian periods, the prices of goods set forth in *kokahō* were supposed to be informed by knowledge of the actual market value of the goods in question. According to the eighth-century *ritsuryō* codes, officials were to use marketplace prices as their guide in fixing price laws, while the ninth-century legal commentary *Ryō no gige* indicates that officials were expected to learn market prices by visiting the market itself.[42] Although the court stopped minting coins after 958, it continued to peri-

---

Heian written materials. Precisely because the documents of that larger body do not survive, there is no way to confirm or disprove this assumption.

40. Another way to reach the same conclusion would be to consider the number of coins documents per volume. In the eight chronologically organized volumes of the *Heian ibun*, the majority (56 percent) of coin documents appear in vol. 1, covering the years 782 to 968. There are a significant number of coin-related documents in vols. 2 (10 percent) and 8 (7 percent), but the coins referred to in vol. 8 are probably Chinese. Coins are almost never mentioned in the intervening volumes. Since the earlier volumes prove that documents mentioning coins tended to be preserved, and since the later volumes contain more documents per year than vols. 1 and 2, the fact that they do not refer to coins confirms that significant coin use stopped during the eleventh century.

41. For examples of price laws, see the *Nihon kiryaku* entries for Tenryaku 1 (947) 11th month 11th day and Kanna 2 (986) 3rd month 29th day.

42. Ihara, "Sōsen yunyū no rekishiteki ishiki," 67.

odically issue price laws in an attempt to fix the values of different goods over the rest of the Heian period.

Kokahō and their significance have been topics of heated debate amongst economic historians over the last fifteen years. On the one hand, these price laws can be seen as signs of the court's resilience and the active assertion of its authority. On the other hand, price laws can be interpreted as the last acts of a court that had lost interest in and control over economic matters.[43] Both positions have some merit, but I find Hotate Michihisa's observation to be particularly persuasive. Hotate's analysis of prices laws reveals that they commonly appeared in the first set of "new proclamations" (shinsei) issued by an emperor. These were specially designated sets of decrees issued by emperors between the mid-tenth and mid-fourteenth centuries. Although given the label "new," in fact they did not necessarily introduce new policies but rather emphasized practices that the court deemed important for proper governance. That the court included price laws in these new proclamations reveals a great deal about the court's approach to formulating economic policy.

A number of possible explanations might account for the decision to issue a price law at a particular moment. For example, if the nobles promulgated a price law at the same time that they issued a new variety of coin, then we might conclude that they sought to set the value of various goods vis-à-vis the new currency. Yet this explanation is difficult to substantiate, since the court stopped minting in the second half of the tenth century but continued promulgating price laws into the Kamakura period. Alternatively, price laws issued during a famine might suggest that they were intended to help keep the prices of commodities affordable during a time of shortage-induced inflation. One price law—that of 1138—was issued after several years of famines and fires, but this appears to have been

---

43. Hotate, "Chūsei zenki no shinsei"; Nakajima, "Nihon no chūsei senka to kokka." See also Mikami, "Kōchōsen no shūen," 43–52, and Ihara, "Sōsen yunyū no rekishiteki ishiki."

the exception rather than the rule.[44] Rather than either of these possibilities, the strongest correlation can be seen in the issuance of price laws and the first *shinsei* of a new emperor. In other words, one part of each new emperor's declaration of sovereignty included a claim of authority over prices. This suggests that Heian elites saw their economic policies as a symbolic means of asserting political authority. Rather than responding to changing prices or to problems with the availability of money or goods, they issued price laws as a matter of course in the eleventh and twelfth centuries.

Kokahō had not originated as exclusively political tools, but by the late Heian period, price laws appear to have been issued with little regard for market conditions. This pattern of issuing price laws as part of an emperor's "new proclamations" had become a powerful institution in the sense that economists use the term—a belief that "defined and limited" Heian economic policies.[45] The institutional concern to assert political authority rather than address changing economic developments would later limit the ability of the late Heian nobility to effectively respond to the large influx of Chinese coins in the twelfth century.

Gold, Foreign Trade, and Bargaining Power

Before considering the reappearance of coins in the twelfth century, let us look briefly at money and economic policy in the international arena. For much of the Heian period, the court prohibited Japanese from sailing abroad or having pri-

---

44. Hotate, "Chūsei zenki no shinsei to kokahō," 2.

45. Avner Greif defines institutions as "the non-technological constraints on human interactions," while Douglass North explains institutions as "the rules of the game in a society . . . the humanly devised constraints that . . . define and limit the set of choices of individuals." Greif, "Cultural Belief and the Organization of Society," 943. See also Aoki, *Toward a Comparative Institutional Analysis*, 4–20; North, *Institutions, Institutional Change, and Economic Performance*, 3–4.

vate dealings with foreigners.[46] As is well known, it decided to stop sending official embassies to China in 894. One reason was deteriorating conditions and concern for safety as the Tang dynasty slowly collapsed. But another factor, as Robert Borgen argues, was that Chinese traders were bringing sufficient quantities of luxury goods to Japan in the ninth century to satisfy the needs of the court and eliminate the economic imperative for diplomatic exchanges (which were also opportunities for trade).[47] The early tenth-century court declared that visits by individual foreign ships were to be limited to once every three years, but trade between the continent and the Japanese islands persisted.[48] The Japanese court attempted (with moderate success) to control this trade by having all foreign visitors handled through the Kōrokan, its customs and immigration office located near Dazaifu in northern Kyushu. Officials claimed the right to inspect and purchase goods on behalf of the state before allowing any "private" trade to take place. As historian Bruce Batten has shown, these exchanges could take months or even years if the merchants missed the seasonal winds that made it possible for them to sail home.[49]

Surviving documents indicate that most Chinese and Korean traders arrived at Dazaifu, though some found it advantageous to avoid the official port and sail instead to Echizen, Satsuma, or Wakasa provinces.[50] Exactly how often trading ships went to alternative ports is difficult to determine because boats docking at other ports were technically illegal and therefore rarely produced official documents. The written refer-

---

46. Heian prohibitions on Japanese sailing abroad are covered in greater detail in Mori, "The Beginning of Overseas Advance," 5–7.

47. The last Japanese diplomatic mission to China took place in 838, but there were plans for future missions until the decision to end official visits to China in 894. For more on this decision, see Borgen, *Sugawara no Michizane*, 228, 240–48.

48. *Sadanobu kōki*, Tengyō 8 (911) 7th month 29th day.

49. Batten provides a detailed analysis of such supervised trade in *Gateway to Japan*, 105–23.

50. For the structure and role of the Dazaifu, see Batten, *State and Frontier in Early Japan*.

ences that make mention of those alternate ports are usually diary entries and other unofficial sources. For example, the Heian noble Fujiwara no Yukinari, in a diary entry from the year 995, records the arrival of a Chinese merchant in Wakasa who was sent on to Echizen.[51] In this sense, trade was not wholly under government control.

When dealing with foreign merchants, gold was the primary medium of exchange. Chinese and Korean traders sought gold, and Japanese elites readily paid it in order to obtain continental goods. To cite just two examples, in 1004, the Chamberlain's Office (Kurōdodokoro) gave 300 *ryō* of gold to the governor of Bitchū province, Taira no Narimasa, so that he could purchase Chinese goods for the court; and in 1014, Fujiwara Takaie sent 10 *ryō* of gold with the monk Seiken to purchase medicines from a Song doctor living in Kyushu.[52] In exchange for gold, Heian elites obtained silk, incense and perfumes, medicines, twill damask and brocade, smelling salts, and other luxury items. They placed great value on these items, as seen both by the high prices they paid in gold and by the formal presentation sessions often arranged to view imported items.[53]

Apparently, the importance of the Chinese merchants as suppliers of such goods was strong enough to allow them to demand high prices and protest directly to the Heian court when they felt that they were being treated unfairly. Consider the case of an exchange-rate dispute between a Song merchant and a Dazaifu official in the year 1000. The Dazaifu official, Fujiwara no Arikuni, sought to pay the merchant, Zeng Linwen, in rice rather than in gold. Citing the official rice-to-gold exchange rates promulgated in imperial price laws, Arikuni

---

51. *Gonki*, Chōtoku 1 (995), 9th month 24th day.

52. *Midō kanpakuki*, Chōhō 6 (1004) 1st month 27th day; *Shōyūki*, Chōwa 3 (1014) 6th month 25th day.

53. *Shōyūki*, Chōwa 4 (1015) 9th month 23rd day; Jian 3 (1023) 7th month 15th day; Chōgen 2 (1029) 3rd month 2nd day. The historian Mori Katsumi first wrote on the obsession with Chinese goods and the resulting "luxurification" (*shashika*) of late Heian society; see his "Sōdōsen no wagakuni ryūnyū no tansho."

offered one *koku* of rice for every *ryō* of gold in the merchant's asking price.[54] However, Zeng insisted that he should receive three *koku* of rice per *ryō* of gold. Arikuni appealed to the Chamberlain's Office for guidance, and officials of that office instructed Arikuni to negotiate for one *koku* five *to* of rice per *ryō* of gold, but Zeng still refused. In the end, the case was brought to the attention of Emperor Ichijō and Minister of the Left Fujiwara no Michinaga, who approved a further compromise of two *koku* of rice per *ryō* of gold (a compromise to which Zeng apparently agreed).[55] In addition to highlighting the bargaining power of Chinese merchants, this case reveals that gold served as the international unit of account in tenth- and eleventh-century East Asia. In other words, even if goods were sometimes paid for with rice, prices were measured and negotiated in terms of gold.[56]

Given the great value that premodern Japanese elites placed on Chinese objects, one might posit that late Heian and Kamakura elites began to import Chinese coins in order to use them for the purchase of luxury goods from continental traders. Mori Katsumi proposed just such a thesis, writing that Japanese began importing coins in the mid-twelfth century to use as a means of payment for trade with the Chinese. Yet there is little evidence to support his contention. Tōno Haruyuki and Ihara Kesao both posit that copper coins were not used as the means of international trade payments until the Muromachi period.[57] Unfortunately, archaeological evidence is not

---

54. During the Heian period, the *ryō*, a unit of weight, was delineated in the *ritsuryō* codes to be approximately 12.5 grams; see the relevant entry in the *Kokushi daijiten*, vol. 13, p. 616. The *koku* was between twelve and thirteen liters; *Iwanami Nihonshi jiten*, 1342.

55. *Gonki*, Chōhō 2 (1000) 7th month 13th day.

56. For another example of the bold bargaining tactics of Song merchants, see the protests of the merchant Zhou Wenyi that he had received too little gold in payment, recorded in *Shōki mokuroku*, Chōgen 5 (1032) 10th month 8th day.

57. Tōno, *Kahei no Nihonshi*, 81. My account of this debate draws upon Ihara's summary in "Sōsen yunyū no rekishiteki ishiki," in Ike, *Senka*, 64–65.

of much assistance in settling this debate. Ōba Yasutoki claims that the unearthing of large value coins (individual Song coins stamped to be worth ten ordinary coins) in Hakata proves that Song merchants used these coins to pay for imported goods for China. Tōno Haruyuki disagrees, contending that large-value coins often had their sides filed down to make them appear similar to regular coins so that they could circulate within Japan.[58] My own findings favor the position of Tōno and Ihara, for as the primary sources cited in the preceding paragraphs demonstrate, gold was the preferred means of payment for Japan-China trade in the Heian period. Furthermore, as will be made evident in the paragraphs below, the late Heian nobility did not favor importing Chinese coins. Nevertheless, small but notable amounts of Chinese coins began appearing in Japan during the twelfth century, despite the opposition of the nobles. Let us now turn to the story of those coins and how they came to Japan.

Twelfth-Century Coins and the Heian Elite Response

After a long absence, coins reappear in the land-sale documents of the *Heian ibun* collection from the mid-twelfth century. The first such record is a document from the year 1150 detailing the sale of a private holding and villa for the price of 27 strings of cash.[59] The coins in question were not the "imperial twelve" produced by the court in the Nara and early Heian periods. Many of those coins had been lost or destroyed by this time, and since no new coins had been domestically produced in almost two centuries, the volume of existing coinage was completely inadequate to support a return to na-

---

58. Ōba, "Hakata ni okeru toraizeni no hajimari," 52–54; Tōno, *Kahei no Nihonshi*, 80–84.

59. *Heian ibun* (hereafter *HI*), doc. 2707, Kyūan 6 (1150) 8th month 25th day. The "string of cash" (*kanmon*) was supposed to include 1,000 coins, though often strings of 980 or even fewer coins circulated as strings. One *kanmon* usually consisted of ten strings of roughly one hundred coins each; the coins were strung together through the square holes in their centers.

tive metal currency.[60] Instead, the 27 strings of cash consisted of imported Chinese money, the very coins that the Heian nobles would condemn as having caused an "epidemic" in the summer of 1179.

Citing this transaction, Mori Katsumi contends that Japanese began importing Chinese copper currency from the middle of the twelfth century to use in trade with merchants from the continent.[61] Mori correctly dates the first documentary reference to coin use, but cash must have actually begun to be imported even earlier. Two pieces of evidence confirm this hypothesis. First, a religious fundraising register from 1151 lists the names and amounts given by supporters to the Hōrakuji temple in Tosa province.[62] Apparently all of the parishioners had ready access to cash, for their donations are in 30- and 50-coin sums, small amounts that suggest coins were already being used for everyday transactions as opposed to land purchases and international trade payments. Second, the strengthening of a ban by the Chinese government on the export of coins from coastal regions in 1155 suggests that the outflow of coins was already a significant problem by the mid-twelfth century—and therefore that it must have begun some time earlier.[63] This document does not name the Japanese as the exporting culprits, though no other country is known to have imported more Song coins by sea. A similar ban from 1199 specifically prohibits the selling of copper cash to Japanese and Korean merchants, but such bans did little to stem the tide of coins flowing into Japan.[64] A Southern Song official

60. Some Japanese coins have been found mixed in with imported Chinese coins from the medieval period, but they are a small fraction of the total volume of medieval coinage. For examples, see Ono, *Zukai Nihon no chūsei iseki*, 179.

61. Mori, "Sōdōsen no wagakuni ryūnyū."

62. *HI*, doc. 2736, Ninpei 1 (1151) 8th month 4th day.

63. This is mentioned in the Chinese chronicle *Jianyan yilai xinian yaolu*, entry for Shaoxin 25 (1155) 5th month 24th day, p. 5384.

64. The ban is Qingyuan 5 (1199) 7th month 24th day and is listed in the *Song shi* vol. 37, p. 725. That the ban extended to Koreans as well as Japanese is curious, since the twelfth-century Korean economy did not use

wrote in the early 1250s that when Japanese boats docked in the Chinese port of Ningbo, all of the coins in the area would disappear overnight, and ships would leave port loaded with nothing but cash as cargo.[65] Such anecdotal evidence does not allow us to settle upon exact dates for the Japanese use of imported cash. It suggests, though, that Japanese first started using Chinese coins in small numbers a decade or two before 1150, and that the demand for currency gradually increased over the next 120 to 150 years.

Mori links the demand for Chinese coins to Heian elites' general desire for Chinese goods, but the rough timeline described above supports an alternative explanation. China during Japan's late Heian and early Kamakura periods was an economic powerhouse. Northern (960–1127) and Southern (1127–1279) Song experienced unprecedented levels of economic growth and commercialization that are widely acknowledged by scholars as having transformed Chinese society.[66] These changes included the full-fledged monetization of the economy. As noted above, copper cash was used in the Tang (618–907), but people also used commodities such as rice and cloth as currency. During the Northern Song, however, both merchants and the government made coins the dominant form of money. The Chinese demand for coins in the newly developing commercial economy was enormous. Northern Song mints produced between one and two billion coins per year during the first half of the eleventh century, yet could not keep up with the twin demands of the military budget and expanding trade. Wang Anshi's reforms stimulated even greater levels of coin production, with a peak of six billion coins reached in the year 1073. Although the casting of six billion coins per

---

coins. Presumably, Korean traders were exporting cash from China in order to sell it in Japan.

65. Ihara, "Sōdai shakai to zeni," 4–18; von Glahn, *Fountain of Fortune*, 54.

66. For example, Mark Elvin refers to urbanization, improvements in farming and water transport, and the increased availability of money and credit as having created a medieval economic revolution; Elvin, *Pattern of the Chinese Past*, 113–78.

year proved unsustainable, annual mint output remained at between two and three billion for much of the early twelfth century.[67]

As China enjoyed this rapid economic expansion, its coins came to travel far beyond state borders. The Song dynasty's rival kingdoms to the north were always interested in importing Chinese cash, both because of the widely recognized high quality of Northern Song cash and because the coins carried the dynasty's prestige. In some cases, the Song paid coins to the northern kingdoms as part of war indemnities. Chinese copper currency was valued in the south as well: upper-class Cambodians reportedly used it as a luxury item, and the people of Java used it as a medium of exchange. Finally, coins traveled even farther afield with merchants. Song coins believed to have circulated in trade have been unearthed in places as varied as Indonesia, India, and East Africa.[68] Among the leading importers of coins were the Japanese, who at first relied on foreign ships but began sailing directly to China for trade sometime after the twelfth century.

During the Heian period, Japanese lacked the shipbuilding skills and navigational information necessary for safe and easy passage across the ocean. Most boats were designed for river use or to hug the coastline. William Wayne Farris believes

----

67. Gernet, *History of Chinese Civilization*, 324–25. Gernet estimates that Northern Song total coin production equaled approximately 200 million strings of cash (i.e., 200 billion coins!). Von Glahn concurs with Gernet's conclusion that the amount of coinage was insufficient and cites references in contemporary documents to "currency famines" (*qianhuang*). Inoue, however, challenges the claim that the coin supply was insufficient. He takes a commodity-money approach, noting an apparent contradiction between the prices of goods generally increasing even as coins were supposed to be in short supply. Inoue argues that in fact there was an *excess* of coins, and that this excess caused inflation. Von Glahn, *Fountain of Fortune*, 49–50; Inoue, "Kokusai tsūka to shite no sōsen," 19–29.

68. See the essays in Rossabi, ed., *China Among Equals*, especially Shiba's chapter on Song trade. Also see Vivier, "Chinese Foreign Trade," especially Chapter 3.

Fig. 3 Northern Song coins unearthed in Japan.
Used by permission of the Bank of Japan Currency Museum.

that they were a continuation of earlier hollowed-out log-and-strakes type vessels that had been used in the archipelago for centuries.[69] Trade with China was dependent on the arrival of ships from the Asian mainland, and Japanese who traveled to China booked passage on Chinese ships. The monk Jōjin did precisely that in the year 1072, buying his way onto a Chinese ship that left from Hizen province.[70] Many others monks, eager to learn more of Buddhism on the continent, followed the same course. Officially, the Japanese imperial court placed a number of restrictions on visiting Chinese merchants, requiring them to dock at Hakata and stipulating how many years they were to wait before coming again. In reality, however, the court's desire for Chinese goods led it to frequently

---

69. Farris, "Shipbuilding and Nautical Technology," 269–70.

70. *Fusō ryakki,* Enkyū 4 (1072) 3rd month 15th day. On Jōjin's voyage by boat, see Borgen, "Jōjin's Travels," 388–89.

violate its own rules by granting "exceptions" to those same merchants.[71] Most germane to a discussion of ships, however, was the fact that the Japanese were dependent on the arrival of foreign trading ships. They rarely tried to sail to the Asian mainland themselves.

Improvements in Japanese shipbuilding techniques, such as keel design and mast placement, eventually allowed Japanese merchants to begin sailing for the continent, though exactly when this occurred is open to debate. Mori Katsumi claims that Japanese sailed their own ships first to Korea in the eleventh century and then to China in the twelfth, but this view is difficult to substantiate. Among his evidence, Mori cites the Song chronicle *Jianyan yilai xinian yaolu*, which records that a ship bearing nineteen Japanese sulfur merchants arrived in 1145.[72] Yet it is not clear whether the ship in question was a Japanese boat or merely a boat carrying Japanese, and even if it was a domestically made vessel, the fact that bad weather carried it to Southern Song suggests that Japanese merchants may not have been the most capable ocean sailors in the mid-twelfth century. Further evidence against Mori's position can be found in the fact that early Kamakura period shipbuilders had not significantly improved in skill or the design of their boats. When the third shogun, Minamoto no Sanetomo (r. 1203–1219), wanted a ship to take him to China, he needed to commission a Chinese priest living in Japan to construct the vessel.[73] In 1254, the *bakufu* issued a proclamation limiting the number of "Chinese vessels" (*Tōsen*) in Kamakura bay to only five, though it is impossible to tell from the *Azuma kagami* entry whether these vessels were Chinese-owned boats, boats

---

71. Batten, *Gateway to Japan*, 105–20; Batten, "An Open and Shut Case," 311–13.

72. Mori, "The Beginning of Overseas Advance," 19–20.

73. Although the priest, Chin Nakei, built the boat, when it was tested in Yuigahama Bay the following year, it proved unable to float, and Sanetomo gave up his dream of traveling to China.

made in China but owned by Japanese, or Japanese boats that were capable of sailing to China.[74]

Rather than Mori's thesis of Japanese boats crossing the Sea of Japan in the Heian period, it is more likely that Japanese did not make all of the necessary ship improvements for safe ocean travel until the second half of the Kamakura period. This is close to, but slightly earlier than, Farris's thesis that real advances in Japanese shipbuilding only occurred after 1300, though I do not see the two proposals as incompatible.[75] By the 1270s, the Japanese had fought off a naval invasion from the Mongols (who had forced the Koreans to build boats for them) and felt confident enough in their ships to propose a counterattack on Korea.[76] Soon thereafter, Japanese merchant ships were making regular calls on Chinese ports, often in search of copper coins. The fact that Khubilai Khan had just tried to invade Japan seems not to have inhibited trade. Yuan records show that Japanese came in 1277 with gold to trade for cash, and two years later four Japanese boats arrived for trade in the port of Keigen. In the early 1300s, Japanese vessels sailed to China with some frequency, hoping to raise cash for temple repairs and construction.[77] And, as is well known, by the mid-fourteenth century "Japanese pirates" (*wakō*) were regularly raiding the coasts of China and Korea.

Unfortunately, we know few details about the sailors and traders who brought Chinese cash to Japan or how it entered the economy. No merchant or shipping records survive. The

---

74. *Azuma kagami,* Kenchō 6 (1254) 4th month 29th day. Farris provides a more detailed discussion of this proclamation and some of the scholarly debate that surrounds it. He believes that the proclamation limited the number to five boats per operator, suggesting that there may have been many more than five boats in total.

75. Farris also notes that Japanese were sailing to China in the late thirteenth century, but sees the most significant improvements in hull design only coming in the fourteenth century ("Shipbuilding and Nautical Technology," 271–75). Perhaps late thirteenth-century success in reaching China drove further innovations in shipbuilding during the fourteenth century.

76. Conlan, *In Little Need of Divine Intervention,* 214–15.

77. Saeki, *Mongoru shūrai no shōgeki,* 196–205.

Taira warrior clan seems to have played an important role in encouraging such trade. Court nobles often complained about Taira no Kiyomori (1118–1181), head of the clan for much of the twelfth century, and his interests in foreign trade and Chinese coins. Kiyomori helped build up the ports along the Inland Sea, especially near his residence at Fukuhara (present-day Hyōgo), and encouraged ships to dock there. He had close ties with Chinese merchants and hosted a meeting between Retired Emperor Go-Shirakawa and a Song merchant in 1170. Kujō Kanezane (1149–1207), a member of the Northern House of the Fujiwara, was quite critical of the meeting in his diary, noting that there were no cases of a Japanese emperor personally meeting with a foreigner since the early tenth century.[78]

The Taira involvement in Asian trade began with Kiyomori's father, Tadamori (1096–1153), who probably developed a taste for foreign trade when he served as governor of Echizen, a province along the Sea of Japan coast that was occasionally visited by foreign merchant vessels. Tadamori later crafted a strong base in western Japan when he was sent there to deal with pirates in 1129 and 1135. His hunger for imported goods even emboldened him to claim that he operated with the retired emperor's authority when he forced government officials from Dazaifu to allow him first access to a Chinese merchant ship that had landed in Kyushu.[79] Although these incidents suggest that the Taira were actively involved in foreign trade, they make no mention of Japanese ships. Kiyomori probably still relied on foreign vessels to bring Chinese coins and other goods to Japan.[80] Furthermore, these incidents offer no insight into the means by which coins were distributed once they reached Japanese ports. Nor, since the Taira were destroyed in the Genpei civil war, can they explain the con-

---

78. *Gyokuyō*, Kaō 2 (1170) 9th month 20th day.

79. *Chōshūki*, Chōjō 2 (1133) 8th month 13th day.

80. Farris notes that Kiyomori and ex-Emperor Takakura each rode on Song junks in 1179 and 1180, respectively. "Shipbuilding and Nautical Technology," 268.

tinued importation of coins to Japan in the late twelfth and thirteenth centuries.

It is also not clear how many coins were brought to Japan in the twelfth century. The best estimates that we can make require extrapolating back from archaeological and documentary evidence of later centuries. Japanese archaeologists have unearthed buried caches containing tens of thousands of coins from the medieval period. Often buried in vases or other porcelain containers, these coins, referred to by scholars as *bichikusen*, have been uncovered as far north as Hokkaido and as far south as Kyushu. The earliest examples date to the mid-thirteenth century, but the types of cash included — primarily Northern Song coins — are consistent with the types known to have been brought to Japan in the twelfth century. However, the volume of currency importation is best suggested by the large number of coins found on a merchant ship that sank off the coast of Korea in the late Kamakura period. The ship, believed to have been heading to Hakata from the Chinese port of Ningbo, contained various porcelains, red sandalwood, silver vases, lacquerware, and more than eighteen tons of copper cash — over eight million coins.[81] If twelfth-century ships brought over even half as much currency — and that seems reasonable, given that coins also served as ballast — then we can safely assume that the amount of cash in circulation must have increased rather quickly.

As for documentary evidence, thirteenth-century writings highlight the role that elites eventually came to play in bringing coins to Japan. An entry in the diary *Minkeiki* reveals that the Kamakura courtier Saionji Kintsune sponsored ships that brought 100,000 strings of cash to Japan in the 1240s, and Hōjō Tokimune, who later became shogunal regent, is reported to

81. Tokyo kokuritsu kakubutsukan et al., *Shin'an kaitei hikiage bunbutsu*, 81–83, and Suzuki, *Shutsudo senka no kenkyū*, 64. This boat is also discussed in Tōno, *Kahei no Nihonshi*, 77–78. Wooden tablets (*mokkan*) found on board date the ship to 1323, though some Chinese scholars suggest it may have sunk as late as the 1350s. Whether or not similar levels of coin importation took place in the late twelfth century, of course, is impossible to tell.

have sent an envoy to China in the 1260s to purchase Chinese coins with gold.[82] Of course, records of these individuals' actions survive precisely because they held prominent positions in government. The boat captains, sailors, merchants, and market managers, who were just as integral to the importation and spread of coins, have not left behind comparable accounts of their activities. And while politically powerful figures such as the Saionji and the Hōjō may have become actively involved with coins in the thirteenth century, such was not the case for the twelfth century. Copper currency met with fierce resistance from the Heian nobility as it reemerged in Japan.

In order to understand this twelfth-century elite opposition to imported cash, let us look at the text *Gyokuyō* to see how the nobles regarded money. *Gyokuyō* was the diary of Kujō Kanezane. Kanezane had connections to the most prestigious noble families. In addition, he built strong ties to Minamoto no Yoritomo and the newly established Kamakura *bakufu*. In part due to Yoritomo's support, Kanezane became regent (*sesshō*) and later chancellor (*kanpaku*), but he lost high office when he fell out of Yoritomo's favor in 1196. His diary, which spans the years 1164 to 1203, offers readers a first-hand account of important events such as the rise and fall of the Taira and early court-*bakufu* relations. *Gyokuyō* also presents an insider's perspective on the debates of late twelfth-century elite lawmakers, and it is to those debates on money that we now turn.

The first detailed discussion in *Gyokuyō* of Chinese coins comes in the year 1179. In the excerpt below, from the 7th month 27th day of that year, Kanezane listens to the opinion of a top advisor, Kebiishichō official Nakahara Motohiro, and provides his own thoughts on the status of Chinese coins in Japan:

Motohiro spoke with me about transactions using coins, stating "Recently, it is reported that coins from the land of the Tang come into

---

82. *Minkeiki*, Ninji 3 (1242) 7th month 4th day; this is discussed in Ōyama, *Kamakura Bakufu*, 379–80. The reference to Tokimune appears in Delmer Brown, *Money Economy in Medieval Japan*, 11.

our court and are used greedily in buying and selling. The private minting of coins (i.e., counterfeiting) is one of the eight severe crimes under the *ritsuryō* legal codes. Although the coins currently being imported are not counterfeit, using them is the same as using counterfeit coins. Truly the use of these coins should be banned. Although the Chamberlain has issued letters of instruction to this effect in the past, the ban has not been carried out. There is no justification for this!"

I agree with Motohiro's opinion. Reviewing price laws of years past—those of the Tenryaku [947-957], Ōwa [961-964], Kanna [985-987], and Enkyū [1069-1074] eras (during the Chōkan [1163-1165] era we started to compose a price law to cover these matters but it was never finished)—among these, the price law of the Enkyū era is the most detailed and is best suited to serve as a guide for these times.

We summoned a market official and asked about the law of selling in the marketplace. According to the official, under the law of the market, the seller aims for a high price and the buyer seeks a low price. Then they negotiate and reach an agreement. This is known as the law of the market.[83]

This entry reveals much about the state of the nobles' thinking about coinage, including the fact that cash had been a major topic of debate at least since the mid-1160s, as seen by the reference to the unfinished Chōkan price law.

Of particular interest is Motohiro's claim that the imported coins should be banned because they are the equivalent of counterfeit money. Although Motohiro recognizes that the coins in question are the legal product of a state mint, the state in this case is a foreign power (Song China).[84] Therefore the coins were seen as a threat to Japanese imperial political authority. In most of premodern East Asia, the right to mint and set the value of currency was an imperial prerogative and a way of asserting kingly authority. Richard von Glahn describes this thinking as follows: "In China, as elsewhere, the authority

---

83. *Gyokuyō*, Jishō 3 (1179) 7th month 27th day.

84. Although Motohiro refers to the coins as coming from the land of the Tang, this is merely a conventional way of referring to China. Motohiro would have been well aware of the current Chinese dynasty.

to issue money remained a closely-guarded sovereign privilege. The state exercised greater direct control over money than over virtually any other facet of the economy."[85] This high regard for money led the rival Chinese kingdoms of the tenth century to each issue their own currencies as part of their efforts to assert sovereign independence. It also influenced thinking on money in Japan, as seen in the Japanese decision to mint coins based on Chinese models. For the nobles of the Heian court, coins produced by a foreign power were the same as coins minted by domestic counterfeiters—in either case, the minter did not hold the right to produce coins for the Japanese realm and was seen as challenging the authority of the Japanese leadership. Kanezane and Motohiro viewed this matter as a political issue rather than an economic one.

Later debates in *Gyokuyō* over the fate of coinage seem to confirm this interpretation. For example, Chinese coins were the topic of a *sengi*, the highest administrative meeting of nobles, during the third month of 1192. Kanezane recorded the discussion in *Gyokuyō* as follows:

Next, there was a *sengi* to determine whether or not to prohibit the use of currency. Although a final decision was not written out, the nobles were of one mind in declaring that coins should be banned. Only the Palace Minister spoke up to advocate a different course of action, arguing "It is inexcusable that the imperial police have not enforced the price laws! First, we should order them to carry out the previous edicts that already address this problem. Only if this matter falls outside the existing laws would I then agree that we should forbid the use of coins." The Minister of the Left replied, saying "Coins should be banned, but if we do not issue a new edict that includes a price law, then in the end, the problems will not stop with a halt in the use of coins. The merchants will use other goods as money and their law-breaking will go unpunished, which would be terrible."[86]

---

85. Von Glahn, *Fountain of Fortune*, 1, 24–26.
86. *Gyokuyō*, Kenkyū 3 (1192) 10th month 1st day.

This excerpt presents a fascinating perspective on issues of money, authority, and elite opposition to coin use in late twelfth-century Japan. First of all, the entry indicates that the nobles were united in their opposition to Chinese cash. Not a single high official saw any advantage to defending copper currency, suggesting that elites had little personal investment in the importation or use of cash. Second, the *Gyokuyō* passage shows that the nobles were confident that their legislative proclamations could solve the problem. If they issued the appropriate commands, and the imperial police did their job, then all would be made proper. The nobles never questioned whether or not the police could actually enforce their commands or whether there were economic factors that would have made banning coins difficult or perhaps even impossible.

Third and most important, the entry reveals that the officials' primary concern was for maintaining their political authority. Only one voice—that of the Palace Minister—was raised in opposition to the proposal to ban coins. He did not speak up to challenge the intent of the proposal, instead arguing that previous orders regarding coins should be enforced before new legislation was issued. Rather than pass another law he insisted the police be made to fulfill their duties. The Minister of the Left shared the Palace Minister's concern over the court's political authority, though he felt that a new proclamation was needed immediately. His more practical approach held that new edicts containing price laws were necessary even if they replicated earlier laws because the merchants' disregard for the law must be stopped. The aim of both the Palace Minister and the Minister of the Left was to ensure that different groups (the police and the merchants) followed the will of the court.

The elite opposition to coins might also be explained as a reaction to problems of inflation. According to this view, the large influx of imported coins increased the money supply (in the same way that counterfeit coins would), which in turn reduced the value of coins and caused higher prices (inflation). Economist Kozo Yamamura favors this interpretation, emphasizing the importance of inflation and dismissing the nobles' concern over the foreign nature of the coins.[87] Certainly it is logical to conclude that there was inflation at this time, for prices should have risen as the volume of coins in circulation and the frequency with which they were used increased.[88] Yet it is difficult to accept that inflation was the primary motivation behind the nobility's opposition to coins. First of all, it is very unlikely that the nobles were directly cognizant of a rise in prices. Their high status isolated them from everyday concerns such as the cost of goods in the market. As the 1179 passage reveals, the nobles' understanding of the market was quite poor; Kanezane finds even a simple explanation of bargaining to be newsworthy enough to record in his diary. Second, we must consider the other points that are described as problematic by Motohiro and Kanezane, such as that previous letters of instruction issued by the court were not heeded, and that the coins are symbols of a foreign state power. These reflect concern over political authority, not rising prices, and lead me to conclude that the motivation for the ban on Chinese coins lay in protecting the imperial right to mint coinage and set its value.

The nobles' concerns, seen in these *Gyokuyō* entries, eventually led to action. According to an 1193 entry in the legal compendium *Hossō shiyōshō*, a price law making coins illegal was promulgated in the eighth month of 1192. Yet the use of coins continued unabated, for the same entry notes that "of its own accord, the exchange of coins has not stopped. How can this

---

87. According to Yamamura, the late twelfth-century court justified banning coins by citing "such inconsistent facts as that imported coins were no more legal than the prohibited, privately minted coins and that the use of coins caused undesirable price fluctuations." Yamamura, "The Growth of Commerce," 359.

88. The classic economic formula to describe inflation is $M \times V = P \times G$, where M represents the quantity of money, V is the velocity with which money circulates in the economy, P stands for the prices of goods, and G represents the gross domestic product. During the twelfth century in Japan, M increased as coins were added to the economy, and V increased as those coins were used more frequently. Thus, P (prices) presumably also increased to keep the equation in equilibrium.

be since a price law has been fixed in the marketplace?"[89] The same entry notes that the ban was reissued in 1193, but repeated court efforts at regulating the use of copper cash would continue to fail. Coins largely replaced cloth and silk as a major unit of exchange by the early thirteenth century, and went on to supplant rice within the next hundred years.[90] As will be discussed in the chapters to follow, the Kamakura *bakufu* came to approve of coin use, and even those living and working on estates eventually came to own Chinese cash.

There were numerous incentives for those who were not Kyoto high elites to use imported coins. Cash presented obvious advantages over silk, cloth, and even rice. Unlike those alternative currencies, coins did not spoil and could be transported without concern for the weather. Coins also had the advantage of being of relatively even quality; even when the government attempted to declare some coins to be worth more than others, people appear to have used coins as if they were of uniform value. Surely these were important factors that led individuals to import and use coins. Yet these advantages are always present when comparing metal currency to agricultural goods for use as money. Why did coins become so popular in the late twelfth century?

To begin with, the twelfth century represented a special moment for the Japanese in that there was a ready supply of Chinese cash available due to the massive scale of Northern Song minting. In fact the vast majority of coins found in Japan—approximately 85 percent of those unearthed and at-

---

89. *Hossō shiyōshō*, Kenkyū 4 (1193) 7th month 4th day.

90. In a widely cited study, Tamaizumi Tairyō looked at land-sale deeds over the course of the Kamakura period. He found a significant shift from the use of rice to the use of coins as follows (*Muromachi jidai no denso*, 143):

Years	Rice (percent)	Coins (percent)
1186–1219	60.3	39.7
1220–1283	30.1	69.9
1284–1333	15.8	84.2

tributed to the medieval period—are Northern Song issues.[91] Even after acknowledging that only a fraction of the total Song coin production made it to Japan, the supply of coins was far superior to what the Japanese court had been able to produce in earlier centuries. But if the timing of China's boom in money production set the stage for the widespread adoption of coins in Japan, then the collapse of the Northern Song dynasty in the 1120s opened the curtain. The Southern Song was unable to produce massive amounts of coinage because most of the mines were in north China. Instead, they turned to other forms of currency, including convertible paper money. This alleviated some of the demand for copper cash and made it easier to export coins.

Merchants could potentially reap large profits from trade in copper coins. Yamamura and Kamiki have thoroughly analyzed the relative values of gold, silver, and copper in China and Japan during Japan's medieval period and concluded that the value of gold to copper was significantly higher in China than in Japan. According to their findings, one *ryō* of gold in China was worth five to six times as many copper coins as the same amount of gold in Japan during the twelfth and thirteenth centuries.[92] This meant that someone from the Japanese islands could obtain more copper coins in China than in Japan for the same amount of gold. It also meant that the Chinese had reason to sell coins, since the gold they could get from the Japanese was worth more in their markets. While merchant records from the twelfth century have not survived, it is known for later centuries that merchants could indeed reap large profits from the importation of coins from China.[93]

---

91. Yamamura and Kamiki assembled a table combining the analyses of unearthed coins performed by Irita Seizo and Kobata Atushi, concluding that 85 percent of Chinese copper coins found in Japan were from the Northern Song. Yamamura and Kamiki, "Silver Mines and Sung Coins," 338.

92. Yamamura and Kamiki, "Silver Mines and Sung Coins," 343.

93. An excellent discussion of imported coins and goods in Muromachi-period Japan can be found in Wakita, "Bukka yori mita Nichi-Min bōeki."

Yet if a large supply of money could prove so profitable, why did late Heian elites not consider minting their own coins? One reason, of course, was the continuing problem of an inadequate supply of copper. New sources of copper ore were not found until the late medieval period.[94] Another common explanation is that the twelfth-century court lacked the state power necessary to back its own currency. As mentioned above, though, the court remained quite confident in its own authority; it is unlikely that members of the court would have thought that they lacked the necessary power to produce coins. A third theory holds that the court abandoned minting because, without any major wars or construction projects during the latter half of the Heian period, it had no need to raise funds via coin production. This seems, however, a problematic assumption at best. One need only consider the many fires that led to major rebuilding projects during the regency of Fujiwara no Michinaga or the three years of violence and devastation wrought by Taira no Tadatsune's rebellion (1028–1031) to realize that the Heian court wrestled with both costly building projects and destructive wars.[95]

Rather than look to the court's weaknesses as a way to explain its decision not to mint coins, we must look for the incentives that led the court to act as it did. The times were difficult for courtiers faced with the upstart *bakufu* and its Taira forerunners, so political pressures for conservatism and stability likely outweighed other pressures to change. The nobles had little direct involvement in or concern for the details of trade. They were still receiving most of the income due from their estates at this time, and so felt little economic concern. However, having overcome a challenge to their political au-

---

94. In fact, by the fifteenth century, the Japanese were exporting raw copper to Ming China in exchange for copper coins. Von Glahn, *Fountain of Fortune*, 90–91; Yamamura and Kamiki, "Silver Mines and Sung Coins," 358.

95. Tadatsune's rebellion left the provinces of Awa, Kazusa, and Shimōsa on the verge of famine. Governors of those provinces claimed to be unable to meet provincial tax obligations for years afterward. Friday, "Lordship Interdicted," 347–48.

thority from Taira no Kiyomori in the 1170s and early 1180s, the nobles faced a new threat in the form of the Kamakura *bakufu*.[96] Consequently, it was more important to members of the nobility to assert their political authority than it was to ensure that the exchange value of goods listed in court price laws was tied to the actual value of goods in the marketplace. Nobles repeatedly insisted upon an idealized exchange rate of 1 *koku* of rice to 1 *kanmon* of copper coins, despite the fact that actual values of both rice and coins varied tremendously over the course of a year. It is well known that the price of rice was high in the months leading up to harvest season and then fell after the harvest was brought in. Furthermore, it was not uncommon for droughts, floods, or other natural disasters to result in poor harvests that drove prices higher and diminished the purchasing power of metallic currency. Finally, coins' buying power must have also fluctuated with their availability, particularly in the twelfth century when Chinese coins were first being introduced to Japan and not yet available in every region. In the midst of such conditions, merchants would have suffered great financial losses if they had followed the court's idealized rate of 1 *koku* to 1 *kanmon*. Thus, court price laws were ineffective as economic policy.

Given all of the factors described above, it made economic sense to import coins even if government figures opposed such moves. Importers were greatly aided by the willingness of merchants and lower-ranking officials on both sides of the Japan-China trade to break the law for the sake of profit. As mentioned above, Chinese traders and port officials readily turned a blind eye to the export of their country's currency, despite Song government efforts to prevent the loss of coin. On the Japan side, it has already been noted that the Kebiishi-

---

96. Kiyomori rose to a position of great prominence in the court, becoming prime minister and having his grandson made emperor. Not only did the nobles associate him with foreign trade and the use of Chinese copper coins, but they also saw him as a threat to their authority. See Hurst, "Insei," 632–37; also Mass, *Yoritomo and the Founding of the First Bakufu*, 17–23.

chō proved ineffective in carrying out the court's regulation of money. Time and again, Japanese nobles cited the failure of the Kebiishichō to enforce price laws and coin regulations as hindering court efforts at restoring propriety to the market-place.

In some instances, Kebiishichō agents were the cause of the problem rather than merely an ineffective part of the solution. At such times, they not only failed to enforce the ban on coins but instead promoted coin use in the marketplace. Consider the case of the Ōtsu Shrine–affiliated merchant Rishō, who was imprisoned by marketplace officials of the imperial police in 1200.[97] It seems that these Kebiishichō officials sought to use coins to purchase some of Rishō's goods, but Rishō refused to accept the copper currency because it was illegal. The Kebiishichō officials insisted, claiming that the ban on coins did not apply to them, and when Rishō continued to refuse, they forcibly took his goods and imprisoned him. Rishō's shrine had to appeal to Enryakuji, one of the most powerful Buddhist institutions, which in turn protested to the imperial court in order to secure his release. As a result of the suit, the superintendent (*bettō*) of the Kebiishichō, Fujiwara no Kimitsugu, was relieved of his post, while the top market official, Fujiwara no Yoshimune, and seven of his subordinates were exiled.[98] In this case the guilty Kebiishichō agents were brought to justice, but it seems reasonable to assume that merchants did not always resist market agents so vigorously and that abuses of this type were not uncommon. Evidently cash held such a potential for profit that some of the court's own anti-coin enforcement agents were willing to risk severe punishment for the chance to use coins in the marketplace.

---

97. The event is described in the entries from Shōji 2 (1200) 5th month 24th day to the same year 6th month 25th day in *Katei yōryaku, Kugyō bunin,* and *Hyakurenshō.*

98. Fujiwara no Yoshimune was exiled to Oki Island and his seven underlings were sent to "Emishi Island" (present-day Hokkaido).

Conclusion

By the early thirteenth century, Chinese cash had attained a secure foothold in the Japanese economy. Over the next several decades, it would displace silk and cloth as a primary means of payment and exchange. By the end of the Kamakura period, transactions formerly carried out in rice would also come to be carried out more and more frequently in terms of coin. (This process, known as *daisennō*, will be discussed in Chapter 4). The means by which coins achieved this status reveal much about changes in late Heian and Kamakura society.

First of all, the importation of Chinese coins in the late twelfth and thirteenth centuries represented a new trend in the Japan-China trade. In earlier times, traders brought goods to Japan: primarily luxury items such as art, incense, or medicines intended for elite consumption. But coins were not luxury items. They functioned less as pure commodities and more as a medium of exchange or store of wealth. In other words, most people used cash to facilitate transactions and obtain other goods—at least those are the most common recorded references to their use. With the exception of a few instances in which coins were melted down for their copper content, imported cash was valued for its monetary characteristics: fungibility, limited availability, transportability, and more. As its value rose, the relative importance of other Chinese goods fell. Limits in Japanese shipbuilding technology meant that most of the coins to enter Japan in the twelfth and early thirteenth centuries must have been brought to the archipelago on Chinese or Korean vessels, but at some point in the second half of the thirteenth century, Japanese seafaring vessels improved enough to allow Japanese merchants to bring coins directly to Japan themselves.

Second, there was a shift in the relationship between the government and money. Nara and early Heian coins were produced by elites and sponsored by the government. Officials of the highest rank determined their value, albeit with limited success. Late Heian and early Kamakura coins, however, circulated quite independently of the central government and elite officials, with the possible exception of Taira no Kiyomori. Those coins were produced overseas and defied efforts by the Japanese court to fix their value. Members of the nobility, who primarily saw coins as an extension of their political authority, found themselves increasingly unable to exert any effective influence on the emerging medieval economy.

Finally, coins played a key role in the creation of the new medieval economy by facilitating exchange between elites and non-elites outside of the confines of government taxation and the *shōen* system. For merchants and traders, coins could be obtained cheaply in China and imported for significant profit. For those selling goods or agricultural products in local and regional markets, the relatively uniform quality and long-term stability of coins made them more desirable than rice or silk. Although some scholars have emphasized the "charm-like" appeal of coins or the power of the Chinese government as a backer of currency, it would be a mistake to ignore the obvious advantages that coins held over other commodities that might be used as money.[99]

Thus it was a combination of factors—quality, technology, availability, government intransigence, and more—that led to the reemergence of copper cash in twelfth-century Japan. The influx of coins began as a trickle sometime before 1150 and had grown to a rivulet by 1200. Although the overall volume of late twelfth-century coin use was still small, nobles found it impossible to dam the stream. During the second half of the thirteenth century, the influx grew to a raging torrent pouring into Japan as coins replaced first cloth and later rice as the primary medium of exchange. In the next chapter, we explore the most important site for monetary exchange, the market, and analyze the social and economic factors that contributed to the spread of metallic currency in early medieval Japan.

---

99. Amino Yoshihiko has written about coins serving as magical charms, and Adachi Keiji argues that Chinese state backing was key to the success and stability of copper coins in medieval Japan. Amino, *Rethinking Japanese History*; Adachi, "Chūgoku kara mita Nihon kaheishi."

TWO

Making Change:
The Spread of Money and Markets

Jōen, a Tōji priest writing in 1269, sympathized with the plight of the peasants on Tara estate. Earlier that year the warrior appointed to the estate, Wakasa Tadakiyo, had demanded that the peasants supply him with charcoal, rice bran, vegetables, fodder for his horses, and other items during his upcoming term of guard duty in the capital. The peasants filed a complaint with Jōen, the central administrator for the estate, objecting to the large sum of money that Tadakiyo was demanding of them. For after each item on the list of goods that the warrior expected the peasants to provide him with, in smaller writing, was a monetary figure. These items included:

Horse fodder	100 coins worth
Rice bran	40 coins worth
Firewood	50 coins worth [1]

Although it might appear that Tadakiyo was expecting to receive actual goods, in fact he was using his upcoming term of guard duty as an excuse to tax the peasants for cash. Com-

---

1. These figures represented taxes to be levied per *tan*, a unit of land. Prior to Toyotomi Hideyoshi's land survey of the late sixteenth century, one *tan* was roughly 1,200 square meters, but varied from region to region.

menting on the complaint, Jōen took pity on the peasants and found in their favor. "Taxing them in hard-to-come-by cash," Jōen wrote, "will lead to the impoverishment of the peasants. It is an unacceptable condition."[2]

Jōen evidently believed that cash would be particularly difficult for the estate residents to obtain, but by the time of this incident, the Tara peasants had probably already encountered coins. With an active market nearby and merchant boats linking Tara to several other estates and ports along the Japan Sea coast, Chinese currency would not have been unfamiliar. Nor was Tara estate unique in this regard. Over the course of the thirteenth century, money and markets spread from the capital across the provinces and came to be used by people from many walks of life. Estate managers sold agricultural surplus—and sometimes even the tax goods they owed to central elites—in markets for cash. Warriors demanded coin payments from farming communities and struggled with proprietors to control the marketplace. Religious professionals served as market agents and collected monetary donations from people in the countryside. The nobles' opposition to the use of cash, described in the previous chapter, had little effect in stopping its circulation. By the early fourteenth century, money and markets became common, if not yet everyday, parts of life.

This chapter explores how money and markets spread through provincial Japan in the Kamakura period. Although it is tempting to speak of a "money economy" at this time, one must be careful not to overstate the case. Only in the Edo period did monetization and commercialization penetrate to every corner of society. As noted in the Introduction, the overall level of monetization in Kamakura was never as extensive as it became in Edo, nor were the means by which money earned acceptance identical. For while Edo monetization can

---

2. The list of what Tadakiyo demanded from the peasants, their petition to the Tōji, and Jōen's response can all be found in *KI*, docs. 10432, 10443, and 10476, respectively.

be attributed to urbanization, travel (particularly of the large official daimyo embassies of the *sankin kōtai* system), and the Tokugawa peace (which allowed commerce to prosper), none of these factors was present in the Kamakura period.[3] Precisely because of such differences, though, early medieval economic history presents an interesting contrast with the early modern. The spread of money and markets in this earlier period suggests the possibility that medieval commercial activities laid the groundwork for—and thereby contributed to—the more complete commercialization that took place in the Edo period. In addition, analysis of these phenomena offers another glimpse into how economic growth and the demand for cash undermined traditional authority and forced changes in the structures of elite rule.

The first two sections of this chapter provide a history of the market from the eighth through the fourteenth centuries. After the official market system collapsed in the Heian period, urban elites turned to private tribute for the distribution of goods while everyone else relied on merchants, trade, and local markets. By the early medieval period, these local markets became the most important sites for the use of cash in the countryside. The third section explores why provincial land managers and even, to a limited extent, peasants came to use coins in the Kamakura period. It analyzes the roles played by merchants, warriors, religious institutions, and provincial community members themselves in promoting rural monetization. In the fourth section, I turn to the response of government authorities, focusing on Kamakura *bakufu* economic policy. Together, the sections of this chapter demonstrate that money and markets became commonplace as much due to the actions of middle-level figures such as estate managers, provincial warriors, and traveling merchants as they did to elites such as *bakufu* officials and estate proprietors.

---

3. Thomas Smith attributed the rise of the rural commercial economy in the early Edo period to peace, improved transportation, and the rise of castle towns (i.e., urbanization). Smith, *Agrarian Origins*, 67.

The Market in Ancient Japan

During the Nara and early Heian periods, market exchange appears to have been tightly controlled by central officials with only limited opportunities for buying and selling outside of designated districts. Provincial capitals sometimes became sites of exchange as well, though under the control of officials appointed by the court bureaucracy. Drawing upon Yoshida Takashi's work, William Wayne Farris contends that since most trade items were tax goods and transport required government assistance, government officials were the most important merchants of the Nara period. He calls attention to evidence of regional trade but concedes that it was less important than what took place in the central Kinai region, the most economically advanced part of the country and the location of Japan's early capitals.[4] The primary structure for economic exchange, at least as reflected in documentary sources, was the payment of taxes and tribute from the provinces. The early Japanese state designed this system to funnel goods into its cities and major shrines and temples, where central elites lived as consumers.

In the capital, elites and elite institutions could exchange goods and see to their redistribution by means of official markets. Just as the imperial court had minted copper-alloy coins as part of its attempt to remake itself on the model of Tang China (described in the previous chapter), so too the court mimicked the capital of Chang'an by incorporating official markets into its urban centers. Chang'an, which may have been the most populous city in the world at the time, had two major markets, each taking up nine city blocks and having access to canals that linked them to the Wei River in order to facilitate the movement of goods.[5] Just as in earlier Chinese

----

4. See Farris, "Trade, Money, and Merchants," 309, 322. Farris also notes some unofficial market activity, such as a reference in the *Izumo fudoki* to a daily market near a popular hot spring, but the lack of surviving documents makes it difficult to say much more about those markets. As he concludes, "Evidence of private commercial activity continues to be sparse," 322.

5. Xiong, *Sui-Tang Chang'an*, 165–69.

capitals, the markets were situated in parallel east and west locations.

The first such Chinese-style capital in Japan was built at Fujiwara by Empress Jitō in the 690s. Fujiwara included eastern and western markets, though on a much smaller scale than those found in Chang'an. Markets were an essential part of later Japanese capitals as well, appearing in Heijō-kyō (modern Nara) as well as the two short-lived capitals of Kuni-kyō and Nagaoka-kyō. The concerns of merchants appear to have been considered in planning these capitals. For example, although little is known about Kuni-kyō, which became the capital in 740, merchants reportedly favored its location on the Kizu River because of the ease of transporting goods. Perhaps due to their influence, the city's markets were completed before Kuni-kyō was abandoned in 744.[6] When the court moved to Heian-kyō (modern Kyoto) in 794, the east and west markets followed in the seventh month of that year.[7] As was the case in China, the official markets were strictly regulated. Each market area was enclosed, with access restricted and supervisors in place to monitor the quality and prices of the goods sold as well as check weights and measures.[8] Regulations stipulated that merchants could not offer their wares before noon or after sunset, and each market was only open for half of the month. In addition, there were restrictions on the types of goods that could be sold at each market, with only a few essential items such as oil and rice available at both. Other regulations, such as a ban against women and men selling goods from the same stall and a requirement that written signs precisely indicate what goods were available for purchase, are found in ninth-

---

6. Piggott, *Emergence of Japanese Kingship*, 254–55. However, merchants' desires to keep the capital at Kuni-kyō were ignored when Emperor Shōmu moved again in 744. Farris, "Trade, Money, and Merchants," 321.

7. *Nihon kiryaku*, Enryaku 13 (794) 7th month.

8. Farris provides a detailed breakdown of market officials for the Nara period; "Trade, Money and Merchants," 304–5. See also McCullough, "The Capital and Its Society," 161–69.

and tenth- century sources and therefore may have been new rules created to address specific problems.[9]

In spite of the attention that government officials were supposed to have paid to their markets, the system soon ran into problems. The Heian western market in particular failed to attract many buyers and sellers, most likely because of its location in the less favored half of the city. Following the Chinese model for capital cities, Kyoto had been designed with symmetrical eastern and western halves laid out in a grid-like pattern. But from the time of its founding, the western half suffered from poor drainage and never attracted as many residents. It soon came to be thought of as a much less desirable place to live. In 835, officials tried to bolster the western market by awarding it some of the goods formerly approved for sale only in the eastern market, but the complaints of eastern market officials led to policy reversals and the western market continued to decline. Location was not the only issue, however, for the eastern market did not fare much better. As the *ritsuryō* state began to pull back from the close regulation of its early days, and as nobles began utilizing alternative means of supplying goods for their households, the official markets began to wither.

Of course, this did not leave the city without any means of providing for itself. The most prominent noble and religious houses relied upon private supplies of tax goods from their provincial estates. It is important to recognize that estates did not merely provide rice. In fact they supplied a wide spectrum of items, such as silk, cotton, oil, paper, fish, chestnuts, vegetables, and more. Consider, for example, the list of goods that the Hōshōgon'in, a small temple located within the Tōji temple complex, received from the estates for which it served as pa-

---

9. The eastern market was open the first fifteen days of the month and its counterpart for the last fifteen days of the month. Complete lists of the 51 items authorized for sale in the eastern market and the 33 items approved for sale in the western market can be found in Mori, "Sōdōsen ryūtsū e no kiban," 20–21. Later sources include *Ryō no gige* (especially vol. 9), issued in the 830s, and the *Engishiki* (especially vol. 42), issued in the 960s.

tron: rice, oil, straw mats (*komo*), incense, pounded rice cakes (*mochi*), silk, cotton, other types of cloth, and laborers.[10] Patrons and proprietors took advantage of the natural endowments of their estates, collecting iron and lacquer from mountain-based estates such as Niimi and Ōyama while requiring sea salt and fish from coastal estates like Yugenoshima and Tara.[11] However, as varied as these estate-provided supplies may have been, they were insufficient to provide for all of each proprietor's needs. Some form of barter or trade was still necessary to allow most residents in the capital to obtain a desirable mix of goods.

As activity at the official markets dwindled, shops began to spring up in areas outside of the official market districts. At first these sellers sought and received special permission from market authorities, but by the tenth century, officials were apparently in such disarray that approval was no longer needed.[12] Including these unofficial businesses, the total market area of the city grew to more than three times what it had been when Heian-kyō was founded in 794. There were half-hearted attempts at restoring the official markets as late as the twelfth century, but these failed, and the areas around Third and Fourth Avenues became major business districts.[13] Streets associated with specific commodities took on descriptive names such as Oil Lane (Abura no kōji) or Brocade Street (Nishiki kōji).

---

10. *Tōji hyakugo monjo*, "re" box, doc. 1-1, Heiji 1 (1159) intercalary fifth month, in *Okayama kenshi*, vol. 20, doc. 108, pp. 139–40.

11. For more on the varied output of early medieval estates, see Sasaki, *Shōen no shōgyō*, and Amino, *Chūsei saikō*. Katsuyama describes the Heian and early medieval tribute system in a more recent work, *Chūsei nengusei seiritsushi*. The most vocal advocate for revising the view that medieval Japan's economy was centered on rice has been Amino; in English, see his "Commerce and Finance in the Middle Ages."

12. Mori, "Sōdōsen ryūtsū e no kiban," 21; McCullough, "The Capital and Its Society," 168.

13. Fujiwara no Sadanaga, in his work *Jakuren hosshishū*, describes one such failed effort at restoring the official markets that was attempted in the late 1180s by the superintendent of the imperial police, Fujiwara no Takafusa.

Around the same time, merchants based in the capital began acquiring continental goods from Chinese traders to sell
as luxury items in the city while others traveled into the countryside to supply and purchase from regional markets. These
merchants were bridging figures linking the more economically developed urban centers with rural estates. Some had
connections to elite institutions, but they used those connections to facilitate forms of trade that operated outside of the
traditional tax and tribute systems. The prosperous merchant,
as described in the mid-eleventh-century text *Shin sarugakuki*,
traded in both foreign and domestic goods, including perfumes, medicines, animal hides, brocades, betel nuts, dyes,
and much more. His travels took him all over Japan, from the
northeast to the southern islands, and kept him away from
home for most of the year.[14] By the end of the Heian period,
merchants of the type parodied in the *Shin sarugakuki* were
making stops at the periodic estate-based markets that had
begun to spring up around the countryside.

Although the author of *Shin sarugakuki* describes a male merchant, women were important players in trade and commerce
as well. They were involved in continental trade, as is shown
by a Song reference to male and female Japanese merchants
in 1145.[15] For the Kamakura period, documentary evidence reveals that women headed trade guilds in Kyoto and ran whole-
saler operations involving the shipment of goods such as "dye
ash" (*kōnohai*).[16] Illustrated materials depict women in a variety of trades, especially those connected with textiles. Four
different *shokunin uta awase* – illustrated scrolls of poems with
matching depictions of the people who supposedly created

---

14. Summary based on an excerpt from *Shin sarugakuki*, as translated by
and quoted in Batten, *To the Ends of Japan*, 193. Although the *Shin sarugakuki*
is a fictional text, it is believed that the characters described therein are com-
posites of real Heian individuals and that the text provides reliable (even if
exaggerated) insight into Heian lifestyles.

15. The reference to male and female merchants comes from *Jianyan yilai
xinian yaolu* and is discussed briefly in Chapter 1.

16. Wakita, "Chūsei josei no yakuwari buntan," 113.

the poems—survive from the medieval period. They show women engaged in everything from the selling of firewood and silk floss to weaving and brewing sake.[17] Although the scrolls were not actually created by the working-class people depicted in the illustrations, they still offer insight into the prominent roles women held in trade and commerce. Even nunneries became involved with the market, producing prepared or semi-prepared foodstuffs such as *sōmen* and *udon* for consumption by the commoners of Kyoto.[18] And, as can be seen in the thirteenth-century Fukuoka market scene of Ippen's scroll (described below), women were active in the newly emerging local markets.

Medieval Markets

These new markets developed slowly, meeting infrequently at first. Many began by meeting only once or twice per month, in keeping with the limited demand of the economically undeveloped countryside. By the late twelfth century, *sansai-ichi* markets that met three times per month began to appear in a few places. Often the meeting days followed a pattern, such as *yokka-ichi*, which met on days that ended in fours (that is, the 4th, 14th, and 24th). The earliest documentary reference to such markets is from the year 1142, referring to a "days ending in nine" market on the north bank of the Aeba River in Ōmi province. Other examples include Yano estate's Naha market, which met on the 1st, 11th, and 21st, and the *yōka-ichi* market in eastern Ōmi province, which met on days ending in eights. As with the use of copper cash, there was a marked increase in such markets over the course of the thirteenth century. Although Toyoda Takeshi notes that three-times-per-month markets did not become truly widespread until the mid-fourteenth century, *sansai-ichi* developed much earlier in some areas—

---

17. On *shokunin uta awase*, see Tabata, "Women's Work and Status in the Changing Medieval Economy," 101–11.

18. Wakita, "The Medieval Household and Gender Roles," 88.

close to twenty are known to have been operating by the end of the thirteenth century.[19]

These early medieval markets were located near roads or rivers for the easy transportation of goods. The land on which they were erected was usually exempt from annual tribute dues; in some cases, it was land unfit for farming or land that was inhabited by beggars when the market was not in session.[20] The Kusado sengen market and the Niimi estate market, for example, both originated on small islands just off shore (though by the end of the medieval period, land had filled in and connected each island to the mainland). In eastern Japan, the Tomono market was situated near the Hikuma River and the Kamakura kaidō, a major highway. Elite proprietors surely had some influence in the selection of such market sites, but equally if not more important were the needs of those actually engaging in trade. They favored locations that were not already encumbered with tax obligations as well as locations near rivers or the coast that greatly facilitated transportation since it was far easier, quicker, and more efficient to move large loads over water than land.

In the later medieval period, as the volume of commerce increased, markets began meeting more frequently. *Sansai-ichi* became *rokusai-ichi*, markets that met six times per month. Often they would space out the days so that a given market might meet on days ending in threes and eights, or fours and nines. Such markets were not common until the mid-fifteenth century, though some earlier examples can be found, particularly at government seats or urban centers. Kōfukuji, a major temple located in the city of Nara, hosted a north market in

---

19. Toyoda, *Chūsei no shōnin to kōtsū*, 470–72; Yamamura, "The Growth of Commerce," 364.

20. Illustrations of the Niimi estate, including the location of the market, are in Ishii, *Chūsei no mura o aruku*, 46–48. The Kusado sengen market is the focus of a major display at the Hiroshima Prefectural Museum; see http://www.mars.dti.ne.jp/~suzuki-y/index_e.html (accessed January 28, 2011). On the Tomono market, see Ihara, *Chūsei no ikusa, matsuri, totsukuni to kawari*, 40–41.

the mid-Kamakura period, added a south market toward the end of the period, and further added a central market in the early Muromachi period. By the late fourteenth century, one of the markets was open on any given day.[21] Distinct meeting days were sometimes employed to allow competing market interests to use the same space. One such case is Niimi estate, where the proprietor held a "days ending in two" market and the local warrior held a "days ending in three" market.[22] It was in these markets that provincial estate managers and even some peasants began to encounter cash.

Descriptions of Kamakura period provincial markets are rare, but those accounts suggest that the marketplace had a lively, bustling atmosphere. For example, the author of the travelogue *Tōkan kikō*, writing in the mid-twelfth century, described the market near Kayatsu no shuku in Owari province as full of people, arms laden with purchases, and voices crying out, "Today is market day!"[23] Perhaps the most valuable source for trying to picture the early medieval market is the *Ippen shōnin eden* (Illustrated Scroll of the Wandering Priest Ippen). Founder of the Ji sect of Buddhism, Ippen spent much of his life traveling around Japan to popularize his teachings. The scroll, commissioned by Ippen's followers shortly after his death in 1289, tells of his trials, tribulations, and triumphs in propagating his interpretation of Buddhism. In one famous section of the scroll, the climax takes place in a Bizen provincial market. The sequence begins with a shrine priest who comes home to discover that while he was away, his wife met Ippen and was converted to Ippen's faith. Angrily, the priest grabs his sword and sets out to teach Ippen a lesson. He and his servants confront Ippen in the nearby Fukuoka market.

---

21. Toyoda and Sugiyama with Morris, "The Growth of Commerce and the Trades," 134.
22. Nagahara, *Shōen*, 260–61.
23. *Tōkan kikō* in the *Nihon koten zenshū*, vol. 106.

Fig. 4 Detail from the Fukuoka market scene, *Ippen shōnin eden*.
Note the buyers and sellers holding strings of cash in the market stall.
Used by permission of Shōjōkōji Temple.

The accompanying illustration (see Fig. 4) is one of the best surviving images of a medieval marketplace.[24]

As we might expect, the market was located near a river. In the foreground, goods are being unloaded off of two boats while a merchant approaches the marketplace, his back and his horse both laden with wares. Scattered around the market itself are five long stalls (*kariya*), some consisting solely of pillars and a roof, others with one or two walls, but all with open fronts to allow the display of the goods for sale. The shoppers can choose from a wide range of items: birds, fish,

---

24. *Ippen shōnin eden*, 98–99. Because it is one of the few contemporary images of a medieval marketplace, this scroll's illustration of the Fukuoka market was used by designers at NHK, Japan's national public broadcasting organization, when they created a Kamakura-period set for the 2001 broadcast of the historical drama *Hōjō Tokimune*.

rice, cloth and silk, shoes, pottery, masks, and more. It is a scene full of motion, with children running and men and women in a variety of costumes speaking animatedly. In the middle of it all, Ippen faces the angry priest, who is starting to draw his weapon. Yet the other marketgoers, busy in their transactions, take no notice of the violent confrontation about to take place. At the center, in front of a stall where two men are selling footwear, a woman holds out a sample of silk to a prospective buyer, a man holding a string of cash. Farther back and to the right, another cloth seller in a bright-orange kimono appears to be checking the number of coins on a string while a woman seated in front of her examines her purchase. In this marketplace, Chinese cash is the medium of exchange.

The Ippen scroll includes one additional depiction of a marketplace: the Tomono market of Shinano province.[25] At first, the image presents a startling contrast. Unlike Fukuoka, the Tomono market is shown as empty. Off in the distance we can see three figures, balancing boxes on their heads, walking toward the market, but no one is buying or selling anything. The main marketplace features the same type of crude huts that were used as sales booths in the earlier depiction of the Fukuoka market, but the Tomono stalls are nearly deserted. The only living beings aside from Ippen and his companions are a few wild dogs and a beggar, who is preparing to throw a stone at two of the animals that have started to fight with each other. Modern viewers might mistakenly conclude that Tomono was a failed market, but to the contrary, later sources suggest that it was as successful as any other early medieval market. Rather the scene in the Ippen scroll shows a day when the market was not in session, for like other medieval markets, Tomono met only on certain days of the month. When not in session, the space was open for use by others ranging from beggars to itinerant priests.

It is precisely this seemingly open quality that led the historian Amino Yoshihiko to propose that medieval markets were

---

25. *Ippen shōnin eden*, 110–11.

places of "unattachedness" (*muen*).[26] According to Amino, such places (and the people who occupied them) were free from the duties, obligations, and hierarchy that dominated most of medieval Japanese society. He contends that markets were liminal places where ordinary ties could be broken. They were not located at the intersection of roads and rivers solely for the ease of transporting goods, nor were they situated at places that beggars favored merely because such land was available (though surely those factors also played a part). Rather, cash transactions involved cutting the ties between the seller and the thing being sold. Thus, Amino proposes that market locations were special because of their functions as places where attachments were broken. He has made similar contentions about money itself, arguing that a commodity must sever its links with the secular world in order to serve as money.[27]

Amino's observations are quite provocative, but we should not be too hasty in concluding that markets were free from authorities and obligations. Rather than consider markets as places of "unattachedness," it may be more productive to recognize them as sites that competing powers struggled to control. As I show in the remainder of this chapter, there were numerous efforts to control markets and cash. In the provinces, local warriors often strove with other authorities to dominate regional markets. Merchants, sometimes religious affiliates themselves, frequently favored setting up markets near the outer gates of temples in part because they sought to ward off competing authorities. In the city of Kamakura, *bakufu* officials struggled to control urban markets and to develop an effective policy for taxing commercial goods. These groups often had only limited success—and sometimes failed—in their ef-

---

26. Amino, *Muen, kugai, raku.*

27. Amino, "Kyōkai ryōiki to kokka." In English, see his "Commerce and Finance in the Middle Ages" and *Rethinking Japanese History.* Tonomura found the location of the *yōka-ichi* market at the intersection of different territorial units, administrative districts, and agricultural environments to support Amino's argument regarding the liminal nature of the marketplace; Tonomura, *Community and Commerce,* 113-15.

forts to regulate market activity. But, as the next section demonstrates, their efforts to promote and control market activity also helped facilitate the spread of money to the countryside.

Why Switch to Cash?

In general, rising agricultural production is seen as the engine of early medieval economic growth. This increase in agricultural productivity was the result of several new innovations that appeared during these years. Of course, the story is not one of uninterrupted success. Improvements spread gradually, varied by region, and were not always enough to prevent periodic famines, especially in the late Heian and early Kamakura periods.[28] But the long-term trend, especially from the second half of the Kamakura period, was one of improvement. One development was the introduction of new strains of rice imported from the Asian mainland, especially Champa rice, which proved heartier and more resistant to flooding, insects, and disease than traditional Japanese rice. It also tended to mature more quickly, probably facilitating double cropping in later centuries. Another development was the greater use of iron tools and draft animals. Farris, drawing upon a range of documentary and illustrated sources, has shown that these started to become more widely available during the late Heian and early Kamakura periods.[29] Improved irrigation techniques also contributed to the boost in production. Kristina Troost has described late Kamakura and Muromachi period steps such as leveling of the soil, the intermixing of raised and lowered fields for more effective drainage and flood control, and the creation of artificial "saucer ponds" that served as reservoirs, all of which helped those estates to collect a surplus above

---

28. Examples include the Kangi famine of 1229–32 and the Shōka famine of 1257–60. See Farris, *Japan's Medieval Population*, 33–57.

29. Farris, *Japan's Medieval Population*, 72–73. Farris also provides more detailed descriptions of the benefits of Champa rice and other innovations in the same work, 129–48.

what was required for self-sufficiency and tribute taxes.[30] The advent of double cropping, in which the same field was planted twice in the same year, further helped increase agricultural productivity.

References to these types of innovations can be found in documents from the thirteenth century. A land conveyance from 1296, for example, states explicitly that the peasants were harvesting rice in the summer and *mugi* (wheat or barley) in the fall.[31] A Kamakura *bakufu* decree from 1264 also makes direct mention of double cropping. In this case the document is an order to vassals in Bingo and Bizen provinces, calling upon them to stop taxing the second harvest of peasants who double crop.[32] If the laws were followed and second harvests were exempt from taxation, then peasants should have been able to truly enjoy the fruits of their added labors. Yet even in cases where both crops were taxed, two yields meant more food for personal consumption as well as surplus for the market.

Modern historians have, quite correctly, held these kinds of agricultural improvements to be the driving force that powered the medieval economy. Tabata Yasuko wrote, "Medieval Japan saw a marked expansion in commodity circulation and the cash economy (as) people . . . collected or purchased surplus yields, which had been made possible by the increase in agricultural productivity."[33] Kozo Yamamura described the growth of agricultural production as "the foundation on which the commerce of these periods flourished."[34] Troost called attention to an "intensification of agriculture" in the fourteenth century that had a "revolutionary impact on people and social organization,"

---

30. Troost, "Peasants, Elites, and Villages in the Fourteenth Century," 94–95.

31. *KI*, doc. 19099, Einin 4 (1296) 7th month, 21st day.

32. *Kamakura bakufu tsuikahō*, doc. 200, Bun'ei 1 (1264) 4th month, 26th day.

33. Tabata, "Women's Work and Status in the Changing Medieval Economy," 115. See also Yamamura, "Introduction," 3; Totman, *A History of Japan*, 146–48; and Troost, "Peasants, Elites, and Villages in the Fourteenth Century," 91–109.

34. Yamamura, "The Growth of Commerce," 376.

including the expansion of commerce.[35] Farris saw these improvements as heralding the start of significant, steady population growth in the medieval period. Double cropping almost always involved planting a different type of food for the second harvest, either because the first product would not grow out of season or because an alternative type of plant was needed to avoid soil exhaustion. Therefore, as Farris persuasively argues, the increase in food production as well as the greater variety of foods led to noticeable improvements in the physical health and nutrition of commoners.[36] And as these scholars all note in their research, there was a clear link between increased agricultural output and involvement in markets that used cash. The provincial production surplus created opportunities for estates to sell their produce in markets and participate in an expanding commercial economy.

Rural markets were not places of barter, but relied on money to facilitate exchange. As noted earlier, silk, rice, and other commodities all served as money in Japan at different points in time, but in the thirteenth century, the conflation of pressures (direct or indirect) from a number of different groups promoted the use of Chinese coins as the currency of the market. Historical records show that the leading members (*hyakushō* and *myōshu*) of peasant communities from Tara estate in coastal Wakasa province to Ategawa estate in mountainous Kii were using cash in their local markets.[37] But how did the metallic currency of a foreign dynasty come to be so widely used in such transactions? In fact, it was not any one group but rather a variety of constituencies—from merchants to local warriors, religious institutions to village communities—that favored coins and played a part in the monetization of medieval markets.

---

35. Troost, "Peasants, Elites, and Villages in the Fourteenth Century," 91.

36. Farris, *Japan's Medieval Population*, 128–32.

37. As Thomas Conlan notes, early medieval *hyakushō* were provincials of sufficient status to have a surname and serve in local office. *Myōshu* had rights over taxable lands. Both resided in agricultural communities, though they enjoyed higher status than an ordinary peasant who worked in the fields. Conlan, *State of War*, 108–16.

Many of them succeeded because of backing from powerful elite patrons such as Enryakuji, while others were responding to directives issued by the Kamakura *bakufu*. They reveal precisely how urban elites and rural actors all contributed to the increase in monetary use.

MERCHANTS

Traveling merchants played a key role in the economy because of the links they created between the capital and the provinces. Some were based in the city of Heian, but others were estate villagers with special status such as *yoriudo* (freemen who commended their services to religious institutions) or *jinin* (also read *jinnin*). The original *jinin* appear to have been lower employees working at shrines, leading to the rendering of the term in English as "shrine sextons." However, from late Heian times this category broadened to include a much wider range of people with shrine affiliations, including all sorts of craftsmen and merchants.[38] Their connections to powerful religious houses allowed them to move freely across various political borders independent of the regulations of Kamakura or Kyoto appointees. One need only look at the case of the shrine-affiliated merchant Rishō (described in the previous chapter) to see the importance of such connections. When Rishō was wrongly jailed by the imperial police, only his shrine affiliation led a powerful temple like Enryakuji to intervene on his behalf and ultimately secure his release. Other merchants sought and obtained special authorization from the court or the *bakufu* to allow them to pass through tolls without paying fees. For example, the shogun's chancellery issued a *kudashibumi* edict in 1212 granting metalworkers an exemption from market, port, toll, and other fees.[39]

As Kyoto was entirely a city of consumers, merchants were able to realize large profits by supplying produce from the

---

38. Miura Keiichi, "Villages and Trade in Medieval Japan." For more on *jinin*, see Toyoda, *Chūsei no shōnin to kōtsū*, 235–327.

39. *KI*, doc. 1943, Kenryaku 2 (1212) 9th month.

countryside. Of course, in times of difficulty, some were quite critical of merchants for taking advantage of people in need. Fujiwara no Atsumitsu, an official of the early twelfth century, described them in rather negative terms for precisely that reason:

> The great merchants of the capital obtain goods from close by and sell them for three times as much in the distant provinces, or they lend a little in the spring and take in a large profit in the fall. . . . The poor people [in need of food and commodities] cannot endure the merchants' strength. With no other recourse, they run away from their homes or sell their wives and children.[40]

Writing during a time of famine, Atsumitsu was no doubt affected by the frustrations of seeing high food prices and desperate commoners. But these same merchants played an essential role in supplying goods to the city and in bringing cash to provincial communities.

People engaged in long-distance trade had a vested interest in promoting the use of coins, for it was extremely expensive to ship bulk goods overland. Tales from *setsuwa* collections offer evidence that merchants in the mid- to late Heian conducted their transactions using bulk goods. For example, the early twelfth-century compilation *Konjaku monogatarishū* describes a wealthy merchant who, intending to purchase mercury in the provinces, sets out from the capital with one hundred horses loaded with rice and silk to use for payment. Historians Mori Katsumi and William McCullough draw upon such tales to suggest that barter was the primary mode of exchange in the late Heian period.[41] These scholars are correct in noting that rice and silk were often traded for other goods at this time, but they are incorrect in assuming that the ex-

---

40. *Honchō zoku monzui*, Hōen 1 (1135) 7th month 27th day.

41. McCullough, "The Capital and Its Society," 164; Mori, "Sōdōsen ryūtsū e no kiban," 24. Many of the *Konjaku* tales were likely composed decades or even centuries before they were written down, so it is possible that the story in question reflects eleventh-century (or earlier) conditions. On the tales, see Ury, *Tales of Times Now Past*, 1–23.

changes were barter trades. In late Heian society, rice and silk functioned as money. Unlike chestnuts, lacquer, paper, fish, or other items that were primarily intended for consumption, rice and silk were often kept as a means of storing wealth and/or changed hands numerous times as media of exchange. It was also around this time that Chinese coins began to be imported, and tales from some of the same *setsuwa* collections make mention of merchants who became wealthy through trading in coins.[42] The advantages of easier portability and longer durability must have been obvious to merchants on the road.

Although we lack direct proof that merchants tried to persuade those associated with rural markets to accept cash, circumstantial evidence strongly suggests that the use of coins spread from the capital region to the countryside. Kamakura-period land sales reveal that coins were used in a significant percentage (25 percent or more) of transactions in the central Kinai region by the second decade of the thirteenth century. During the same years, coins were used in only a tiny fraction of transactions outside of the Kinai. In those areas, coins did not come to be used in over 25 percent of transactions until roughly two decades later.[43] As merchants were the key group involved in trade between the Kinai and other regions, it is no surprise to find that they used metallic currency. Even those salesmen lacking important temple connections or other forms of status transacted in large amounts of cash. For example, a lawsuit from 1311 makes mention of a traveling salesman who was robbed and murdered after entrusting 30 *kanmon* (30,000 coins, a sizeable sum) to a friend. The murdered man was not a person of importance, nor does he appear to have enjoyed any connection to a major temple or shrine. In fact, his name is not even listed in the legal document, which concerns a dispute between the murdered man's father and a money-lender who had previously lent him the even larger sum of

---

42. Ury, *Tales of Times Now Past*, chapter 16 tale 17, p. 102.
43. Takizawa, "Kamakura jidai zenki no kahei," 229.

260 *kanmon*.[44] Given the ready availability of coins and the desire of merchants to ease the transport of goods by switching
to cash, we must look to them as agents in the promotion of
rural monetization.

WARRIORS

With the founding of the Kamakura *bakufu* in 1185, its leader,
Minamoto no Yoritomo, secured the right to confirm or dis-
miss provincial warriors in their posts as estate stewards (*jitō*).
One of Yoritomo's goals was to restore peace after the five-
year civil war that brought him to power, and so he ordered
stewards to follow local precedents and obey the orders of
civilian estate proprietors.[45] With few exceptions, warriors
were not placed on estates that had lacked a resident warrior
prior to 1185. This changed in 1221, however, when a coalition
of disaffected parties led by the imperial house attempted to
destroy the Kamakura *bakufu*. Although *bakufu* armies won
the day and the leaders of the revolt were exiled, Kamakura
officials, determined to keep a much closer watch on the provinces, placed their appointees on far more estates than before.
In particular, estates whose patrons or proprietors had been
on the losing side were now assigned *jitō* without regard for
precedent. The terms of appointment were quite different
for these stewards. Relying on individual estate custom had
proven contentious, so in an effort to avoid legal (or other)
battles over warriors' rights to income, the *bakufu* decided that
new stewards' income would be limited to one-eleventh of an
estate's wet- and dry-field produce (or its equivalent).[46]

———

44. The legal decision, which went against the lender and awarded the
traveling salesman's 30 *kanmon* to his family, is found in the *Tōdaiji monjo*,
Shōwa 2 (1313) 4th month 21st day.

45. On the establishment of the *jitō*, see Mass, *Yoritomo and the Founding of
the First Bakufu*, 121–30.

46. Stewards were also given the right to levy a tax of five *shō* per *tan* of
land. *Kamakura bakufu tsuikahō*, doc. 10, Jōō 2 (1223) 7th month 6th day.

Many *jitō* found these terms to be too constrictive, for they faced a number of financial pressures. At the most basic level, they struggled to operate in an economy that was commercializing and expanding more rapidly than their incomes, which were bound by estate custom. Others brought the trouble on themselves through gambling losses and money borrowing, which, according to the sources, appear to have been major problems. Of course, the growing economy posed challenges for many people during the Kamakura period. Unique to the *bakufu*-affiliated warriors, however, were the special cash levies that the shogun sometimes demanded of them. These levies were supposedly used for temple repair or construction, various ceremonies, or even to cover the costs of entertaining the shogun. Warriors were also sometimes required to help underwrite the costs of court rituals, as is seen in a 1241 decree that stipulated a tax of 200 *mon* per *tan* to help pay for the emperor's *dajōe* ceremonies.[47]

Most burdensome was the obligation of *bakufu*-affiliated warriors (*gokenin*) to perform periodic guard duty (*ōban'yaku*) in Kyoto or Kamakura. Documents reflect that stewards across Japan, whether newly appointed or from pre-1221 positions, levied taxes on the peasants of their estates to cover the costs of their travel to those cities. In some cases, such as that of Wakasa Tadakiyo (cited at the start of this chapter), warriors used guard duty as a pretext to levy taxes for personal gain. Other examples also reflect warriors' readiness to abuse their taxing privileges. On one occasion, the manager of Sasakibe estate found it necessary to file a suit on behalf of the estate's peasants against the resident *jitō* in 1238.[48] The complaint lists a number of problems that the *jitō* had caused, among them his imposition of special taxes to fund his upcoming trip to

---

47. *AK*, Ninji 2 (1241) 9th month 10th day. See also *KI*, doc. 5490, in which a *gokenin* is ordered to pay 470 coins to Rokuhara for the construction of a temple, and *KI*, doc. 5407, in which a *gokenin* is ordered to pay 500 coins and provide a laborer, purpose unstated.

48. *Kamakura bakufu saikyōjōshū*, vol. 2, doc. 7, Katei 4 (1238) 10th month 19th day.

the capital and his insistence that the peasants bring a horse to Kyoto for him to ride back to the estate when his service was completed. Disputes such as this one were all too frequent during the thirteenth century as *gokenin* found their financial positions either unsatisfactory or untenable.[49]

Greed compounded by economic stress led *jitō* to disrupt traditional estate-proprietor relations. As noted in the Introduction, much of the scholarship on this period has focused on disputes between civilians and warriors over land. Such disputes certainly were a dominant theme of the Kamakura age, but battles over income, money, and markets also preoccupied the people of this time. Let us consider another case involving Tara estate, Wakasa Tadakiyo, and Jōen. Approximately twenty years before the case discussed at the opening of this chapter, Jōen filed a legal suit against Tadakiyo with the Kamakura *bakufu*. He accused Tadakiyo, among other crimes, of having taken part of the estate's annual tribute dues in order to repay a personal cash loan.[50] Tadakiyo's embezzlement reflected not only his apparent need for money, but also revealed how a warrior could threaten traditional estate relations by appropriating resources owed to the proprietor.

Efforts at appropriation by *gokenin* included attempts to control emerging provincial markets. Many chose to build their residences near waterways and road junctures in order to capture the gains of trade.[51] Others actively contended for authority over the marketplace. For example, on Ishiguro estate in Etchū province, the *jitō* Sadayori tried to claim the exclusive right to open a market from the estate's proprietor and from two local temples, while on Miiri estate in Awa province, various parties contested for control of the fields on which the market was held. The Yuasa family, whose members served as

---

49. Sekiguchi, "Shōen kōryōsei keizai no hen'yō to kaitai."

50. *Tōji hyakugo monjo*, Hōji 1 (1247) 10th month 29th day. *KI*, doc. 6893.

51. The *jitō* residential compound located next to the market on the Kamakura period map of Okuyama estate in Echigo province is one of many such examples. On the location of warrior residences, see Ishii, "Chūsei no kyokanshi to kasen."

gokenin and as proprietors in Kii province, managed to insinu-
ate themselves into most of the estates along the Arita River.
By doing so, they became important players in the region's
lumber trade since the only practical way to ship timber out
of the region was on the river.[52] These efforts at capturing
markets were the direct result of the demands placed upon *jitō*
and *gokenin* for cash.[53] With warriors under such pressure to
increase their incomes, inevitably they would turn to the estates on which they were stationed to satisfy their monetary
needs. Estates that were unable to stop such actions through
legal appeals were forced to sell their produce for cash, bringing them into direct contact with merchants and the market.

Warriors promoted rural monetization in other ways too.
For example, those in the countryside forced people to change
the way they thought about the value of their belongings. As
part of their duties, *jitō* were expected to investigate crimes
and punish offenders.[54] Theft was a crime that they often in-
vestigated, and over the course of the thirteenth century, they
began distinguishing different levels of punishment for thieves
based on the monetary value of the goods that had been stolen.
According to a *bakufu* legal proclamation of 1231, someone
caught stealing goods worth 200 coins or less was required to
repay double the amount in question, but was otherwise not
punished. Stealing goods valued at 300 coins or more, however, was considered a "serious crime" (*jūka*) and resulted in
the arrest of the thief and his or her immediate family. This
two-tiered system was expanded into three levels in 1253, with
amounts and punishments as follows:

---

52. Kira, "Kii no kuni Yuasashi no ryōshusei to soma," 203–38.

53. *Kamakura bakufu saikyōjōshū*, vol. 1, doc. 106 and 111. Sekiguchi Tsuneo
analyzes these and other cases, concluding that "along with challenging the
authority of the local managerial class over fields and properties, *jitō* showed
an extraordinary interest in markets which we must consider related to the
demand for money." Sekiguchi, "Shōen kōryōsei keizai no hen'yō to kaitai,"
144–45.

54. Except for capital crimes such as murder and treason, which the *shugo*
was to investigate.

VALUE OF STOLEN GOODS	PUNISHMENT
300 coins or less	repayment in double
between 300 and 500 coins	repayment in double, plus 2,000-coin penalty
over 600 coins	thief imprisoned, but family not punished

Bakufu-affiliated warriors were ordered to enact these policies in the provinces, forcing those outside of Kamakura to think about the value of goods in terms of money.[55] Of course, warriors had their own "cash consciousness" raised by being threatened with monetary punishments themselves. For example, *jitō* found guilty by the *bakufu* of purposefully obfuscating their income status could be penalized 5 *kanmon*. *Gokenin* who reported one month late for guard duty faced a fine of 10 *kanmon* (10,000 coins).[56] The imperial court, having come to acknowledge the pervasiveness of copper cash, also began levying monetary fines. In a pronouncement of 1263, the court laid out guidelines that included cash penalties for a range of crimes from fighting and injuring someone with a sword to rape and adultery.[57]

Warriors further contributed to the monetization of the provincial economy through their handling of tribute and taxes. As conflicts between warriors and central proprietors became more frequent over the course of the thirteenth century, some proprietors despaired of ever resolving their disputes through the courts and instead made contractual agreements (*ukesho*)

---

55. *Kamakura bakufu tsuikahō*, doc. 21, Kangi 3 (1231) 4th month 20th day, and doc. 284, Kenchō 5 (1253) 10th month 1st day. These are also discussed in *Chusei seiji shakai shisō*, vol. 2 (Iwanami shoten, 1981) and in Kasamatsu's chapter "Nusumi," in *Chūsei no tsumi to batsu*, 71–88.

56. *Kamakura bakufu tsuikahō*, doc. 152, Ninji (1240) 11th month 23rd day, and doc. 153, 28th day. The *mon* was the counter for coins, and the *kanmon* was the counter for strings of 1,000 coins. Hence, 20 *mon* equaled 20 coins, while 20 *kanmon* equaled 20,000 coins. Of course, one must keep in mind that strings did not always contain exactly 1,000 coins; they sometimes circulated with as few as 980 or 970 coins.

57. "Jingikan kudashibumi," Kōchō 3 (1263) 4th month, 30th day, in Kasamatsu et al., eds., *Chūsei seiji shakai shisō*, vol. 2, 24–32.

with *jitō*. According to these contracts, the *jitō* would deliver a certain percentage of the annual tribute to the proprietor, in exchange for which the proprietor would not contest the *jitō*'s authority on the estate. Many of these arrangements from the thirteenth century provided the *jitō* with the option of paying either in goods or in cash. One well-known case comes from Okuyama estate in Echigo province, where the *jitō* entered into a contractual agreement to pay 100 *koku* of rice or substitute a cash payment of 60 *kanmon* annually to the proprietor.[58] Still other proprietors, unable to work with warriors at all, opted to divide their land holdings (*shitaji chūbun*) between themselves and local warriors, in effect splitting estates into two. In either arrangement, warriors usually had the advantage because they lived on the estates, whereas elite proprietors almost always resided some distance away, in temples or cities. With warriors actually collecting the produce and/or taxes, they had the ability (if not the legal authority) to decide how rents would be collected and payments made to proprietors. As the Kamakura period progressed, those warriors increasingly sought cash as part of their income.

RELIGIOUS INSTITUTIONS

It is difficult to characterize the complexity of medieval Buddhist views of money and the market in any succinct way. Indeed, a proper treatment of this topic would surely lead to a book of its own. Therefore, this brief chapter subsection will only highlight a few notable ideas. In Japanese Buddhist thought, the market was sometimes used to symbolize mundane concerns and everyday life. An excellent example can be found in the *Ten Oxherding Pictures* of the Chinese Zen master Guoan Shiyuan (J. Kakuan Shien), consisting of ten illustrated scenes with accompanying text, composed in the twelfth century. The pictures depict a man in search of enlightenment, which is represented metaphorically as an ox. Over the course

---

58. Mass, "*Jitō* Land Possession in the Thirteenth Century," 167.

of the first seven scenes, the man succeeds in capturing the elusive ox, only to then realize that both ox and self are illusions. In earlier versions of this story, which contain only eight scenes, the final illustration contains a single large circle symbolizing the unity of all things. Guoan, however, felt that eight stages could not adequately convey the process of reaching enlightenment. He added two additional pictures, including a final scene in which the enlightened man returns to the ordinary world to help others find the path. The image of the "ordinary world" is that of the marketplace. There, the enlightened man acts in seemingly irreligious ways: he drinks alcohol, mingles with the crowd, and talks to innkeepers and fishmongers. In this conceptualization, the market is a place full of distractions, home of those who remain unenlightened and caught up in the world of everyday concerns and desires.[59]

In reality, markets were often established at the gates of temples and shrines, most likely because those were locations that attracted a variety of people. Such markets are referred to as *monzen ichi* (literally, "front-of-the-gate markets"). The peasants of Tara estate, mentioned at the outset of this chapter, bought and sold goods in just such a market. Onyū market was a *monzen ichi* established in front of Wakasahime jinja, an important shrine that dates to the early eighth century. The location was conducive to trade as several other estates were located in the vicinity, including Imatomi, Miyagawa, Kunitomi, and Tamaki estates. It was also beneficial because the market lay on the trade route between Obama Bay on the Sea of Japan coast and Lake Biwa, which was connected to the market networks of Kyoto. But only in the thirteenth century did the location come to host a market worth mentioning in documentary sources. The first written reference to Onyū market is from a 1243 dispute in which the *jitō* was trying to

---

59. Phillip Kapleau writes of the market in the *Oxherding Pictures* as representing "the defiled world." *Three Pillars of Zen*, 323–25. On the images (particularly in the Chinese Buddhist context), see Sørensen, "A Study of the 'Oxherding Theme.'"

extract cash from Tara residents. As this case illustrates, cash was already in use by the mid-thirteenth century and it had some connection to the rise of rural markets. Of course, there was another reason for establishing the market in front of the Wakasahime jinja. With both the provincial *shugo* and the civilian government office (*kokufu*) nearby, the shrine could offer some protection to Onyū from its powerful neighbors who might otherwise attempt to tax or control the marketplace.[60]

The Buddhist and Shinto communities of medieval Japan included people with varying beliefs and practices, but religious institutions and individuals generally played a positive role in provincial monetization. Many were quick to embrace the emerging cash economy. As noted above, *jinin* and other lay religious figures sometimes worked as merchants, utilizing their special status to move easily throughout society. In fact, some appear to have specifically sought religious affiliation precisely because it facilitated their business travels. And, as is well known, major temples such as Enryakuji and Kōfukuji became the leading moneylenders of the age, managing large operations and stationing agents throughout Japan during the medieval period.[61] The attitude of religious figures in medieval Japan was quite different from that found in medieval Europe. The Christian Church viewed moneylending and commercial transactions with suspicion. Its concern appeared in an iconographic shift whereby greed replaced pride as the worst of the seven deadly sins, and the church made usury by Christians illegal.[62] In contrast, Buddhist monks generally did not oppose usury on religious or doctrinal grounds, and in many cases, they embraced the use of cash. Their contributions to the spread of money in this period cannot be overstated.

---

60. Sasaki, *Shōen no shōgyō*, 31–35.
61. Tonomura, *Community and Commerce*, 24–25. For more on Enryakuji's role as a moneylender in the Muromachi and *sengoku* periods, see Gay, *Moneylenders of Late Medieval Kyoto*.
62. Little, "Pride Goes before Avarice," 16–49.

Along with the key role played by elite institutions such as Enryakuji, however, this study seeks to highlight the provincial activities of non-elite figures in promoting monetization. Consider the monk Insai, who received a 3-*tan* parcel of land from a woman with the surname Fujiwara to support readings of the Lotus Sutra on the anniversary of her death. This would seem to signify the establishment of a sacred trust, an exchange of land for prayers that involved no money and created an enduring legacy for someone after her passing. Yet in 1187, Insai *sold* this land to his own disciple, receiving 30 *kanmon* for the property and presumably excusing himself from the obligation for sutra recital.[63] As discussed in the previous chapter, the oldest surviving documented sale of land for cash comes from the 1150s, so monks such as Insai, operating only decades later, may have been among the first to embrace the new cash economy. Such transactions were to become increasingly common over the course of the medieval period.

Further evidence for the use of money in unexpected places comes from the guidelines for monks at An'yōji temple in Bizen province. According to the institution's rules, those who failed to participate in certain temple rituals faced monetary penalties. For example, those who did not take part in *genkurabe*, the comparison of supernatural powers achieved through meditation and religious training, were required to pay 100-*mon* fines.[64] The monks, who composed the rules and voted to adopt them, must have used coins if they subjected themselves to cash penalties. At the same time, if monetary penalties were the only repercussions that non-participating monks faced, then the rule in effect commodified participation, since it allowed monks to use cash to buy their way out of taking part. This may seem surprising, for we tend to think of monks as individuals who have renounced personal possessions as part of their training to achieve enlightenment. Yet the rules indicate

---

63. *KI*, doc. 221, Bunji 3 (1187) 3rd month 19th day.
64. *Okayama kenshi*, vol. 19, doc. 1157, Kenji 3 (1277) 7th month 12th day.

that monks were actually using money while undergoing religious training. Clearly there were some differences between expressed ideology and actual practice. Gregory Schopen, writing about Buddhist monks in India, persuasively argues that we should not be surprised to find that they used money. The reason for the surprise, he contends, is that much of the scholarly work on Buddhist institutions has relied on scripture rather than on archaeological evidence. The latter shows that coins were not uncommon in Indian monasteries, regardless of any ideal of giving up one's personal possessions.[65] The same must have been true in Japan.

Less surprising, perhaps, is that monks and temples used cash in their dealings with the outside world. For example, they used money to pay skilled workers, builders, and performers, such as the dancers and musicians who performed during religious ceremonies.[66] They also came to rely on cash donations from supporters as a source of revenue, especially through financial pledge drives known as *kanjin* campaigns. There had been similar campaigns in the past, such as the eighth-century fundraising efforts to finance the construction of Tōdaiji. But *kanjin* campaigns took on new importance for temples and shrines in the twelfth and thirteenth centuries because of the evolution of the early medieval economy.[67]

In earlier times, temples primarily relied upon the state and the nobility to cover their expenses. Emperors, their consorts, members of the Fujiwara, and other nobles all directly supported temples and shrines or else bequeathed rights to income from estates which the religious houses could use to support themselves. But as warriors began encroaching on land rights, temples found that they could no longer rely on their estate incomes alone. Nor could they turn to the nobility to make up the difference, since the nobles also derived much of their in-

---

65. Schopen, *Bones, Stones, and Buddhist Monks*.

66. *Okayama kenshi*, vol. 19, doc. 1243, indicates that the Tōdaiji paid three *kagura* performers by converting tribute to cash.

67. Goodwin, *Alms and Vagabonds*, 13–14.

come from landed properties. Consequently, temples began to solicit donations from the general public. Fortunately for them, the timing coincided with the growth of the economy and the spread of cash in the provinces. As Janet Goodwin describes, an "economic revolution . . . involving increases in agricultural productivity and the use of money" took place in the late Heian and Kamakura periods, and religious institutions tapped into that revolution by drawing on new sources of support: rural land managers and prosperous cultivators.[68]

Not everyone within the Buddhist community approved of temples' new reliance on and involvement with the monetary economy. Some, for example, criticized the ways in which *kanjin* campaigns were carried out. Mujū Ichien, a prominent Tendai priest of the thirteenth century, complained of temples that were "brought to completion with fraudulent 'donations' levied as taxes on people's houses." He also disapproved of those who engaged in religious begging for alms, claiming that "even animals dislike having people beg things from them."[69] Indeed, as Mujū decried, sometimes "donations" were actually taxes levied on people's homes. Such was the case with the 300-coin-per-*tan* tax for shrine construction issued by Emperor Go-Horikawa in 1229.[70] Temples as estate proprietors also had a mixed record of support for the commutation of taxes. While some temples welcomed cash payments, others that insisted upon receiving tribute in kind rather than in cash might be seen as having inhibited the growth of a money economy.[71] Thus it is hard to generalize the role of religious institutions in monetization. Some, such as Enryakuji, quickly took to the use of cash in the thirteenth century while others opposed its introduction.

---

68. Goodwin, *Alms and Vagabonds*, 40–41.

69. Both quotations are taken from Robert Morrell's translation of Mujū Ichien's *Shasekishū*, 8:23. See Morrell, *Sand and Pebbles*, 229–33.

70. *KI*, doc. 3855, Kangi 1 (1229) 7th month 28th day.

71. For example, in the mid-thirteenth century Tōdaiji announced that it would only accept payments in kind from estates supporting certain ceremonies. Piggott, "Hierarchy and Economics in Early Medieval Todaiji," 72.

PROVINCIAL ESTATE MANAGERS
AND PEASANT COMMUNITIES

The people living in the provinces were not merely passive re-cipients of monetization initiated by merchants, warriors, and religious institutions. Many eagerly took to money and chose to sell their goods in local markets. Yet because those living in the countryside left behind fewer written records, it is difficult to determine exactly who within provincial communities fa-vored the use of money and who opposed it. The documents that have survived do not reveal which members of those communities won and lost. Scholars can only turn to temple-maintained tax registers, receipts and correspondence from officials living on the estates, and legal documents explicating suits that involved provincial warriors. These materials offer glimpses into life on estates and public lands in thirteenth-century rural Japan, but are limited in what they can reveal about the lives of common peasants. Those who used coins were most likely estate officials (*shōkan, gesu, azukari dokoro*) and the leading cultivators (*hyakushō* and *myōshu*, both of whom were of sufficient status to hold office or have taxation rights).[72] Documents composed directly by the lower-status members of peasant communities (i.e., those who actually worked in the fields) are extremely rare. Consequently, in the paragraphs below, it is necessary to write about the actions of provincial communities without being able to easily distinguish among community members of different status.[73]

---

72. Conlan, *State of War*, 108–16.

73. In addition to the challenge of distinguishing between on-site estate officials and other residents, it is difficult to distinguish among people of dif-ferent status within the agricultural community. At the very least, one might expect to find *hyakushō* (provincials with surnames who held *shiki* or public office), *genin* (commoners without surnames or land rights), and *hinin* (those of such low status that they might be forced to live outside of the village proper). Nagahara, *Shōen*, 146–47; Conlan, *State of War*, 251–54. How these different groups gained or lost with the increasing use of money is a topic for future research.

Even given these limitations, there is much that these sources can reveal about the use of money by provincial communities during the Kamakura period. For example, we know that people living in the thirteenth-century countryside possessed money because we see that warriors were able to take it from them. Sometimes they used taxes to take money from the peasants. In addition to the types of levies described above, in which *gokenin* sought cash to cover the cost of their obligations to the Kamakura *bakufu*, other forms of monetary taxation began to spread, including "housepost levies" (*munabechisen*) — cash taxes whose assessment was based on the number of pillars in the family dwelling. Although they became common only in the late fourteenth century, the first appearance of such a tax dates to 1293. That year, the *bakufu* ordered its agents to levy a 10-*mon*-per-household tax on residents of Settsu province to help fund temple repairs.[74]

But aside from taxes, warriors sometimes simply confiscated private monies held jointly by peasants. These were known as *tanomoshi*, which commonly involved a number of villagers each contributing a small sum of cash per month into a collective fund. Each of the members was able to borrow in turn from the total amount collected. Unscrupulous warriors who discovered such funds were quick to seize them, as is demonstrated by a manager's written response to the complaints of the peasants on his estate against their *jitō*.[75] Warriors appropriated cash for their own special events, as can be seen in the testament of Shibuya Jōshin, a warrior who lived on Iriki estate of Satsuma province. Jōshin's will included instructions for his sons on the appropriate means of managing their lands after his death, including how much cash to levy from each of the different peasant communities under their control when great hunts (*ōniwa onmaki*) were held. From Jōshin's description, one

---

74. Mass, *Kamakura Bakufu*, 185–86.
75. *KI*, doc. 12184, Kenji 1 (1275), 12th month.

can sense that these villagers regularly used money and that his sons would have no difficulty taxing them in cash.[76]

This supposition is further confirmed by one of the rare documents that reflects the concerns of ordinary villagers: the complaint filed by the peasants of the Kamimura village on Ategawa estate against the resident warrior in 1275. The document, in barely legible *katakana* script, was presumably written by a member of the community or someone living close by. It is most famous for its account of the warrior's treatment of the residents: according to their complaint, when the men absconded (a common technique, similar to a strike) in protest against the warrior's demands, he arrested and mutilated a number of the women and children. But also among the thirteen points of complaint are several that refer to the warrior taking money from the community, such as his levying a cash tax of 400 coins on "hidden" fields even after the peasants had already paid the proprietor.[77] Another document, from Shimomura village of the same estate (and dated just one year earlier), indicates that wealthier peasants were able to use cash to buy their way out of having to perform physical labor for the estate's upkeep. Thus, coins were quite convenient for those who could afford them.[78]

Peasants' use of money can also be confirmed by the efforts of religious institutions to collect coins from the countryside. *Kanjin* campaign fundraisers sought donations among both rich and poor, urban and rural communities. Kujō Kanezane recorded in his diary that mendicants from Tōdaiji sought donations from houses throughout the capital, including even the compound of the retired emperor.[79] We might suspect that the same individuals who approached nobles and the imperial

---

76. The will of Shibuya Jōshin is preserved in the *Iriki-in ke monjo*. It can also be found in the *KI*, doc. 6485, Kangen 3 (1245) 5th month 11th day. It calls for 100- and 200-coin sums to be collected when great hunts are scheduled.

77. Kuroda, *Mimi o kiri hana o sogi*, 15–20.

78. *Kōyasan monjo*, Bun'ei 11 (1274) 2nd month 3rd day.

79. *Gyokuyō*, Yōwa 1 (1181) 10th month 9th day.

house did not also visit rural communities, but other members of their order may very well have done so, since numerous *kanjin* campaigns, such as the Tōshōdaiji campaign of the 1250s, solicited cash from provincial estate dwellers.[80]

Proprietors' rules for estates and their managers provide another indication of coin use on provincial estates. These rules, like those of the *bakufu* for the warriors described earlier, imposed cash penalties against criminals. For example, in 1275, the temple at Kōyasan issued regulations to the managers of three of its estates in Kii province.[81] One clause stipulated a 5-*kanmon* penalty against the manager if he knew of a crime but failed to act. Another clause instituted a prohibition against killing birds, fish, and animals, with a 5-*kanmon* fine for violators. Surely Kōyasan would not have called for such penalties if there had been no cash on the estates.

These signs of monetization do not allow us to see how prevalent the use of cash among medieval villagers may have been, nor do they reveal what percentage of a community consisted of coin wielders. Presumably cash use varied by region and was most common in those communities situated close to local markets. Even within those communities, one would suspect that only those who had enough land (or fishnets, or other means of income) to produce surplus for sale in the market would have held money. Yet there is considerable evidence to support the claim that cash was no stranger to some early medieval communities by the second half of the Kamakura period. Illustrated materials frequently depict men of commoner status with a belt pouch (*koshibukuro*) at the hip. This was the place where they kept copper coins and other personal effects.[82] Fourteenth-century peasants, even those living in less prosperous villages, sold woodwork, charcoal, and fire-

---

80. Goodwin, *Alms and Vagabonds*, 111–12.

81. The estates in question were Sarukawa, Makuni, and Kōno. The document, *KI*, doc. 12148, Kenji 1 (1275) 11th month, was the Sarukawa official's acknowledgement of the orders.

82. Hotate Michihisa refers to these pouches an essential part of an adult's attire in the medieval period; see his *Monogatari no chūsei*, 214–28.

wood to acquire cash. And often the residents of a village included one or more purveyor-merchants, individuals who brought knowledge of money and the market back to their home communities. [83] As these examples suggest, growing numbers of commoners were coming into contact with coins by the end of the Kamakura period.

Money, Trade, and the Kamakura Bakufu

Although various groups in the countryside contributed to the increased acceptance of cash in regional markets, nobles in the imperial court were less open to its use. The court continued to pursue its attempts to control money and markets, repeatedly debating the money problem and banning Chinese coins. Imported currency was discussed or prohibited in 1189, twice in 1192, twice in 1193, and again in 1195. The people of Kyoto, at least, knew of these currency prohibitions, as revealed by Rishō's refusal to use coins in the market incident of 1200 (described in Chapter 1). But as that incident also revealed, the court's efforts at market regulation proved difficult to enforce.

Meanwhile, the newly established Kamakura *bakufu* was slow to get involved in issues of commerce. Initially, *bakufu* officials left monetary matters to the imperial court. Minamoto no Yoritomo displayed little interest in Chinese coins or trade. Not only did Yoritomo fail to issue any new commercial regulations, in some instances he did not even support established trade procedures. Consider his handling of an 1187 dispute between Dazaifu, the official port of entry to Japan for foreign ships, and Shimazu estate of southern Kyushu. As noted in Chapter 1, continental merchants were supposed to sail to Dazaifu and receive clearance there before engaging in trade with the Japanese. Consequently, when a Chinese merchant vessel sailed directly for Shimazu in violation of Japanese legal pro-

---

83. Nagahara Keiji mentions villagers selling firewood, etc., in his chapter "The Medieval Peasant," 328. He draws heavily upon Ōyama, *Nihon chūsei nōsonshi*, 288–319. Finally, Miura Keiichi discusses purveyor-merchants living in rural villages in his article "Villages and Trade in Medieval Japan," 64.

cedures, Dazaifu agents under the direction of Amano Tōkage
(a Yoritomo appointee) confiscated goods that Shimazu officials had acquired through trade with the Chinese. Estate officials appealed to their proprietor, the Konoe noble family, and
the Konoe persuaded Yoritomo to order the return of the confiscated goods.[84] As this case illustrates, Yoritomo was less concerned with enforcing proper trade policy than he was with
maintaining his political support.

Yoritomo's successors in Kamakura gradually became more
involved in economic policy formulation. Even though the
nobles in the capital never relinquished their right to set prices
and regulate trade,[85] Kamakura came to take the lead in such
matters, in part out of necessity as the warrior capital increased
in size and economic significance. When the *bakufu* was established in 1185, it had not been clear whether the institution
would survive much beyond the civil war from which it was
born. As the samurai government demonstrated its staying
power, however, the city of Kamakura began to grow and
merchants flocked to the warrior capital. In 1216, the *bakufu*
placed limits on the number of merchants allowed to operate
there. In 1223, it issued a series of regulations for boats sailing
along the coast, many of which shipped annual tribute dues
(*nengu*) and commercial goods throughout the Japanese islands.
Although Kamakura had only been a city of consequence for
a few decades, it had already come to attract a large number
of these ships. The author of the travelogue *Kaidōki* observed
"hundreds" of ships moored in the Kamakura port of Yuigahama as he passed through in the late spring of 1223. The next
day, viewing one of the city's markets, he noted "a hundred

---

84. This incident is recounted in Ōyama, *Kamakura bakufu*, 375.

85. For example, the nobles continued to periodically issue price laws
(*kokahō*, a court practice described in Chapter 1). Thirteenth-century court-
issued price laws are mentioned in the chronicle *Hyakurenshō*, entries for
Kangi 2 (1230) 6th month 24th day and Kenchō 2 (1250) 6th month 13th day.

merchants' houses" crowding the streets.⁸⁶ We should not take the author's numbers literally, but the *Kaidōki* account suggests that commerce had come to occupy an important place in the warrior capital.

Whereas the imperial court's currency prohibitions might be seen as having been antagonistic toward merchants and money, mature Kamakura *bakufu* policy cannot be described in that way. In 1232, for example, shogunal regent Hōjō Yasu-toki (1183–1242) acted upon a suggestion from those soliciting religious donations to improve his city's port facilities by authorizing the construction of docks on Wagae Island in the bay.⁸⁷ These and other examples show that the *bakufu* was not hostile to commerce. Rather, they highlight an important characteristic of *bakufu* economic policy: that, as the *bakufu* matured, it increasingly sought to control commerce. In 1251, having failed to limit the number of merchants in Kamakura, the *bakufu* tried instead to limit the areas in which merchants could operate. It declared seven sections of the city open for business and ordered merchants to take care of their neighborhoods by not tethering oxen along the roads and being sure to clean the streets.⁸⁸ Interestingly, one of the seven approved merchants' areas was the small port island of Wagae, suggesting either that the new docks were doing well or that the *bakufu* hoped to bolster their use by forcing merchants to conduct business there.

Bakufu efforts at control were not limited to establishing business districts. The warrior government also attempted to regulate prices within the city. In 1253, it passed a number of measures including its own set of price laws for Kamakura.

86. *Kaidōki*, entries for Jōō 2 (1223) 4th month 17th day and 18th day. The author of the *Kaidōki* is not known, though some scholars have proposed the scholar Minamoto no Mitsuyuki (1163–1244).

87. *AK*, Jōei 1 (1232) 7th month 12th day, 15th day. The project was apparently completed in less than a month, as indicated by the entry for the same year 8th month 9th day.

88. *Kamakura bakufu tsuikahō*, doc. 272, Kenchō 3 (1251) 12th month 3rd day.

Noting that prices had been rising in recent years, the edict fixed them as follows:

> Charcoal: 1 horseload = 100 coins
> Firewood: 3 bundles = 100 coins
> Miscanthus reeds: 8 bundles = 50 coins
> Straw: 8 bundles = 50 coins
> Rice bran: 1 bag = 50 coins [89]

The edict went on to bemoan that lumber merchants operating at Wagae Island were failing to follow size regulations and trying to sell unusable-sized pieces of lumber. It called for stricter enforcement of the size regulations, threatening punishment for violators.

It is difficult to tell whether or not the *bakufu*'s official prices were in keeping with the market value of the products for sale. Since the decree began by censuring recent high prices, it seems safe to assume that those goods cost more on the unregulated market. Apparently the *bakufu*'s efforts at price regulation proved problematic, however, for after just one year Kamakura revoked most of the provisions of the 1253 decree.[90] The reasons for the *bakufu*'s reversal are not clear. Perhaps market officials in the warrior capital, in contrast to the ineffective imperial police in Kyoto, had been strict in enforcing the price guidelines and trade had suffered. Regardless of the reason, such legislation and its quick retraction highlight a second characteristic of *bakufu* commercial policy: confusion.

This confusion is also apparent in the warrior government's policies on tolls.[91] Toll stations had been in place along major roads of the realm since the creation of the *ritsuryō* state in the seventh century. The primary function of those posts was to maintain security. As they came under local control in the late Heian and Kamakura periods, however, provincial authorities

---

89. *Kamakura bakufu tsuikahō*, docs. 296 and 297, Kenchō 5 (1253) 10th month 11th day.

90. *AK*, Kenchō 6 (1254) 10th month 17th day.

91. In discussing tolls, I have drawn primarily upon Toyoda, *Chūsei no shōnin to kōtsū*, 398–403.

began to turn posts into toll stations, which they used to tax merchants shipping goods to market. Rather than serving a national good such as security, toll stations functioned primarily for the benefit of local institutions. The same was true for waterways, as port authorities transformed temporary levies for harbor maintenance into permanent taxes that became important sources of income for temples, shrines, and provincial warriors. Similar river tolls set up and manned by *gokenin* allowed provincial warriors to exert significant influence on regional trade.

The *bakufu* vacillated in its reaction to these developments. Starting in the 1210s, it first prohibited *jitō* from establishing toll stations but cancelled the ban due to warrior objections the following year.[92] *Bakufu* policy went back and forth on tollgate regulation. On the one hand, Kamakura officials seem to have allowed *gokenin* to collect revenue from tolls as long as no problems arose. On the other hand, the *bakufu* was quick to ban tolls when they were seen as troublesome or, at the time of the Mongol invasions, when they were perceived as an impediment to the quick movement of warriors and supplies ordered for the defense of Kyushu.[93] Note that tolls were not a source of direct revenue for the *bakufu* itself. In actuality, major temples such as Kōfukuji and Tōdaiji were the most active in erecting toll barriers for profit. The Kamakura warrior government got involved because it policed the actions of its affiliated warriors and needed to ensure the easy passage of people and goods throughout the country. Seen in that light, the *bakufu* remained consistent in not taking an active role in commerce but rather primarily working to preserve peace and order.

Confusion over *bakufu* policy extended to more than whether or not tolls were permitted. By the early fourteenth century, problems emerged over exactly what types of goods could be subject to tolls. Historians have long believed that, as a general

---

92. *AK*, Kenryaku 2 (1212) 9th month 21st day.
93. Toyoda, *Chūsei no shōnin to kōtsū*, 400.

rule, commercial goods were taxable whereas *nengu* owed to proprietors were exempt from tolls. However, as Chapter 4 of this book will explain, recent research shows that the distinctions between commercial and *nengu* goods began to blur as more and more goods were converted to cash in provincial markets. Increasingly over the course of the Kamakura period, the *bakufu* found its fledgling economic policies unable to handle the new developments of an emerging monetary economy.

Conclusion

This chapter has covered a wide range of topics: the collapse of the official market system, the pressing demands of warriors for cash from provincial communities, and the increasing circulation of copper currency in the countryside. In each case, economic growth proved damaging to traditional economic relations within the framework of the old imperial tax system. Reliance on private tribute rather than the redistribution of state taxes via the official market was another step in the weakening of the early Heian *ritsuryō* state, while in the provinces, agricultural communities found advantages in trade and markets that freed them from dependence on central proprietors. Meanwhile, warriors disrupted the tribute economy by pushing the boundaries of their authority to tax estate residents for cash. Yet as proprietors often had little recourse other than the courts to stop warriors, the result was a shift in the provincial balance of power from civilian proprietors based in temples or the capital to local warriors. In the face of such developments, both elite proprietors and Kamakura *bakufu* officials had to wrestle with the tension between older ideas of authority and the economic needs of a new age. Finally, the peasants themselves gained a relative measure of independence from central elites as they found the strength to press for better terms of tribute payment.

But lest the picture appear too rosy, not everyone in the countryside gained from these changes. Peasants found that samurai could be oppressive figures in their lives. As for those provincial warriors, although some pushed for cash out of

greed, others found their financial situations to be quite difficult. Their demands for cash, such as Wakasa Tadakiyo's levy
on the peasants of Tara estate, interfered with traditional civilian estate management and forced many agricultural communities to trade their produce for money. The Kamakura *bakufu*
knew of its agents' abuses, calling them "greedy for cash," and
tried to prevent further warrior outrages in 1260 by instituting
standard levy rates for *gokenin* on guard duty.[94] Even so, as we
will see in the next chapter, the inability of some warriors to
secure adequate levels of income would continue to be a problem for the *bakufu* throughout the thirteenth century.

---

94. The *bakufu* authorized *gokenin* to tax 300 *mon* per *tan* along with one
horse and two laborers for every 50 *tan*. AK, entry for Bun'ō 1 (1260) 12th
month 25th day.

THREE

Virtue, Vice, and Self-Interest: Money and the Kamakura Bakufu

In 1297, the Kamakura *bakufu* issued edicts declaring that the outstanding monetary debts of its direct retainers, known as *gokenin*, were to be forgiven.[1] They did not need to repay loans and could even reclaim lands that they had lost prior to 1297 due to defaulting on their debts. The same legislation barred their creditors from turning to the courts to enforce loan agreements, proclaiming that the *bakufu* judiciary would refuse to hear lawsuits brought by non-retainers over cases of debt default. Seemingly intended to provide relief to financially troubled *gokenin*, the *bakufu* edicts of 1297 were referred to as orders of "virtuous rule" (*tokusei*).[2]

---

1. The text of the edicts is published in the *KI*, doc. 19416, Einin 5 (1297) 7th month 22nd day. *Tokuseirei* have been the subject of numerous scholarly studies in Japan; perhaps most famous is Kasamatsu Hiroshi's *Tokuseirei: chūsei no hō to kanshū*, in which he proposes that there was an expectation in medieval Japanese society that property would eventually return to its owner even if sold. In English, *tokusei* are mentioned in passing in a number of works (see citations below), but there has been no full-length treatment since Brown's 1949 article "The Japanese *Tokusei* of 1297."

2. *Tokusei* and *ontokusei* are compounds that appear in medieval documents. The word *tokusei* is composed of two characters: *toku* 徳 meaning "virtue" and *sei* 政 meaning "government" or "administration." Modern scholars

Although the legislation's authors may have thought of themselves as virtuous for trying to aid *bakufu* retainers, in fact the amnesty proved to be an unmitigated disaster. It sent the economy into a chaotic downturn. Property changed hands multiple times as various parties reclaimed and resold lands that they had previously alienated. Confusion over how the edicts were to be applied and who was eligible allowed non-*gokenin* to reclaim lands as well. Moneylenders were unable to collect payments or safely extend new loans. As a result, even *gokenin*, the supposed beneficiaries of the legislation, suffered as they found their ability to borrow severely restricted. Presumably it was these conditions that led the Kamakura *bakufu* to repeal the provisions of the 1297 *tokuseirei* within a year of their promulgation.[3]

What factors led Kamakura officials to make such a drastic intervention on behalf of their retainers? This problematic initiative not only disrupted the economy, but it was also inconsistent with earlier *bakufu* practice of maintaining neutrality in legal disputes rather than favoring Kamakura-affiliated warriors. Had *bakufu* leaders changed their thinking on such matters? If so, what led to the change, and why did their action take the form of a debt amnesty? General histories of Japan and some scholarly writings offer an easy answer to these questions.[4] They argue that the costs of defending Japan against invasions by the Mongols in 1274 and 1281 forced samurai defenders to exhaust their financial resources, borrow money, and put up their land holdings as collateral. The *bakufu*-led forces successfully defended Japan, but the government had

---

employ the term *tokuseirei* to describe regulations issued in the name of virtuous rule. Hence, the term "virtuous government orders" is a literal translation of *tokuseirei*.

3. No explanation is given in the relevant documents to account for the *bakufu* decision to repeal the 1297 *tokuseirei*. See *KI*, docs. 19608 and 19609, Einin 6 (1298) 2nd month 28th day.

4. See Ishii, "The Decline of the Kamakura *Bakufu*," 130, and Hall, *Japan from Prehistory to Modern Times*, 94, 103. Additional examples are provided in the discussion below.

no means of compensating its followers at the conclusion of the conflict. One of the only actions it could take was to issue *tokuseirei* that protected retainers from moneylenders and allowed them to reclaim lost land holdings. Thus, according to this view, it was the extraordinary event of the Mongol invasions, together with Kamakura *bakufu* concern for the financial well-being of its retainers, that led to the 1297 edicts.

This chapter argues for a more nuanced reading of this late thirteenth-century legislation by placing the famous *tokuseirei* in a broader context. Careful examination of documents that pre-date the Mongol threat shows that the invasions were not as significant, nor the *bakufu* quite as well intentioned, as is implied by the standard interpretation. Instead, reevaluating the 1297 *tokuseirei* in light of other written materials reveals it to be the product of the thirteenth century's evolving economy. I focus on two alternative factors that are central to understanding Kamakura-period virtuous relief orders. First, the *bakufu* was forced to pursue radical economic policies such as debt abrogation by moneylenders' accumulation of retainers' land rights. Moneylenders had been acquiring those land rights for decades, irrespective of the Mongol invasions. Second, the *bakufu*'s struggle for power with the weakened but still active imperial court dictated that the *bakufu* employ notions of virtue in its debt-relief efforts. The widespread involvement of *gokenin* in the evolving, impersonal, market-based economy (described in the Chapter 2) threatened the *bakufu*'s ability to demand service from its retainers. This led Kamakura to appropriate already well-established imperial court notions of virtuous rule in an attempt to stop the breakdown of reciprocal *bakufu*-retainer relationships. According to my view, the *bakufu*'s concern was less for its retainers than for ensuring its own survival.

After critically reassessing the significance of the Mongol invasions as a causal factor behind the decision to forgive debts, this chapter proposes alternative explanations that take into account the importance of reciprocal relationships to the *bakufu-gokenin* system. It also dips into intellectual history by exploring the concept of "virtuous rule" in Japan, arguing that it was the court rather than the *bakufu* which was closely associated with *tokusei* for most of the thirteenth century. Finally, the chapter highlights the role of *bakufu* self-interest in promulgating virtuous government edicts and draws comparisons between the reciprocal relationships of the *bakufu* retainer system and "gift economy" studies that have been used to help explain aspects of medieval European society. Together these sections illustrate how new economic relationships and the spread of money in the thirteenth century forced the modification of existing political and social structures.

Mongols or Moneylenders? Searching for Motives

Until the 1980s, historians generally agreed that the costs of fighting off the Mongol invasions led to the impoverishment of warriors and the need for debt amnesty.[5] Delmer Brown and Kyotsu Hori, the two leading scholars to have written in English about the 1297 *tokuseirei*, were both influenced by this view. Brown observed: "The financial burden [of the Mongol invasions], not only to the military government but also to individual warriors, was staggering. When . . . other measures failed to improve the economic position of retainers, the *bakufu* was forced to consider more drastic methods [i.e., the *tokusei* of 1297]."[6]

Hori seemed to concur with this notion, writing that "forerunners of the more sweeping '*tokusei*' regulations of 1297 . . . [were] intended to serve as reward and compensation at the expense of those who had not directly contributed to the anti-Mongol effort."[7] Japanese scholars have also emphasized the fiscal strain of the invasions, as seen in Hayashiya Tatsusaburō's account of the 1297 decree: "The Einin Edict, which had the highly utilitarian effect of wiping out debts, was meant to succor the Kamakura shogunate's housemen who

---

5. See, for example, Aida, *Mōko shūrai no kenkyū.*
6. Brown, "The Japanese *Tokusei* of 1297," 191–92.
7. Hori, "Economic and Political Effects of the Mongol Wars," 189.

had fallen into severe financial straits in the aftermath of the Mongol invasions."[8] Although these authors did not attribute *tokuseirei* solely to the economic difficulties that followed the invasions, all three held the Mongol attacks to have been key factors. This interpretation has earned widespread acceptance in Japan and is commonly found in standard history textbooks.[9]

Brown and Hori's insistence that the *bakufu*'s inability to pay those who fought against the Mongols necessitated *tokuseirei* seems a logical conclusion, given the nature of Japanese warfare during these years. Early medieval warriors had come to expect liberal compensation for their services on the battlefield. In fact, samurai received appointments to office or land after every significant military clash of the twelfth and thirteenth centuries. When rival court factions vied for power in the Hōgen disturbance of 1156 and the Heiji disturbance of 1159, warriors in the winning coalitions received appointments, titles, and land rights as rewards. Most famously, Taira no Kiyomori, the leader of the victorious samurai faction in each disturbance, gained appointments including the governorship of Harima province and the assistant governor-generalship of Kyushu.[10] The same was true for the Genpei civil war of 1180 to 1185. Yoritomo, leader of the winning Minamoto coalition, confiscated rival Heike-affiliated estates and awarded them to loyal warriors.[11] The Jōkyū Uprising of 1221 provides another example, as warriors who had fought for the victorious *bakufu* received numerous titles and lands while those who sided with

8. Hayashiya, "Kyoto in the Muromachi Age," 26.

9. For example, see Miyahara et al., *Kōkō Nihonshi B Shinteiban*, 60–61.

10. Jeffrey Mass downplays the gains Taira no Kiyomori realized from these disturbances. But Mass is attempting to challenge the notion found in older scholarship that Kiyomori became preeminent in Kyoto at this time by proving that Kiyomori's power was still limited by Retired Emperor Go-Shirakawa. There is no question that Kiyomori realized concrete benefits in land and appointments for his participation on the winning side. *Yoritomo and the Founding*, 18.

11. Yoritomo awarded or confirmed positions, including estate managerships and vice governorships. Mass, *Yoritomo and the Founding*, 73.

the defeated imperial court lost control of an extensive array of estates and temple proprietorships.[12] Finally, Hōjō Tokiyori's destruction of the Miura and Chiba in 1247 allowed him to confiscate and redistribute their lands to his allies.[13] Based on these outcomes, warriors came to expect that combat would lead to direct economic gain for those on the winning side.

Defending Japan against the Mongol-led invasion forces was in fact quite costly for warriors. As the prospect of invasion became imminent, the *bakufu* ordered retainers with titles to land in Kyushu to muster on the western island. This was expensive, as warriors had to cover their own transportation costs as well as provide their own arms and supplies. Following the initial attacks on the islands of Tsushima and Iki in the tenth month of 1274, the *bakufu* ordered additional fighting men to report for duty within twenty days.[14] Many warriors possessed scattered land holdings with their primary residence in other parts of the country, but they were still required to bear the costs of physically relocating to Kyushu so as to contribute to the defense effort.[15] These same warriors also had to expend labor and financial resources to build a stone wall along Hakata Bay to strengthen the country's defensive position. Concern over a threatened third invasion forced these men to maintain their defensive posture well into the fourteenth century.

Both the 1274 and 1281 invasion attempts were successfully repulsed due to a combination of the *bakufu*'s mobilization efforts, Japanese warriors' strength of arms, and the timely arrival of storms that damaged the invading fleet(s).[16] But this

---

12. The imperial house lost the highest level rights-to-income (*honke shiki*) from estates in Kii, Yamato, and other provinces. Mass, *Development of Kamakura Rule*, 38–40.

13. Kondō, "1247 as a Turning Point," 30.

14. For examples, see *KI*, docs. 11741 and 11742, Bun'ei 11 (1274) 11th month 1st day, and doc. 11743, 11th month 3rd day.

15. Institutions and individuals frequently held land rights on a number of estates. Rarely were their holding contiguous; in some cases, the estates in question might be located on completely different islands.

16. Most scholars now think that there was only one storm (at the time of the 1281 invasion), and some believe that Japan's samurai defenders were

fighting differed from the earlier conflicts described in the previous paragraphs because the military effort yielded neither confiscated lands nor titles to divide among the defenders. Petitions from veterans seeking compensation from Kamakura for their service against the Mongols continued for years after the actual fighting.[17] Under such conditions, it was reasonable for modern historians to see *tokuseirei* as an attempt by the *bakufu*, seemingly without any other way to compensate its warriors, to reward *gokenin* by exempting them from obligations to moneylenders and allowing them to reclaim lands lost as loan collateral.[18]

Although this interpretation seems *prima facie* internally consistent, careful scrutiny of other evidence renders it questionable. First, there is little documentary proof that samurai impoverishment stemmed directly from the costs of defending against the Mongols. Consider the case of Takezaki Suenaga, a *gokenin* from Kyushu who led five men into battle against the Mongols.[19] Desperate for some form of financial reward after the fighting, Takezaki decided to directly petition the shogun's officials in Kamakura. Against the advice of his commander on Kyushu, Takezaki sold his horse and armor to pay for his journey to the warrior capital. But Takezaki's financial troubles appear to have had little to do with the fighting itself. He had been in financial straits prior to the invasions, due to a dispute over family land holdings that he lost to a rival.[20] Part of his motivation in travelling to Kamakura was to get those lands (or a comparable holding) back. After the fighting, he took a

----

able to match the Mongols in combat. Ishii, "The Decline of the Kamakura *Bakufu*," and Conlan, *In Little Need of Divine Intervention*, 254–75.

17. Hori notes petitions from warriors for compensation from as early as 1286 and as late as 1307. "Economic and Political Effects of the Mongol Wars," 184.

18. Hori, "Economic and Political Effects of the Mongol Wars," 188.

19. Suenaga's tale is recounted in the *Mōko shūrai ekotoba*, an illustrated manuscript that he commissioned in his latter years. In English, see Conlan, *In Little Need of Divine Intervention*.

20. Ishii, "The Decline of the Kamakura *Bakufu*," 141–42.

calculated risk in selling off his belongings to pay for his journey to and stay in Kamakura in an attempt to gain rewards directly from *bakufu* officials. By the time he reached the warrior capital he was destitute, but it was the expense of the journey rather than the costs of combat that had reduced Takezaki to penury. Thirteenth-century warriors such as Takezaki saw the fighting as a potential opportunity to earn rewards, overlooking the equally possible drain on their finances.[21]

A second problem is that the *bakufu*'s inability to reward its retainers has not been clearly established. A key piece of evidence supporting the older argument was a *bakufu* decree from 1295 that forbade retainers from requesting compensation for their battlefield service during the Kōan years (1278–1188). Historians at one time thought that this decree referred to the 1281 invasion and cited it as proof that the *bakufu* was unable to compensate warriors for their service against the Mongols.[22] However, Hori's research proved that the fighting referred to in the 1295 decree was not the Mongol invasion but rather the destruction of Adachi Yasumori and his followers. In fact, the *bakufu* was still awarding grants in the fourteenth century to those who had driven back the Mongols.[23] The truth is that historians know very little about the state of *bakufu* finances.[24] On the one hand, contemporary documents attest to religious and military petitioners pressing the *bakufu* for compensation. On the other hand, key members of the Hōjō, the family that monopolized power in the *bakufu*, were expanding their holdings

---

21. Of course, it may be that even though the roots of their financial troubles lay elsewhere, the invasions provided an opportunity for warriors to petition for relief and have their claims heard.

22. Sansom, *A History of Japan to 1334*, 451–59.

23. The confusion concerns the term *Kōan gassen* (Kōan war). While the Kōan years include those of the second defense against the Mongols, the fighting in Kyushu was always referred to as the *ikoku gassen* (war against the foreigners) or the *Mōko gassen* (war against the Mongols). It is now generally agreed that the *Kōan gassen* refers instead to the 1285 destruction of the Adachi family. Hori, "Economic and Political Effects of the Mongol Wars," 185–86.

24. Mass, "Black Holes in Japanese History," 171–75.

(and thereby their income) during precisely these same decades.[25] Considering the paucity of evidence in late thirteenth-
century sources indicating that the Mongol invasions left warriors destitute and the *bakufu* unable to pay, other factors likely
played a part in the decision to declare their debts forgiven.

Finally, it should not be forgotten that only some retainers—
those with holdings in Kyushu—were ordered to take part in
the defense of that island. Yet retainers' financial problems cut
across geographic boundaries. In other words, some of the retainers struggling with financial debt did not participate in
the defense of Kyushu. This fact alone suggests that it is mis-
leading to give so much significance to the costs of fighting
off the Mongols.

This chapter proposes instead that the *bakufu* issued *tokuseirei* to address larger problems caused by the spread of money
and markets over the course of the thirteenth century. It is clear
that samurai retainers were using money and that some were
falling into debt as a result. As early as 1226, the Kamakura
bakufu's official chronicle, the *Azuma kagami*, noted that gambling, betting, and usury were widespread. One of its entries
for that year demands that such behavior among retainers
stop, and that the names of those who fail to follow the pro-
scription should be forwarded to Kamakura officials (presume-
ably for disciplinary action).[26] Stories and popular tales also
make reference to the use of cash by samurai. The *setsuwa*
collection *Kokon chomonjū*, which dates to the mid-Kamakura
period, includes several tales that deal with money and gambling. In one such episode, the samurai attendants at the residence of Minister of the Right Kazan-in Tadatsune are con-
sumed with betting on *shichihan* (a dice game), but one older
samurai is so poor that he has no money with which to gam-
ble.[27] When he reluctantly confesses to his wife that he wishes
to play like the others just once, she takes pity on him and sells

25. Kaizu, *Mōko shūrai.*
26. *AK*, Karoku 2 (1226) 1st month 26th day.
27. *Kokon chomonjū*, 242–45.

her robes for 500 *mon*. The husband (with the help of the gods) turns the small sum into 30 *kanmon* in a single day through his good fortune with the dice. He then uses this money to retire, take religious vows, and devote himself to recitation of the *nenbutsu*. The tale is surely fictional — few gamblers, especially inexperienced ones, are able to enjoy such winnings, and the intervention of the gods in aiding the old samurai is miraculous, intended to prove the benefits of proper worship. But in order to make the miracle stand out and the tale's lesson believable, the setting must have been realistic to thirteenth-century readers. This and other tales demonstrate that gambling and the use of cash by low-ranking samurai was not uncommon. Unfortunately for some, as in any society, gambling was more frequently a source of impoverishment than wealth.

Yet the *bakufu* did not attempt to ban the use of coins altogether. As noted in the previous chapter, it expected periodic cash payments from retainers and instructed *jitō* to assess penalties for theft in accordance with the cash value of the goods stolen. Although never institutionalized, the periodic cash levies assessed on retainers often involved considerable amounts of money. For example, a 1240 entry in the *Azuma kagami* reveals a special tax on retainers to pay for the shogun's prayer services (*onritsugan*). The entry notes that an "enormous sum of money" (*bakudai yōto*) is required, and that the levy is a source of anxiety for the *gokenin*.[28] Later in the same entry, there is a reference to "thank you money" (*kōsen*), cash that *gokenin* paid to *bakufu* officials in order to secure appointments. Nor was the use of money amongst warriors restricted to payments to the *bakufu*. As was also shown in the previous chapter, samurai used money when traveling to and from guard duty, and warrior houses taxed estate communities to raise cash for everything from travel costs to subsidizing hunts.[29]

---

28. *AK*, Ninji 1 (1240) 12th month 16th day.
29. "Shibuya Jōshin okibumi," *Iriki-in ke monjo*, Kangen 3 (1245) 5th month 11th day.

Yet retainers' efforts to obtain money led them to endanger their land holdings and thereby threaten the *bakufu*-retainer system. Warriors' income was limited inasmuch as it was a percentage of estate rents. Because rents did not increase as quickly as agricultural output grew, warriors seemed to be always falling behind in the emerging monetary economy. They needed (or simply desired) more cash than their fixed incomes could provide. This led retainers to borrow from moneylenders (*kashiage*) and use their land rights as collateral in order to obtain cash, as can be seen in thirteenth-century warrior correspondence. One warrior writes of repeatedly trying to cover his expenses by borrowing money. "Every time [I borrow], they [moneylenders] take interest [*rizeni*] from me," he writes. Another provincial retainer's letter orders his subordinates to raise cash for loan repayment or else he will have to sell additional lands.[30] In cases where they defaulted on their loans, moneylenders—who owed no service to the *bakufu*—confiscated lands intended to support retainers. Thus Kamakura had good reason to be concerned with its retainers' loss of land holdings irrespective of the Mongol invasions.

Kamakura legal pronouncements throughout the thirteenth century reflect this concern. The Jōei Formulary of 1232, composed by shogunal regent Hōjō Yasutoki, was the earliest warrior codification of laws.[31] Among its rules for proper warrior conduct are several provisions that address monetary and land ownership issues, both of which were elements of *bakufu toku-seirei* later in the century. For example, Article 8 declares that an individual must maintain possession of a land holding for

---

30. *Chibaken no rekishi: shiryōhen chūsei 2*, doc. 14, pp. 1028–29; doc. 19, pp. 1090–91. Many of these documents are incomplete and survive only because the paper on which they were written was reused. Although often difficult to date with precision, these two are confidently attributed by the editors of the *Chiba Prefectural History* to the mid-thirteenth century.

31. The standard annotated version of the Jōei Formulary is in the first volume of *Chūsei seiji shakai shisō*, 7–42. More recent research is in Takahashi, *Goseibai shikimoku*. Though old, a complete English translation is Hall's "The Hojo Code of Judicature," 17–44.

at least twenty years in order to establish clear rights of ownership. This left open the possibility that *gokenin* might reclaim lands taken from them less than twenty years previously. Even more telling, Article 48 states that only hereditary holdings (as opposed to land received from Kamakura) may be bought and sold. In other words, *gokenin* were free to alienate family holdings as they pleased, but lands awarded to them by Kamakura could not be transmitted without the *bakufu*'s approval. This was because *gokenin* were expected to render service to the *bakufu* in exchange for possession of those lands.

Lawsuits are also addressed in the Jōei Formulary, such as in Article 36, which discourages land disputes that cause unneeded burden on the judicial system.[32] These and other legal concepts put forth in the Jōei Formulary seem to have been intended to prevent retainers from losing their land rights. Curiously, the formulary does not employ the term "virtue" in these sections; in fact, the character for virtue appears only once in the entire code, in reference to the virtue of the gods. Kamakura would not employ the concept of "virtue" as a way to describe economic relief for retainers until the second half of the thirteenth century. Yet the policies espoused in the Jōei Formulary are very similar to those that would appear in the virtuous government edicts of the later thirteenth century.

Kamakura continued to issue proclamations that limited lawsuits and prevented the transmission of retainers' holdings in the decades following the issuance of Hōjō Yasutoki's legal codes. In 1240, the *bakufu* decreed that if a *gokenin* paid back more than half of the debt he owed when a loan came due, then his holdings were immune from confiscation. Instead, the loan would be adjusted to give the retainer more time to pay back the outstanding balance.[33] Eighteen years later, Kamakura proclaimed that it would not hear lawsuits over

---

32. See also Article 6, which prevents parties from bringing lawsuits without a letter of recommendation from local tribunals, and Article 29, which prevents multiple suits over the same issue to different Kamakura officials.

33. *Kamakura bakufu tsuikahō*, doc. 139, En'ō 2 (1240) 4th month 20th day.

lands granted to retainers prior to 1242.[34] This stood in sharp contrast with the normal pattern of Kamakura justice up to that point, in which cases were retried numerous times with Kamakura content to serve as the arbitrator.

Other related legislation included a 1239 prohibition against appointing moneylending merchants (*shōnin kariage*) or the moneylending monks (*sansō*) of Enryakuji as deputy *jitō*. Apparently some warriors, unable to pay back loans, attempted to get out of debt by appointing their creditors as deputy *jitō* and allowing them to extract income directly from provincial estate residents. The decree bemoans retainers who appoint moneylenders because they "covet the profits of the moment, without considering the financial problems (they will cause for) the future."[35] The suggestion that retainers were acting out of greed rather than to rescue themselves from debt might have been correct in some cases, but it also reflected the *bakufu's* misunderstanding in 1239 of the desperate financial straits in which its warriors found themselves.

These legislative efforts seem to have had little impact on moneylenders, who flourished in both Kyoto and Kamakura. In Kyoto, a major business district was located between the Seventh and Eighth Great Avenues, bounded on the west by Karasumaru and on the east by Abura no kōji. Commenting on a fire that burned down much of the district in 1234, Fujiwara Teika noted that the area had been home to innumerable moneylending houses that contained "all the wealth of the world." The day after the fire, Teika wrote, the moneylenders received condolences and gifts from other merchants that piled up like mountains and blocked the road.[36] Kamakura also had active merchant districts — according to a decree from 1251, there were seven official business districts scattered through-

---

34. The 1240 and 1258 decrees are both discussed in Brown, "The Japanese *Tokusei* of 1297," 194–96.

35. *Kamakura bakufu tsuikahō*, doc. 120, En'ō 1 (1239) 9th month 11th day.

36. *Meigetsuki*, Bunryaku 1 (1234) 8th month 5th day.

out the city.[37] And, as mentioned in a legal proclamation from 1255, moneylending became rampant within the city of Kamakura itself. The decree banned such activities, comparing moneylenders to thieves. It noted that the former (i.e., moneylenders) use pawnshops to profit from the sale of confiscated collateral and hide the identity of borrowers in the same way that the latter (thieves) use middlemen to sell stolen property and disguise the identity of the proper owners.[38] But such efforts by the *bakufu* to bolster the economic position of retainers had little effect. That point is especially clear in the opening lines of a 1267 proclamation that decries the bad financial position of retainers who have sold or mortgaged their holdings. The decree goes on to prohibit all sales of and foreclosures on *gokenin* holdings. It is so similar to the 1297 virtuous government edicts that Amino Yoshihiko refers to this 1267 debt-abrogation decree as the first medieval *tokuseirei*.[39]

Obviously, the 1267 edict pre-dates the first Mongol invasion by seven years. What led to its promulgation? Amino cites the increasing level of violence associated with land and loans in the mid-thirteenth century. Within the early medieval framework of land rights, different individuals concurrently held distinct rights to income from the same land parcel. Thus, a warrior might possess rights to a percentage of income from a specific piece of land but not possess the authority to determine how the land was to be used.[40] In several instances, Kamakura vassals offered as collateral land over which they did not have the primary rights of management. When they failed to repay their loans, the lenders tried to claim the land, but those with primary rights would refuse to recognize the claims of the

37. *Kamakura bakufu tsuikahō*, doc. 272, Kenchō 3 (1251) 12th month 3rd day.
38. *Kamakura bakufu tsuikahō*, doc. 305, Kenchō 7 (1255) 8th month 12th day.
39. Amino, *Mōko shūrai*, 141–42.
40. This early medieval land-rights system emerged during the Heian period; for more on concurrent rights, see Kiley, "Estate and Property in the Late Heian Period," 109–24. The system had already begun to break down by the end of the thirteenth century; see Mass, "Of Hierarchy and Authority," 17–38.

lenders. Often temple-shrine complexes were involved as participants in these disputes. Temples and shrines frustrated by competing land claims tended either to seek the aid of more powerful religious institutions, thereby turning small disputes into major incidents, or they resorted to violence, in some cases burning down the religious houses of their opponents.[41]

Kamakura could not allow such behavior to continue. Its reaction in 1267 was fourfold. First, it allowed *gokenin* to keep their lands even if they were late in repaying their loans. Second, it forbade land-management contracts known as *wayo*, deals by which warriors would manage land and pay a fixed fee to the civilian proprietor, since such agreements were also often at the heart of disputes.[42] Third, the *bakufu* stopped non-*gokenin* appeals of judicial decisions involving retainers. Fourth, and perhaps most interesting, Kamakura banned women who remarried from conveying land to their new husbands.[43] This clause specifically prevented widows of retainers from bequeathing their holdings to second husbands who were not affiliated with the warrior government. Whereas the first three clauses might be interpreted as the *bakufu*'s efforts at aiding financially troubled retainers, the fourth clause makes it quite clear that Kamakura's concern was to prevent service lands from being transferred to individuals without ties to the *bakufu*.

Why was the *bakufu* so concerned about the fate of its retainers' land holdings? The answer lies in the structure of the *bakufu* itself, which at its core promised land to retainers in exchange for service. Minamoto no Yoritomo's great innovation was that he built independent, reciprocal relationships with local samurai in eastern Japan. Prior to Yoritomo, elites

---

41. Amino, *Mōko shūrai*, 139–40.

42. For more on *wayo*, see Mass, "*Jitō* Land Possession in the Thirteenth Century."

43. For reasons unclear, Takeuchi Rizō listed the clause regarding women as a separate entry in the *Kamakura ibun*, although Amino indicates that it was part of the same 1267 decree. See *KI*, docs. 9837 and 9838, both Bun'ei 4 (1267) 12th month 26th day.

based in the capital controlled all provincial appointments. Some warriors were able to secure posts as estate managers or provincial government administrators, but they held those positions at the whim of central elites. Warriors could not even transmit their offices to heirs without the approval of their superiors in the capital. [44] Because there were more samurai seeking office than there were posts available, it was easy for central elites to replace uncooperative samurai with others eager for official positions. The appeal of Yoritomo was that he offered local warriors an alternative to that system. Yoritomo guaranteed samurai land rights in exchange for their loyalty and service, and thereby built a regional power base independent of Kyoto. Samurai gained greater security over their property rights, while the *bakufu* gained a group of retainers ready and willing to serve.

These reciprocal relationships between the *bakufu* and its retainers formed the cornerstone of Kamakura's power. Yet within decades of the *bakufu*'s founding in the 1180s, changes in the economy had a profound effect on retainers. Their involvement in gambling and their need or desire to purchase goods with money led them to seek larger amounts of cash. Unable to extract such cash from their estate-based fixed incomes, *gokenin* had to pursue one of four options. First, warriors could attempt to increase the size of their estate-based incomes by taking income rights away from the civilian estate proprietors. Second, they could align with the *bakufu* against other warriors and hope to receive in exchange for their military service the land holdings of those who were deprived of their positions. Of course, as Jeffrey Mass has shown, warriors who chose the first option were likely to face a protracted legal battle in which the civilian proprietor would defend his land rights. And the second option, as Kondō Shigekazu argues, was only viable in the first half of the thirteenth century. Following the destruction of the Miura family in 1247 and the

---

44. The Heian system by which central elites controlled provincial samurai appointments is described in detail by Friday in *Hired Swords*.

subsequent redistribution of Miura lands, there were no major land-holding families that were not already *bakufu* insiders.[45] A third option for warriors was to attempt to raise taxes on their estates' villages, a topic discussed in Chapter 2 of this volume. Fourth and finally, they could turn to moneylenders. Kamakura retainers tried all of these alternatives. I will now address the *bakufu*'s response to those who pursued the fourth option.

Virtuous government edicts should be seen as a *bakufu* corrective measure intended to restore *gokenin* lands that had been lost to moneylenders and thereby preserve the *bakufu*-retainer system. Yet why should Kamakura's efforts have been labeled "virtuous"? What factors led *bakufu* officials to choose virtuous government edicts as their form of relief? The next section explores the history of ideas of "virtuous government" in Japan and demonstrates that *bakufu* concern over the power of the imperial court played a large role in its decision to employ virtue as a trope for economic relief efforts.

Virtuous Government and Debt Relief in Early Japan

Japanese notions of "virtuous government" can be found in some of the oldest surviving texts, but clearly draw upon even older Chinese ideas of good government that came to Japan from China no later than the eighth century CE. Among those Chinese philosophers whom the Japanese studied, perhaps Confucius is most closely associated with notions of virtue and good government. In the Confucian *Analects*, compiled between the fifth and third centuries BCE, Confucius discusses the need for virtue in several sections as part of his larger philosophy that the ruler should set the example for his subjects. For example, when asked by a ruler, "Why not kill those who do not know propriety?" Confucius responds, saying: "Why should you need to kill in order to rule? If you seek goodness,

---

45. Kondō Shigekazu, "1247 as a Turning Point," 30–31. See also Mass, "Jitō Land Possession in the Thirteenth Century."

then the people will be good! The virtue of a gentleman is like the wind, while the virtue of a petty man is like the grass; when the wind blows, the grass bends."[46] The Former Han dynasty Confucian scholar Dong Zhongshu was another important early figure who helped shape ideas of virtuous rule. Dong held that the lack of such rule was the cause of natural disasters visited by Heaven upon the Chinese realm—a theme that would frequently appear in Japanese writings as well.[47] However, Hongō Kazuto, who has conducted extensive etymological research on *tokusei*, proposes that ideas of virtuous government in medieval Japan were heavily influenced by the *Chunqiu zuozhuan* (Zuo Commentary on the Spring and Autumn Annals). This text includes discussion of how the weak state of Cheng faced the threat of being taken over by its stronger neighbors of Jin and Chu. Cheng's ruler is encouraged by his advisors to survive by relying on virtue. The advisors tell the king that if he rules with laws alone, the people will only fear punishment, and low and high will become confused, a theme that appears in the *Analects* as well. They urge him instead to rule by virtuous example. This story is written about in detail in Zuo Qiuming's commentary on *The Spring and Autumn Annals*—the only annotation of this Chinese classic known to have been available in thirteenth-century Japan.[48]

As these examples reveal, Chinese political thought held that virtue and benevolence were essential to good state administration. Governments that lacked such qualities would incur Heaven's displeasure, which would manifest itself in the

---

46. *Analects*, 12.19 (my translation). While the Chinese Confucian scholars used the characters 德治 more commonly than 德政, examination of their usage shows that the two are clearly linked. In the *Analects*, 德 and 政 are linked in at least three passages: 2.1, 2.3, and 12.19. *Lunyu yizhu* (Beijing: Zhonghua shuju, 1980).

47. Lowe, "The Religious and Intellectual Background," 708–13.

48. This annotated version was the only one included in the holdings of the Kanazawa Bunko, the library of a branch family of the Hōjō that survived the destruction of Kamakura in 1333. See Hongō, *Chūsei chōtei soshō no kenkyū*, 223–25.

form of natural disasters. Both of these strands of thought can be found in early Japanese writings as well. For example, the eighth-century *Nihon shoki* (Chronicles of Japan), one of the oldest extant Japanese texts, includes the story of Emperor Nintoku, famous for his three-year remission of all taxes when he discovered that the people were suffering from a poor harvest. Nintoku is supposed to have reigned during the fifth century, but as there are no written documents that survive from his reign, it is impossible to substantiate the *Nihon shoki* account. Yet the inclusion of this story in Kamo no Chōmei's well-known late twelfth-century essay "Hōjōki" suggests that virtuous Nintoku was a part of the late classical and early medieval popular imaginary.[49] Even the characters for the emperor's name, 仁德, clearly show Chinese Confucian influence in their combination of *ren* (benevolence; Jp. *nin/jin*) and *de* (virtue; Jp. *toku*).

Ideas of *tokusei* as virtuous or benevolent rule were not just reserved for mythic histories and literary essays. During the Nara period, the female emperor Genmei is reported to have seriously weighed the burden to the people of conscripting laborers and levying supplies because she knew that showing benevolence was a means of confirming her legitimacy.[50] The Heian imperial court also recognized the importance of these notions in administering affairs of state. For example, the ninth-century *Nihon kōki* (Later Chronicles of Japan) records a heated debate before the emperor in 805 between two advisors of the fourth rank.[51] The first, Fujiwara no Otsugu, called for tax reductions as a form of virtuous government for the realm. He argued that the people were suffering from high taxes to support construction projects and the military, and that those taxes had to be stopped in order to pacify the people.[52] The

---

49. Aston, *Nihongi*, 278–79; Kamo no Chōmei, "Hōjōki."
50. Piggott, *The Emergence of Japanese Kingship*, 189.
51. *Nihon kōki*, Enryaku 24 (805) 12th month 7th day.
52. Taxes had been especially high during this period in order to finance wars against the Emishi in the north and build the new capital at Heian (modern Kyoto).

second advisor, Sugano no Mamichi, argued strongly against abandoning current policies. According to the *Nihon kōki*, the emperor chose to follow Otsugu's advice and thereby earned the admiration of the people. As this account was recorded in the *Nihon kōki* within decades of its supposed occurrence, it is far more reliable than the story of Emperor Nintoku canceling taxes, and proves that the remission of taxes was associated with good government during the Heian period.

The Japanese linked virtuous rule with other economic relief policies as well, such as the forgiving of loans and the restoration of lands to their original owners. The *Nihon shoki* includes two references to the canceling of interest due on debts. The first is from shortly before Emperor Tenmu's death in 686 and was probably enacted in hopes of aiding in his recovery from illness, while the second appears during the reign of his widow, Emperor Jitō, and was likely related to mourning rituals.[53] Other virtuous acts listed include the granting of a general amnesty and gifts to the elderly and those unable to support themselves. While these debt cancellations surely had some religious significance, they also highlight the close relationship between virtuous rule and economic assistance. Virtue was also invoked to restore land holdings. For example, an imperial command from the eleventh month of 751 declared that property sold within a certain period of time should be returned to its original owners.[54] Even in this early period, good governance involved protecting the economic well-being of the people.

Tokusei was a major topic of discussion in both the court and the retired emperor's office during the late Heian period. Ichisawa Tetsu observes that officials in the Heian period attributed natural disasters such as famines and earthquakes to a lack of virtuous administration, but that a major shift oc-

---

53. *Nihon shoki*, entries for the seventh month (pp. 463–64) and the twelfth month (p. 477) of 686. In English, see Aston, *Nihongi*, 378, 385. On mourning rituals during this period, see Ebersole, *Ritual Poetry and the Politics of Death*.

54. *Shoku Nihongi*, Tenpyō shōhō 3 (751) 11th month 10th day.

curred with the Genpei war. Specifically, Ichisawa sees a turning point in a report made during the conflict by Minamoto no
Yoritomo to Retired Emperor Go-Shirakawa. In that report,
Yoritomo outlines concrete policies for restoring virtuous administration, including his thoughts on capturing the rem-
nants of his wartime enemies, the Heike and Kiso Yoshinaka.
Yoritomo's report implies that *tokusei* had little to do with the
gods and much to do with man-made policy decisions.[55] According to Ichisawa, Yoritomo's advocacy of policy as a means
of enacting *tokusei* marked the start of a shift in conceptions
of virtuous rule. Kaizu Ichirō also writes of a shift in the defi-
nition of *tokusei* from reliance on the gods and court to reliance
on men and the *bakufu*, though he dates the shift to the late
thirteenth century. What had once been understood to be a reflection of Heaven's displeasure through natural phenomena
came instead to be perceived as the result of human decisions
in the medieval period.[56]

With Yoritomo's formation of the Kamakura *bakufu*, government became a dyarchy, making it necessary for modern
scholars to look separately at how *tokusei* was regarded in
Kyoto, seat of the imperial court, and in Kamakura, headquarters of the *bakufu*. These two capitals made up Japan's "dual
government" during the Kamakura period. There was some
degree of intellectual exchange between the two cities. After
the death of the last Minamoto shogun in 1219, future warrior
leaders were adopted from the noble or imperial families, while
prominent warriors served in the *bakufu*'s Rokuhara office in
Kyoto. Yet their approaches to government reflected distinct
differences in the thirteenth century, in part due to the very
different political fortunes of each city. Modern history books
tend to associate virtuous government edicts with Kamakura's
warrior administration, but the next section will show that the

---

55. *AK*, Genryaku 1 (1184) 2nd month 25th day.
56. The respective interpretations can be found in Ichisawa, "Kuge tokusei no seiritsu to tenkai," and in Kaizu, *Chūsei no henkaku to tokusei*.

court was more active in promoting *tokusei* than the *bakufu* for most of the thirteenth century.

Tokusei *and the Court-*Bakufu *Rivalry of the Thirteenth Century*

An uneasy peace between the Kyoto imperial court and the newly formed *bakufu* came to an end in 1221 when retired emperors Go-Toba and Juntoku mobilized a coalition of disgruntled warriors and other anti-*bakufu* figures in an attempt to destroy the warrior government. They misjudged Kamakura's strength. After receiving Kyoto's declaration of war, armies from Kamakura attacked first and crushed the pro-Kyoto military uprising. Defeated in a matter of weeks, their failure left Kyoto and its supporters weakened. Many of their estate holdings were confiscated and key leaders killed or removed from office. Go-Toba and Juntoku were sent into exile on remote islands, and the current emperor, Juntoku's son, was forced to abdicate. The shogunate not only insisted upon selecting the next emperor but also created a special Kyoto office, the Rokuhara *tandai*, where two of its top officials were stationed so that they could keep watch over Kyoto's affairs. In short, the court's freedom of action was seriously diminished and its prestige was badly damaged. These conditions led to a heightened interest in *tokusei* among the imperial nobility. Under trying circumstances, members of the court turned to concepts of virtuous government in a campaign to clean up inefficiency and abuse in the retired emperor's chancellery.[57] Lacking military strength, they had to rely on ideology and moral righteousness.

Leading this campaign were important Kyoto nobles including Kujō Michiie (1193–1251), who looked to *tokusei* to justify a new role for the court in governing Japan. Michiie had the pedigree to lead the court in this effort, for his grandfather Kanezane had served as both regent (*sesshō*) and chancellor

---

57. Hashimoto, "In no hyōjōsei ni tsuite," 1–18.

(*kanpaku*), and his father Yoshitsune (1169–1206) had served
as regent until his sudden death in 1206. Kanezane helped
raise the young Michiie and, after Yoshitune's death, helped
groom him for high office. Michiie also had the motivation
to work at strengthening the court since he had seen how the
warrior government could meddle in court affairs. His grandfather Kanezane had lost power in 1196 in part because he lost
the support of the shogun Yoritomo. Michiie himself was removed from the post of regent by the Kamakura *bakufu* only
months after taking office in 1221 when the Jōkyū Uprising
failed. Perhaps it was with his grandfather that he first studied
Confucian notions of virtuous rule, for Kanezane had worked
closely with Kiyohara no Yorinari (1122–1189), a leading scholar
of the Tōji and the man who wrote the Japanese commentary
on Zuo Qiuming's *Spring and Autumn Annals*. As mentioned
above, the *Zuo Commentary* was the only version of that Chinese text available in Japan at the time, and it seems to have
inspired Michiie's thinking on government.[58]

Michiie proved to be an astute politician and served as regent again from 1229 to 1232, but his years in office were
marred by frequent famines and natural disasters. Heavy summer rains, flooding, and a typhoon in the late 1220s set the
stage for the Kangi famine, described by William Wayne Farris
as "possibly the most lethal famine in Japanese history." Although speculative, Farris estimates death rates at over 25 percent in some parts of the country and notes that many named
fields, productive prior to the famine, can no longer be found
in the records of land under cultivation after the famine.[59]
The famine was likely the result of unusually cold weather, as
evidenced by *Hyakurenshō* references from the summers of
1230 and 1231 to snow falling in several provinces. Michiie in-

---

58. It was not only available, but widely read. According to Hongō, Fujiwara Yorinaga mentioned the Kiyohara version of the *Spring and Autumn
Annals* as the first book he read. Emperor Hanazono referred to it in his diary, and Kitabatake Chikafusa also cited it. See Hongō, *Chūsei chōtei soshō no
kenkyū*, 225–26.

59. Farris, *Japan's Medieval Population*, 33, 39–42.

terpreted these to be signs of the anger of the gods, brought about by the suffering and confusion of the people. In order to prevent such phenomena, Michiie argued, the court needed to restore order to the world. In his capacity as regent, Michiie pushed the court to reform the imperial appointment system and to hear petty suits brought by the people to help them settle their problems.[60] Following the courtiers' defeat in 1221, key nobles such as Michiie recognized the need for the court to find a new role for itself and show true concern for the people as a way of ensuring its continued existence.[61]

Michiie may have found more than one form of inspiration in ideas of *tokusei*. As noted above, the *Spring and Autumn Annals* taught how reliance on virtue allowed the weaker state of Cheng to survive even though stronger, hostile states surrounded it. Perhaps Michiie interpreted Cheng's situation as mirroring that of Kyoto: the imperial court, the weaker entity, was confronted by the Kamakura *bakufu*, whose victory in 1221 left it able to dictate terms to Kyoto. Michiie may therefore have turned to reform of the imperial government as part of an effort to foster *tokusei* and help his state endure. This interpretation is somewhat speculative, for it would necessitate Michiie granting the *bakufu* the same status in his mind as a rival state (something he presumably would have found objectionable), but it is not incompatible with Michiie's other actions during this time. With their survival in question, it seems reasonable to suspect that Kyoto leaders found hope in this well-known Chinese model.

Michiie's strategy was taken up wholeheartedly by Retired Emperor Go-Saga (1220–1272) and his sons Kameyama (1249–1305) and Go-Fukakusa (1243–1304), who became famous for adjudicating lawsuits. During Kameyama's tenure as a retired emperor (1274–1287), he took over the site that his father had used for literary society meetings and converted it into a court

---

60. Hongō, *Chūsei chōtei soshō no kenkyū*, 75–76.
61. Hongō, "Kamakura jidai chōtei soshō no ichizokumen," 129–31.

for hearing common cases.[62] Nobles sat in judgment, and the retired emperor himself sometimes attended. This institution flourished and became quite refined, with specific days and rituals reserved for certain types of cases and petitioners. Nobles who held the positions of *daijin* and *dainagon* officiated three times per month (on days ending in "ones"), whereas *chūnagon* and other nobles holding lesser offices presided six days per month. The entire process was referred to as the *tokusei* system, and its popularity and sophistication are described in a detailed account from 1284.[63] Through the administration of justice (*ontokusei no sata*), the court forged a new role for itself. Kyoto's involvement in popular legal matters became widely publicized, restoring prestige to the court and perhaps allowing nobles to think that they had taken the moral high ground vis-à-vis the *bakufu*. The *bakufu* was busy with its own concerns, however.

Despite Yoritomo's call to restore *tokusei* in 1184, Kamakura initially did not adopt the term in its edicts or law proclamations. *Bakufu* leaders did make use of the term "virtue" to justify taking arms against the emperor in the uprising of 1221, but that appears to have been an exceptional case.[64] The only mention of virtue in the famous 1232 legal code of Hōjō Yasutoki, for example, is a reference to the virtue of the gods. Of the few other references to *tokusei* in *bakufu* records from the first half of the thirteenth century, most concern the link between *tokusei* and natural disasters. The term appears in the *Azuma kagami* on nine different occasions, with six of the nine entries calling for *tokusei* as a response to strange natural phenomena ranging from comets and earthquakes to fires

---

62. Hongō, "Kamakura jidai chōtei soshō no ichizokumen," 126–32. In the late Heian and Kamakura periods, the retired emperor was often the most powerful man in the court. See Kondo, "1247 as a Turning Point," for a thorough explanation of the relationship between the emperor and retired emperor in the thirteenth century.

63. *Kanchūki*, Kōan 9 (1286) 12th month 3rd day, 24th day. *Zōhō shiryō taisei vol. 35: Kanchūki, vol. 2*, pp. 132–33, 140.

64. Brownlee, "Crisis as Reinforcement of the Imperial Institution," 196–97.

and snow in summer. Clearly *bakufu* leaders sometimes interpreted meteorological phenomena as reflections of the approval or disapproval of the gods, or at least chose to couch their responses to such phenomena in the language of virtuous government.

Over the course of the thirteenth century, however, the *bakufu* began to make moves to assume more of the court's authority. One such area was international relations, which had up to that point been left to the imperial court. When Khubilai Khan sent representatives to Japan in the late 1260s insisting upon diplomatic relations and threatening war, a foreign policy crisis emerged. Imperial officials began drafting a conciliatory reply to send to the Mongols, but Kamakura squelched their efforts and insisted that the *bakufu* alone would negotiate foreign policy matters. Another such area was estate management. Previously, *bakufu* warriors were denied entry into estates that were wholly under civilian control. Such estates that did not regularly have a *bakufu* appointee were known as *ichien shōen*. But when it became clear that the Mongol situation would lead to hostilities, the *bakufu* forced the court to give it the authority to enter those civilian estates and draft men not otherwise affiliated with the *bakufu* for service in the defense effort.[65] The Kyoto court presumably granted the *bakufu* this additional power temporarily, because of the emergency situation. However, since the Mongol threat never went away, the *bakufu* retained this authority until its collapse.[66]

At the same time, the Hōjō, the family that monopolized the position of shogunal regent and was already one of the most powerful families in the *bakufu*, took advantage of the crisis

---

65. See *Kamakura bakufu tsuikahō*, no. 463, Bun'ei 11 (1274) 11th month 1st day, wherein *jitō*, *gokenin*, and *honjo ryōke ichienchi no jūnin* are all ordered to turn out for the defense of Japan. While *jitō* and *gokenin* normally received orders from the *bakufu*, *honjo ryōke ichien* lands did not.

66. Even after the failed invasions of 1274 and 1281, Khubilai Khan threatened a third invasion, and Kamakura *bakufu* forces remained on alert in Kyushu into the fourteenth century.

to further strengthen its own position within the Kamakura power structure. Its actions included appointing relatives to key provincial posts and to positions on the various judicial and administrative councils. Consider the position of *shugo* (military provincial governor). In the early 1270s, only one of the nine Kyushu *shugo* posts is known to have been held by a member of the Hōjō family (the *shugo* for two of the nine are unknown). By the late 1270s, however, six of the nine posts were held directly by Hōjō, and a seventh was held by Adachi Yasumori, the father-in-law of the shogun.[67] It was during these decades that contemporaries began referring to *bakufu* efforts at protecting retainer land holdings as virtuous government edicts. The *bakufu*'s appropriation of court notions of good government can be seen as part and parcel of a larger process by which the *bakufu* took over authority from the court.

Ideas of virtuous government were complex and held multiple meanings for the people of Kamakura-period Japan. Whereas influential nobles including Kujō Kanezane associated *tokusei* with prayers to appease the gods and avert strange natural phenomena, his grandson made *tokusei* into a call for good government. Meanwhile, the *bakufu* was enacting economic relief policies that resembled Japanese notions of virtuous government from the ancient and classical periods. By the second half of the thirteenth century, the retired emperor's new popular court and *bakufu* efforts to prevent *gokenin* from losing their lands were both being referred to as *tokusei*. It was into this setting that the Kamakura *bakufu* issued its virtuous government edicts of 1297, also known as the *Einin tokuseirei*.[68]

---

67. Kaizu, *Mōko shūrai*, 39.
68. The edict was first promulgated in Kamakura as a *Kantō onkotosho* on the 6th day of the 3rd month, and then issued as a *Kantō migyōsho* to the *bakufu* office in Rokuhara on the 22nd day of the 7th month. Although it was common for proclamations to be made first in Kamakura and then reissued as *migyōsho* when they were sent to Rokuhara, the process usually only took days. Why the Einin *tokuseirei* required four months before it was reissued to Rokuhara remains a mystery. Kasamatsu, *Tokuseirei*, 21.

In the first of its three sections, the *tokuseirei* prohibited direct judicial appeals to the *bakufu*. This might seem to be a break with *bakufu* willingness in the first half of the century to hear all cases involving its retainers, yet Kamakura had been taking steps to limit its case load since the 1230s.[69] Lawsuits initiated before the Einin decree and already in the system were to be heard, though. The second section allowed retainers to reclaim lands that they had pawned or sold, and made any future mortgage or sale of *gokenin* lands a criminal offense. Sharp distinctions were drawn between retainers and non-retainers in this section. Retainers could keep any lands that they had acquired, including lands of other *gokenin*, if they maintained possession of the land for twenty or more years, or if they received an official confirmation from the *bakufu*. The twenty-year possession rule is clearly derived from Article 8 of the 1232 Jōei Formulary, described above. Non-retainers were treated quite differently, however. Even if they had purchased or foreclosed on land and maintained possession for more than twenty years, the previous owner could still reclaim property from them. This clause in particular has led some scholars to focus on *tokuseirei* as instruments of restoration, fulfilling a social need to restore things to their original condition.[70]

In the third section, retainers were absolved of any responsibility to repay loans and the *bakufu* declared that it would not hear suits brought against *gokenin* for violating the terms of a loan agreement. From the time of this decree onward, even if a moneylender possessed a previously issued *bakufu* order requiring a *gokenin* to repay a debt, the *bakufu* refused to enforce the order. An exemption, however, was made for *dosō*, a particular type of moneylending house (often rendered

---

69. See the discussion of Articles 6, 29, and 36 of the Jōei Formulary and of the 1258 *bakufu* proclamation earlier in this chapter.

70. The best-known advocate of this view is Kasamatsu Hiroshi, who employs the term *modoshi* to describe the phenomenon of returning things to their original owners or condition. See his *Tokuseirei*, cited above.

as "pawnshops" in English); the significance of this exemption will be explained below.

Although the *bakufu* did not use the term *tokusei* anywhere in its 1297 proclamation, within weeks, landowners and disputants were using that name to refer to the decree.[71] Not only did they use the term to describe the Kamakura edicts, but they also began inserting clauses in land-sale agreements (*baiken*) to preempt or counteract the effects of future *tokusei* actions. For example, when one Nakamura no Shirōjirō purchased the rights to a mountain in 1306, the deed included the following language: "But in the event that *tokusei* is issued by either the nobles or the warriors [*kuge, buke*], it should not apply. Let this serve as proof for the future." Or, in the case of some dry fields sold the same year, the document included this set of phrases: "Even if a country-wide *ontokusei* is promulgated, there should be no variance (from the transaction recorded herein)." These types of exclusions are referred to by scholars as *tokusei tanpo mongon*. Other variations included promises on the part of the seller to refund the purchase price or to assist the buyer in legitimating his claim if the transaction was later invalidated by *tokusei*.[72]

From this time forward, the association of *tokusei* with debt abrogation would become dominant over other ideas of virtuous rule. The Kamakura *bakufu* had taken a court notion of good government for all and narrowed it into a policy that favored only *bakufu* retainers. Yet the 1297 edicts proved no more successful at restoring the financial position of *gokenin* than earlier *bakufu* decrees. As noted at the start of this chapter, land began changing hands in 1297 amidst much confusion as lawsuits proliferated. Many took advantage of this decree

------

71. For examples, see *KI*, doc. 19331, Einin 5 (1297) 4th month 1st day; and doc. 19488, 10th month 22nd day.

72. The two *baiken* cited are *KI*, doc. 22771, Kagen 4 (1306) 11th month 21st day; and *KI*, doc. 22773, same year and month, 23rd day. For examples from the months immediately following the issuance of the Einin tokuseirei of 1297, see *KI*, doc. 19343, 4th month 16th day; doc. 19401, 6th month 23rd day; and doc. 19525, 11th month 11th day.

to reclaim property, and despite the *bakufu*'s ban on lawsuits, many brought cases to the courts claiming that the terms of the *tokuseirei* did not apply to them. Most importantly, the legislation did not address the fundamental problem of *gokenin* with limited landed income living in a society with an expanding market economy.

Self-Interest and Bakufu-Retainer Relations

Should modern scholars view the 1297 *tokuseirei* as a sincere but misguided effort to aid *gokenin*, or were there other factors that led the *bakufu* to issue this legislation? Kozo Yamamura argued that the decision to rescind the decree in 1298 reflected the inability of the *bakufu* to "defy the dictates of a monetized economy." Suzanne Gay interpreted the *bakufu*'s actions as attempting to protect its vassals from the "excesses" of moneylenders.[73] In the final two sections of this chapter, I build upon these scholars' conclusions as I attempt to prove two related points: first, that the *bakufu* issued *tokuseirei* to protect its own retainer control system, and second, that *tokuseirei* represented the *bakufu*'s response to the emergence of a thirteenth-century monetary economy.

The greatest challenge posed by the new economy to the *bakufu* retainer system was that it facilitated transactions between people of different status. In earlier periods, such transactions were forbidden.[74] Land rights were only transferred amongst people of similar status. The ease and anonymity of money-based transactions, however, allowed *gokenin* to borrow from moneylenders and stake their land holdings as collateral. When those lands were lost, retainers were deprived of their primary source of income—the land. But the loss of these lands by *gokenin* did not merely lead to "the impoverishment of the *gokenin*," as mentioned in the 1297 *tokuseirei*; it also resulted in

---

73. Yamamura, "The Growth of Commerce," 376; Gay, *Moneylenders of Late Medieval Kyoto*, 73.

74. Kiley, "Estate and Property in the Late Heian Period," 109–24; Mass, "Of Hierarchy and Authority," 19.

the *bakufu* being deprived of the service of its retainers. This also can be clearly seen in the primary sources, such as a document of conveyance (*kishinjō*) from 1243 that, after providing the description and boundaries of the holding, states:

This land was originally a *gokenin* holding that had been handed down for generations, but because of [financial] need, was sold to another person. In short, after [the sale, the *gokenin*] became unable to support himself [*musoku*]. The shogun's house has previously made pronouncements [condemning] the selling of lands that support *gokenin* service. In keeping with the [shogun's] decree, this land shall be awarded to Ōsumi Daimyōji temple so that it can support prayers for the prosperity of the Kantō.[75]

As the document indicates, the loss of his property left the *gokenin* unable to render service to Kamakura. The *bakufu*'s response, curiously, is not to aid the retainer, but rather to order the land given to a temple so that it might provide service instead. In other words, the *bakufu* did not act as a benevolent ruler guarding the well-being of its warrior constituency, but rather it was first and foremost interested in ensuring that its lands were in the hands of individuals or institutions that would serve.

Although the *bakufu* would never have claimed to disregard the interests of its retainers, in fact a number of instances demonstrate that it had little concern for the fate of individual *gokenin*. Consider, for example, another edict from 1243, in which the *bakufu* addresses the problem of *gokenin* who fail to heed civilian estate proprietors.[76] Technically, retainers were supposed to obey civilian proprietors on estate matters, but since retainers received their appointments from *bakufu*, they often disregarded proprietors' wishes. In this particular edict, as in the conveyance discussed in the previous paragraph, the *bakufu* does not defend its retainers, nor does it proclaim that they are immune from charges of wrong-doing by pro-

---

75. *KI*, doc. 6240, Kangen 1 (1243) 9th month.
76. *Kamakura bakufu tsuikahō*, doc. 210, Kangen 1 (1243) 8th month 3rd day.

prietors. Instead, it asserts three things: first, that civilian proprietors should inform the *bakufu* of problems with *gokenin;* second, that the *bakufu* (not proprietors) will discipline *gokenin;* and third, that if problems recur, only the *bakufu* has the authority to replace the *gokenin* with others. The edict concludes by noting that all duties owed should be rendered without negligence. Thus, the *bakufu* did not care if retainers were replaced; its only concern was to retain the right to appoint and discipline its own followers.

In the *tokuseirei* of 1297, a clear sign of such self-interested thinking on the part of the *bakufu* can be found in the exemption granted to pawnshop moneylenders in the third edict. This clause meant that regardless of virtuous government decrees abrogating debts, retainers could not reclaim items placed in hock with those moneylenders. If the *bakufu*'s primary concern was for the fate of its retainers, would it not have allowed them to reclaim property lost to all types of moneylenders, including pawnshops? The clause challenges the idea that the *bakufu* was paternalistically looking out for its retainers. We are left to speculate on possible reasons for this provision. Perhaps *bakufu* officials had a financial (or other) connection to the pawnshops and did not want to disrupt a source of income or support. The Muromachi *bakufu* taxed pawnshops, but there is no other evidence to support such a connection between pawnshops and Kamakura, so we can only speculate on the nature of the connection. Alternatively, the *bakufu* may have sought to avoid adjudicating loan agreements that involved pawnshops, though why those agreements differed from other types of agreements remains unclear.

The changing economy of the thirteenth century proved to be a particularly difficult challenge for the *bakufu* system of rule. Earlier efforts at banning the sale or transfer of *gokenin* lands had proven ineffective, and the 1297 edicts were to fail as well. Yet the problem continued to demand the attention of *bakufu* officials, for the *bakufu* based its power structure on personal, reciprocal relationships with its affiliates. Impersonal, one-time transactions in the marketplace deprived the *bakufu* of the service due on lands formerly held by *gokenin* and led to drastic legislation such as the Einin *tokuseirei*. I turn to this problem of impersonal relationships, drawing upon the gift economy model, in the final part of this chapter.

Reciprocal Relationships and Gift Economy

This book contends that rising *bakufu* interest in *tokuseirei* paralleled the increase in the use of money and the spread of markets in thirteenth-century Japan. On the surface, this claim might not seem new, for Delmer Brown has already credited the "disrupting forces of an expanding exchange economy" as contributing to warrior difficulties in the years leading up to the 1297 edicts.[77] Yet as noted in the Introduction, my interpretation differs from Brown's in significant ways. Brown's analysis is informed by notions of an economic progression in which money is preceded by barter. But the Japanese economy prior to the twelfth-century reemergence of coins was neither based on barter nor was it primitive. Furthermore, unlike Brown, I argue that the *bakufu* valued personal, reciprocal ties with its retainers, at least when it sought service from them. Tensions between personal *bakufu*-retainer relationships and impersonal, single-interaction land purchases resemble those that accompanied the transition from "gift economy" to "profit economy," which some scholars have successfully employed in better understanding medieval European society.

The "gift economy" framework, widely discussed by historians and anthropologists, may be said to originate with the writings of French anthropologist Marcel Mauss. He saw premodern societies as having complex economies in which gift exchange was a primary means for the circulation of goods. He wrote: "In the economic and legal systems that have preceded our own, one hardly ever finds a simple exchange of goods, wealth, and products in transactions concluded by individuals. . . . [Rather] collectivities impose obligations of ex-

---

77. Brown, "The Japanese *Tokusei* of 1297," 189.

change and contract upon each other."[78] Giving is personal and creates obligations, according to Mauss. The gift always retains something of the giver with it and therefore necessitates the return of an equal or greater gift by the recipient. This system may strike modern readers as burdensome because it means that gifts come with obligations. But Mauss saw it as positive, for it allowed people in those societies to build and maintain long-term relationships. Examples of such giving can still be found in modern society, but impersonal, one-time transactions that lack reciprocity have displaced gift exchange as the primary means for the circulation of goods.

Mauss largely drew upon ethnographic accounts of native North American and Pacific Islander societies in conceiving of his theory of the gift. However, he also claimed to see gift circulation in early and medieval Europe, supporting his position with examples from Germanic law and Old Norse verse. Many historians of medieval European society have taken up Mauss's argument. Georges Duby, for example, described a shift from gift to profit economy over the eighth to twelfth centuries. Duby wrote of a society "shot through with an infinitely varied network for circulating the wealth and services," in which gifts were the primary items of exchange. According to Duby, commerce was a fringe activity at this time, tangential to the gift economy. It was left to Jews and foreigners, while barter was practiced on a large scale.[79] Trade grew with government control under the Carolingians and with the peace of the eleventh century, and cash was increasingly used to pay wages and facilitate market exchange. By the twelfth century, according to Duby, money, commerce, and paid labor were becoming more common. Although Duby does not quote Mauss directly nor use the term "gift economy," his findings were inspired by Mauss's description of a transition from a gift-based to a profit-based economy.

---

78. Mauss, *The Gift*, 5.
79. Duby, *Early Growth of the European Economy*, 56, 61–64.

Lester Little most clearly articulated these ideas in his research on the impact of tenth- and eleventh-century commerce
upon European society.[80] Little examined the shift during
those centuries from a gift economy to a developing profit
economy in which money and markets made impersonal, one-
time transactions increasingly easy. Compared to earlier times,
goods were evaluated for their value in currency rather than
for their prestige value or for the connections between buyer
and seller that they created. According to Little, this shift to
a profit economy led to changes in the religious orders, many
of which had long held that profit was to be frowned upon.
He attributes the emergence of the Friars as powerful religious
figures in the late medieval period to their willingness to offer
spiritual guidance in a period of growing commerce and urbanization. Barbara Rosenwein also employs the gift-economy
model in her study of land acquisition by the monks of Cluny.[81]
She finds that gift exchange and land *donations* involved a
"necessary generosity" and helped to cement personal relationships between the donor and the monastery, while land *purchases* were impersonal, did not lead to long-term relationships, and were motivated by the desire to accumulate land
and wealth. Both of these authors conclude that the shift from
largely gift-based to profit-based economy produced tremendous changes in medieval European society.[82]

The kinds of relations described by these scholars as having
occurred in medieval Europe share something with the approach to relations taken in traditional East Asia. The Chinese

---

80. Little, *Religious Poverty and the Profit Economy*, 3–8, 61–69.

81. Rosenwein, *To Be the Neighbor of Saint Peter*, 44–45, 95–99, 103–8.

82. Of course, the gift-economy model has its critics. Many scholars have
found problems in Mauss's claim that the gift itself, i.e., the actual object
given, has a spirit that requires it or its equivalent be returned to the giver.
See Lévi-Strauss, *Introduction to the Work of Marcel Mauss*, and Godelier, *The
Enigma of the Gift*. Other recent criticism proposes that Mauss was actually
writing about contemporary Europe and disguising his argument with examples from "primitive" societies. See Geary, "Gift Exchange and Social Science Modeling."

tribute system, which was the basis for formal diplomacy, trade, and international relations for much of the region's history, incorporated elements quite similar to those of the gift-economy model in that lesser rulers (or their representatives) presented "gifts" of tribute to the Chinese emperor, who was then bound to reciprocate by bestowing "gifts" in return. I contend that we can also apply these ideas to the study of relations between lord and retainer, *bakufu* and *gokenin*. In early medieval Japan, as described above, Minamoto no Yoritomo created an authority independent of the established imperial system by forging direct ties with warriors on the land — something that had never been accomplished before.[83] He put an end to violence and turmoil in the provinces during the 1180s by bestowing "gifts" of appointments to his retainers. In exchange, they were obliged to offer service when called upon. In neither case was the exchange a voluntary one. Sometimes Yoritomo accepted as a retainer someone not well known (or even necessarily trustworthy) simply because that individual was the most powerful warrior on the estate in question. This was especially true in western Japan, where Yoritomo had few vassals from the Genpei war years. And as for the service of the retainers, those who ignored or disobeyed a *bakufu* order risked losing their positions. The clearest example of such service was Yoritomo's decision to invade Ōshū in 1189. The ensuing war became a litmus test of warrior loyalty. Those who did not muster were automatically suspect and, in some cases, deprived of their positions.[84] This became the new Kamakura control system, one based on gifts and reciprocal relationships. Such a control system was necessary, for as Jeffrey Mass has written, "Warriors without rewards and without organizational controls to keep them in check were more apt to abuse than use for constructive purposes their newly acquired pow-

---

83. For more on Yoritomo's rise to power, and his use of confirmations and awards to secure retainers, see Mass, "The Kamakura *Bakufu*," 52–58.
    84. Ibid., 63–65.

ers."[85] For the warrior government, these reciprocal relationships were the key to preserving power.

Maintaining these ties was vital to the effective functioning of the *bakufu* during Yoritomo's lifetime and became even more important to the *bakufu* after his death in 1199. Although the position of shogun passed to his sons, Yoriie and Sanetomo, true power came to reside with their mother's family, the Hōjō. When Sanetomo died without an heir, the Hōjō filled the shogun's seat with an adopted heir from Kyoto while they continued as the *bakufu*'s leading family. Yet because the Hōjō were only related to Yoritomo by marriage, their claim to lead the *bakufu* was open to challenge. Hiraga Tomomasa, a member of the Shinano Genji, became the focus of a plot in 1205 to make him shogun rather than Sanetomo. And in 1219, Ano Tokimoto, one of Yoritomo's nephews, rebelled, claiming that his blood tie to the *bakufu*'s founder made him the best individual to rule upon the death of his cousin, the third shogun, Sanetomo. The legitimacy of the Hōjō as regents was dependent upon the legitimacy of the shogun, and the shogun's legitimacy in turn resided in his direct relationships with his retainers. Therefore, the Hōjō adopted two large policy goals: first, to perpetuate and strengthen exclusive relationships with warriors at all costs and, second, to employ notions of virtuous governance — *tokusei* — in their administration.

To maintain exclusive reciprocal relationships, the Hōjō took steps to ensure that retainers were reminded of their connections to Yoritomo and dependent upon Kamakura for their positions. Continuing a policy begun by Yoritomo, the Jōei Formulary explicitly forbade warriors from accepting appointments from Kyoto. Even former warriors who took religious vows were required to get a letter of recommendation from Kamakura before receiving an imperial appointment.[86] In ad-

---

85. Mass, *Warrior Government*, 92.

86. Jōei Formulary, Articles 39 and 40. As for Yoritomo's policy, it was supposedly Yoshitsune's acceptance of a commission directly from Go-Shirakawa that led to the final falling out between the two brothers.

dition, the *bakufu* tried to use historical memory to reinforce connections between warriors and Yoritomo—and through him, the Hōjō. As depicted in the *Azuma kagami*, Yoritomo seems to spend much of the Genpei War confirming and redistributing lands as rewards to retainers who have performed services for him. Even popular tales such as the *Heike monogatari* emphasize Yoritomo's role as bestower of rewards to loyal fighters. These tales shift attention away from the warrior and his immediate superior and instead emphasize the direct relationship between warriors and Yoritomo, the ultimate source of rewards.[87]

As for *tokusei*, the *bakufu* attempted to portray itself as virtuous in the eyes of its retainers through the very same actions. That is to say, by rewarding men promptly for loyal service, Kamakura claimed to exercise virtuous rule. In addition, Hōjō Yasutoki, author of the Jōei Formulary, set out to improve society through efficient judicial administration.[88] Through these efforts at ensuring reciprocal relationships and administering virtuous rule, the Hōjō created a social and economic system for warrior society that was complex, obligatory, and had many of the qualities that one would expect to observe in a gift economy. According to the Hōjō, even the gods relied on reciprocal relationships, as described in the first article of the 1232 law codes: "The majesty of the gods is increased by the worship of men, while the fates of men are satisfied by the virtue of the gods."[89] People needed to maintain the shrines, and in exchange the gods would provide good fortune to people. In the

---

87. Watson, "Warriors Rewarded."
88. Steenstrup, *Hōjō Shigetoki and His Role in the History of Political and Ethical Ideas in Japan*, 29. The Hōjō may have intended to conduct virtuous rule by means of a good legal system, yet one must wonder, since in Confucian writings, virtue is always set out as distinct from (and inferior to) laws as a method of governance. See the references to the *Spring and Autumn Annals*, above.
89. Jōei Formulary, Article 1. Takahashi, *Goseibai shikimoku*, 89. The translation is mine.

thirteenth-century view of the world, such reciprocal relationships were commonplace.

Against this background, however, money-based transactions in land were becoming more common, and *bakufu* efforts to stop *gokenin* from selling their holdings or using them as collateral were unsuccessful. The economic boom of the thirteenth century meant that *gokenin* had to deal not only with Kamakura but with moneylenders and commoners as well. These were individuals from outside the lord-retainer network who were, nonetheless, capable of purchasing or confiscating the land rights that made the network function. If Kamakura allowed these outsiders to interfere in the lord-retainer relationship, then the basis for Kamakura authority would be called into question. Under such circumstances, *tokusei* must have seemed the perfect vehicle for legislation to reassert the *bakufu's* individual, reciprocal relationships with its retainers. It was neither a *bakufu* invention to alleviate the financial difficulties of warriors who fought the Mongols, nor was it legislation with the best interests of retainers at heart. Rather, *tokusei* was a concept already linked to good government and the restoration of property that Kamakura tried to use for its own ends: the defense of its "gift economy" system of personal relations from the encroachments of a "profit economy."

Conclusions: Vice, Virtue, and Self-Interest in Kamakura Japan

Seen in this light, the *tokuseirei* of 1297 and similar legislation from the mid-to-late thirteenth century should be recognized as the conflation of vice, virtue, and self-interest. *Gokenin*, unable or unwilling to adhere to *bakufu* proscriptions against selling their land or using it as collateral, perpetrated the vice by gambling, dealing with moneylenders, oppressing peasants, and violating the legal edicts of the Kamakura *bakufu*. The warrior government tried to legislate a solution to this problem by invoking virtue—that is, the concepts of good government that were commonly associated with *tokusei*. Yet at its core, *bakufu* policy was inspired by self-interest—virtuous government edicts reflected the *bakufu*'s interest in perpetuating lord-retainer relations and ensuring that warriors rendered service. In many cases, this dovetailed quite nicely with legislation aimed at alleviating the financial stress of *gokenin* and other *bakufu* affiliates. But in other instances, the *bakufu* was quite willing to allow retainers to lose their lands or even to reassign retainer lands to other entities (such as shrines) better able to render service.

It was precisely because *tokusei* was an old, established concept that it had value to Kamakura. But warrior ties to the *bakufu*, built on the logic of a gift-exchange system, proved difficult to maintain in the face of a growing profit-driven monetary economy. The Hōjō would continue to wrestle with this problem for the remainder of the Kamakura period, trying unsuccessfully, for example, to create a new group of retainers, the *miuchibito*, who owed allegiance directly to the Hōjō family rather than to the *bakufu*. The breakdown of personal, reciprocal relationships, however, would continue throughout the medieval period, well after the destruction of the Hōjō family and its government in 1333. And as the *bakufu*'s system of governance began to be challenged, changes in agricultural production and the spread of regional markets contributed to the growth of regional trade, with dire implications for the classical system of estate management. It is to that topic that we turn in the next chapter.

FOUR

Coins, Taxes, and Trust

in the Fourteenth Century

The newly appointed estate manager faced a difficult situation when he arrived to take charge of Ōyama estate in Tanba province in 1315. The peasants of one of the estate's agricultural communities were refusing to pay their annual tribute dues (*nengu*) in rice, as was expected of them by the estate's temple proprietor, Tōji. Instead, the peasants insisted that they wanted to pay in cash. The previous estate manager had allowed them to commute their dues, they claimed, and so precedent had been set. Tōji officials did not agree; they had never authorized such a change, and the previous manager's decision to allow cash payments was likely one reason for his dismissal. In a letter informing his superiors of the situation, the new manager wrote that because the peasants had no document establishing their right to pay in cash, their request should be denied. Yet the economic power of the agricultural community proved difficult for Tōji representatives to suppress. Although the immediate outcome of the 1315 dispute is not known, documents dated two years later indicate that the community was paying its dues with coin by 1317.[1]

---

1. *Kyōō gokokuji monjo*, docs. 263 and 273. These documents are also discussed in Ōyama, *Nihon chūsei sonrakushi*, 304–11.

This chapter looks at how and why the economic developments of the thirteenth and fourteenth centuries transformed relations between center and periphery in medieval Japan. Elites at the center had to make choices. Those who embraced change—Kōfukuji with its toll stations, for example, or Enryakuji with its network of moneylenders—flourished in the newly emerging economy. Their command of cash resources not only gave them secure sources of income but also afforded them greater influence in political affairs. But those central institutions that still relied on government taxes or provincial estate tribute found themselves at a disadvantage. Tribute was the lifeblood of those urban elites, who had for centuries relied upon it to provide for many of their needs. As explained in Chapter 1, this system worked successfully in earlier times. During the Nara and Heian periods, nobles and temples enjoyed the ability to insist upon certain combinations of goods from the provinces. For those few goods that they could not obtain directly from their properties, redistribution took place at the capital's official markets.

Provincial figures had far fewer options in the Nara and Heian periods. They were required to provide certain goods as tax or tribute payment, and when they were unable to produce those goods, they had to find other means of obtaining them. Bizen provincial officials complained of this very situation in 796. Although they were expected to satisfy part of their tax obligation with iron, they did not produce iron and were forced to trade for it with a neighboring province.[2] *Shōen* managers wrestled with similar problems during these years because the limited availability of local and regional markets made it difficult for them to obtain some goods. Circumstances changed in early medieval times, however, as the spread of regional markets and the switch to copper cash made alternative types of exchange possible. As the leading members of late thirteenth-

---

2. Farris, "Trade, Money, and Merchants," 311–12. Obviously such trade was not impossible, but it must have come at a high cost for the Bizen officials (hence their complaint).

century provincial communities began selling agricultural surplus in local markets and handling Chinese coins, it was only a
matter of time before they began pressing for changes in the
annual tribute dues system as well.

Two major changes to the *nengu* payment system can be
traced to the period from the late thirteenth to the early fifteenth centuries. The first major change was a shift to tax
commutation: that is, from paying taxes in goods to paying in
cash. In some cases, proprietors requested that their provincial
estates convert tax obligations into cash payments. But in
others, it was local estate managers who pushed for commutation, forcing reluctant proprietors to concede control over
the means of payment. Tōdaiji was one of the first major proprietors to wrestle with this problem. As Joan Piggott notes,
"The monks had difficulty setting and enforcing adequate exchange rates between payments in kind and in coin."[3] They
preferred to receive goods rather than cash, as seen by their
decision in 1251 to only accept payments in kind from those
estates supporting the temple's Hokke Ceremony. It was the
provincial properties (more specifically, provincial managers)
that desired to pay in cash. Traditional proprietors had to address such problems with increasing frequency over the course
of the next 150 years. I will analyze the motives of the various
parties involved in the commutation of *nengu* and try to determine what factors contributed to its popularity. In other words,
who pushed to use cash in tribute payments, and why?

The second major change was the widespread employment
of a money remittance system — "bills of exchange" — by merchants and estate managers to forward cash over long distances. This innovation was a major improvement over paying dues in goods or coins because it drastically reduced the
risks and costs of shipping over long distances. As with commutation, some central elites were quite open to this new form
of transfer — as long as it worked. There were risks, though,
because bills of exchange required placing trust in a form of

---

3. Piggott, "Hierarchy and Economics in Early Medieval Tōdaiji," 72.

paper money that lacked the backing of any central authority. I will analyze how this system functioned without state authority to ensure that bills of exchange were honored and what steps managers and proprietors took to minimize the risks of buying bad bills. In addition, I will use that analysis to draw insights into the status of merchants in medieval Japanese society.

Tax Commutation

Monetization was a catalyst for change. Urban elites with access to good markets but limited by what their estates could produce might instead push to receive payments in cash and use the money to purchase goods in the markets. This surely became even more important for some traditional proprietors as provincial warriors began to interfere with increasing boldness in the payment of tribute from the countryside. For those based in the provinces, monetization had a much more significant impact than merely facilitating the sale of agricultural surplus in the marketplace. Having come to use cash in markets to sell excess produce, estate managers and peasants began to push to pay their annual tribute dues in currency as well. Instead of paying urban elites in rice, silk, paper, lacquer, and other goods demanded by temples and nobles, estates petitioned to pay the equivalent value of those goods in Chinese coins. This process of tax commutation, known as *daisennō* (literally, "substituting with cash payments"), was sometimes insisted upon by elite proprietors. In other cases, however, it was a concrete manifestation of the growing power of the countryside vis-à-vis traditional absentee landlords. Depending on the circumstances, each side might have legitimate reasons for favoring *daisennō*. But in earlier times provincial figures had little ability to push for change, whereas in medieval times they sometimes demanded changes, often successfully.

By the early fourteenth century, the most powerful figures in the countryside were the estate managers (*shōkan, gesu,* or *azukari dokoro*) and stewards (*jitō*). Warriors alone could serve as stewards; their appointments had gradually become hereditary over the course of the thirteenth century. Warriors might also hold estate-manager posts, but those positions were more frequently awarded to civilians—for example, a temple might designate one of its monks to manage its property. Because they lived on or near estates, managers and warriors were in a far better position to assume leadership of local communities than were the absentee landlords who served as estate patrons (*honke*) and proprietors (*ryōke*). Families that secured hereditary positions and were careful to cultivate positive relations with the estate's residents often had the strength to stand up to the estate's proprietor.

One such family was the Ōe of Kuroda estate in Iga province. Members of the Ōe family held the *gesu* managerial position for many generations, dating back at least to the late twelfth century. As managers, they were expected to handle tax collection, manage the budget, and supervise other economic affairs for the estate's proprietor, Tōdaiji. The length of their service on the estate, as well as their detailed knowledge of local conditions, enabled Ōe Kiyosada, the manager at the end of the thirteenth century, to push for a switch to cash payments of *nengu*. As part of his tactics against the temple, Kiyosada mobilized local warriors and withheld taxes from Tōdaiji. The temple officially deposed Kiyosada from his post and exiled him, but estate residents favored the Ōe family, and soon Kiyosada's son had been appointed to the managerial position. Resistance continued for years.[4] As this case illustrates, provincial managers and warriors such as the Ōe could effectively wield their local influence to dictate payment terms to central proprietors.

Kiyosada was not unique in this regard. The assistant *jitō* of Tomita estate in Owari province, for example, enacted a switch to *daisennō* even though the proprietor contested the move.[5] And in a similar case from Yano estate in Harima prov

---

4. This case is discussed in greater detail in Nagahara, "The Decline of the Shōen System," 268–69.

5. *Kamakurashi-shi shiryō-hen 2*, Shōō 3 (1290) 9th month 12th day.

ince, a long-standing managerial family, the Terada, clashed with the estate's proprietor, Tōji, in the early fourteenth century. Among other things, the amount of the estate's tribute dues and means of payments were at issue. One of the reasons Terada could resist so effectively was that he had strong commercial ties with others in the area around Nawa Bay, a nexus for trade between the San'yō and Inland Sea regions. As historian Lorraine Harrington explains, "Terada had the economic and political resources sufficient to be a formidable enemy on the land."[6] Ultimately, the conflict could only be settled in 1323 with the use of military force. As these examples demonstrate, provincial figures had a number of advantages when challenging traditional proprietors. Unlike absentee landlords, resident authority figures such as provincial warriors and managers had the advantage of better information about crop conditions and market prices. And those who did not abuse the local residents could often develop stronger relationships with the peasants and count on their loyalty.

Managers and stewards were not the only provincial figures pushing for change. In a few instances, peasant communities found the strength to directly demand tax commutation from their proprietors. Ōyama estate, described at the beginning of this chapter, was one such community. Kamikuze estate in Yamashiro province was another. In the late fourteenth century, estate residents petitioned the proprietor, Tōji, to allow them to make their annual tribute payments in cash. The temple approved the residents' petition in 1398, stipulating a substitution rate of 50 coins per bundle of straw.[7] Of course, it is not always easy to determine whether the push for tax commutation came from the central proprietor or the local community. Consider the case of Yano Estate, the Tōji property in Harima Province mentioned above. In 1353, the estate manager wrote to the temple, proposing to switch *nengu* payments from rice to cash. The proposal claimed that payments made

---

6. Harrington, "Social Control and the Significance of the *Akutō*," 234.
7. *DaiNihon shiryō*, series 7, vol. 3, Ōei 5 (1398) 11th month 28th day.

in rice were burdensome to the farmers and were difficult to transport via boat.[8] In that particular instance, the estate manager used claims of saving costs and effort to justify his appeal for *daisennō*, but he did not force anything—the proprietor agreed to the change. In fact, the Yano estate manager may have suggested it as part of a cost reduction measure to please his superiors back at the temple. In this case, both sides may have benefited from switching to payments in cash.

In general, the Kamakura *bakufu* took no issue with estates switching the means of tribute payments. The *bakufu* itself did not rely on *nengu* as a source of income. When the *bakufu* was established in the late 1180s, the imperial court in Kyoto handled matters of estate *nengu*. Kamakura only needed to get involved if there was a dispute between one of its vassals and a proprietor. But Kamakura displayed heightened interest in all aspects of government following the Jōkyū Uprising of 1221, and its willingness to follow the court's lead eroded. Furthermore, as the *bakufu* placed more warriors in *jitō* positions around the country, it had to deal with a growing number of disputes over estate management and *nengu* payment. As a result, warrior officials became actively involved in setting economic policy. In 1226, they forbade the use of cloth in tribute payments and instead promoted the use of coins.[9] Agricultural communities, a few of which had sought to use coins from even earlier dates, now jumped at the opportunity. Sōma estate in Shimōsa province used the *bakufu* legal system to secure its right to pay the Toyouke Daijingū Shrine, its proprietor, in cash rather than in cloth. According to a settlement of 1227, the estate agreed to pay 40 *mon* in cash for every *tan* of cloth that was owed. Interestingly, the document refers to stopping payments in "illegal cloth" (*fuhō junpu*), surely a reference to the *bakufu* pronouncement of a year earlier. In addition, it is important to note that the proprietor preferred to

---

8. *Tōji hyakugō monjo*, "no" box, Bunna 2 (1353) 11th month, in Kodama, ed., *Shiryō ni yoru Nihon no ayumi*, 351–52.

9. *AK*, Karoku 2 (1226) 8th month.

be paid in kind. Apparently the shrine had agreed earlier to receive cash payments of 30 coins per *tan* but found that it could not acquire cloth of the same quality on the open market, and so it tried to force the estate to make payments in cloth again. The *bakufu* ordered a compromise solution, raising the rate of payment to 40 coins per *tan*.[10]

Such cases were rarely settled with ease, however, and the two sides were back in court again the following year. The shrine had two complaints this time. First, Toyouke Daijingū claimed that it was not receiving the proper amount of cash for every length of cloth it was owed. On this point, the shrine appears to have been correct, for the rate inexplicably seems to have reverted to 30 coins per *tan*. Second, the shrine argued that Sōma estate was not paying its miscellaneous duties (*zatsuji* or *zōji*) at the proper rate. According to the shrine, the estate was supposed to supply it with fish, or, when fish could not be caught, the estate could substitute cloth at a specified rate. The estate's *jitō* represented the estate in the legal proceedings. He replied to the shrine's charges by claiming that the people living on the estate had been told a different rate and that the shrine's representative had abused residents while conducting his investigation. In its decision, the *bakufu* ordered the estate to pay in fish and that if fish could not be provided, substitution rates were to be determined by the current trading price on the open market.[11] There are three points worth noting in this case. First, the proprietor, Toyouke Daijingū, could not impose its will on one of its own estates without turning for help to the *bakufu* court system. Second, although *jitō* are often described in the literature as having caused problems on estates, in this instance the *jitō* argued on behalf of the local community against the estate's proprietor. Third and perhaps most interestingly, in its pronouncement the *bakufu* relied on the market to determine substitution prices.

---

10. *KI*, doc. 3649, Karoku 3 (1227) 8th month 16th day.
11. *KI*, doc. 3777, Antei 2 (1228) 8th month 3rd day.

Over the course of the thirteenth century, the Kamakura *bakufu* tended to support provincial efforts at switching payments to cash except when it came to goods that the *bakufu* itself preferred to receive in kind. One important commodity that the *bakufu* refused to allow commuted payments on was silk from northeastern Japan. After the *bakufu* defeated the Ōshū Fujiwara in 1189, it retained direct control of Mutsu province in the northeast. Only top members of the Hōjō, the family that monopolized the *bakufu* regency, were appointed to rule that region. Mutsu was known for producing fine silk of high value and was required to use that silk in fulfilling part of its annual tribute obligations. In 1239, however, the silk-producing communities sought permission to pay cash instead, citing the 1226 *bakufu* ban on cloth payments as a precedent. We can only assume that the Mutsu silk producers felt that they could get higher prices for their silk on the open market. The *bakufu* was quite harsh in its denial of the petition, charging the peasants with having "forgotten their obligations" and being engaged in "evil scheming." The denial went so far as to declare that no coins were to be carried east of the Shirakawa inspection station, as if the *bakufu* could keep coins out of northeastern Japan altogether.[12] Kamakura was much more powerful than the Toyouke Daijingū—it was able to dictate terms of payment, and for some years thereafter, Mutsu continued to provide silk. Nonetheless, the conversion of payments from goods to cash was a process that could not be held off forever, and at least one estate (Yoshima, located in the southern part of Mutsu province) had formally switched by 1271.[13]

During the first half of the Kamakura period, *daisennō* was limited to a few estates, but the practice became widespread between 1270 and 1370. Of the 227 cases of *daisennō* mentioned in the documents of the chronological primary source compendium *Shiryō sōran*, historian Sasaki Gin'ya found that 83

---

12. *Kamakura bakufu tsuikahō*, doc. 99, Ryakunin 2 (1239) 1st month 22nd day.

13. Sasaki, *Chūsei shōhin ryūtsūshi no kenkyū*, 352.

percent of them were initiated during that hundred-year period. He also observed some regional variation. In the San'in, Kantō, and Tōhoku regions, only one estate each switched to coins before 1300, which suggests that there may have been some regional differences in the speed with which cash was adopted.[14] Of course, it is also possible that this discrepancy is merely a by-product of the limited data that survive from those regions. By the fourteenth century, however, multiple estates in every region of Japan were commuting their dues to cash. Assuming cash was available in local markets for provincial managers to obtain, conversion represented a fundamental change from the traditional tribute system, since provincial figures gained a degree of freedom from central proprietors. But was this freedom granted from the political center or petitioned for by rural residents?

Commutation: A Local or Central Phenomenon?

In the Ōyama, Tomita, and northeast regional examples described above, people living on provincial estates—*jitō*, residential estate managers, and peasants—pressed for the right to pay *nengu* and other taxes in cash. But there were cases in which proprietors were the ones calling for payments in coin. One of the earliest known examples comes from the properties of the Yoshida Shrine. At the same time that the Sōma estate was winning the right from Toyouke Daijingū to pay in cash, the Yoshida Shrine was ordering agricultural communities located within its holdings to make monetary payments in support of the construction of the Great Shrine at Ise. The order stated that "although precedent dictates that payments should be made in cloth, that obligation is now nullified and all should pay in rice, or if rice is not available, then pay in coins."[15] In

---

14. Based on data from table 46 of Sasaki's *Chūsei shōhin ryūtsūshi no kenkyū*, 352–62. For more on the timing of widespread coin use and an alternative interpretation of Sasaki's data, see Ōta Yukio, "12–15 seiki shotō higashi Ajia ni okeru dōsen no rufu," 20–48.

15. *KI*, doc. 3505, Karoku 2 (1226) 7th month.

this instance, the proprietor declared an end to traditional payments of cloth and insisted on receiving either rice or cash. The order came less than one month before the *bakufu*'s 1226 ban on cloth payments, though it is unclear whether the Yoshida Shrine was anticipating Kamakura's prohibition. This case was unusual for the first half of the thirteenth century, and the preference for rice over coins reveals that Chinese currency was not yet the preferred means of payment for everyone. But similar instances of proprietor-ordered payment substitution were to become increasingly common in years to come. They raise the question of which side—central proprietor or provincial estate—played the more important role in the shift from goods to cash tribute payments.[16]

Ono Takeo, writing in the 1940s, posited that *daisennō* was instituted by elites seeking cash to spend in the capital. He saw elite proprietors placing the demands, and provincial estate managers and *jitō* handling the sales of estate produce for cash. In Ono's model, the *jitō* was an agent of the proprietor and the cultivators themselves played no part in the switch to metal currency.[17] Although evidence that *jitō*, estate managers, and even cultivators sometimes pressed for *daisennō* against the wishes of the proprietor has made Ono's exclusively top-down view obsolete, the importance of proprietor demands to receive commuted taxes cannot be ignored. Toyoda Takeshi and Sasaki Gin'ya expanded upon Ono's research, proposing several reasons why proprietors sometimes insisted on receiving payments in cash. The most significant reason appears to have stemmed from the increased availability of goods in Kyoto's unofficial markets. Elites wanted cash in order to purchase goods in Kyoto rather than to have to rely on the goods forwarded from their own estates. A second, related reason came from some elites' realization that they could get more cash by selling the tribute goods owed to them in local markets

---

16. Yamamura summarizes this debate in "The Growth of Medieval Commerce," 368–71.

17. Ono Takeo, *Nihon shōensei shiron*.

rather than in those of the capital. In these cases, the proprietor found that certain goods yielded higher cash returns if sold in regional markets close to the estate rather than in the markets of the capital. Obviously, this would not hold true in every case, but depended on the goods and the markets involved.[18]

Information was the most important factor if a proprietor hoped to profit by ordering its estates to convert their payments to cash. It required careful attention to prices and conversion rates, as was reflected in the monk Jitsuen's report to his Tōji superiors in 1346. In the report, he recorded the various amounts of *nengu* received from a particular territory within Yano Estate. Some of the payments are listed in cash, apparently having been converted years ago, and others are listed in rice but with cash conversion rates after each entry, suggesting that these payments had only recently been converted. Jitsuen's careful accounting of exchange rates is of particular interest. In one instance, he took a separate piece of paper and pasted over outdated exchange information; in another, he indicated that he had someone named Igabō investigate prices in Kyoto for him.[19] Through such research, Jitsuen ensured that the Tōji received everything that it was due. Not all proprietors, however, had such meticulous agents.

On the other side of the equation, there were powerful reasons for provincial estates to favor converting goods to cash. Sasaki Gin'ya identified five types of estates that pushed for the use of cash. First, there were estates where the on-site administrator or *jitō* had a strong grip on the local marketplace and could take advantage of his position to profit from goods-to-cash exchanges. Second, there were estates such as Kamikuze that were located very close to the central Kyoto markets and could easily convert their goods to cash. For these estates, easy access to major markets meant that they had all the more incentive to produce items that would sell rather

---

18. Toyoda, *Chusei Nihon shōgyōshi no kenkyū;* Sasaki, *Chūsei shōhin ryūtsū-shi no kenkyū*, 250–70.

19. *Aioi shishi*, vol. 8.1, doc. 145, Jōwa 2 (1346) 4th month 16th day.

than items stipulated by their proprietors. Third, some coastal estates produced goods that were easily sold for cash and difficult to transport long distances. For example, communities along the Japan Sea in Wakasa province were often expected to provide seafood to their proprietors but found it safer and easier to sell the seafood locally and provide cash to the proprietors instead. Fourth, some estates, such as Yano and Ōyama, were situated on the regular circuits of urban merchants and therefore had the sources of information necessary to be sensitive to changing market conditions. Fifth and finally, many eastern estates favored using cash because of the high costs associated with shipping goods overland all the way to Kyoto or Nara.[20]

What becomes apparent when considering Sasaki's groups is that in each case the provincial community had an opportunity to decrease transaction costs by switching to cash payments. Some had an advantage in information, such as the estates on regular merchant routes. Others, such as the eastern estates, realized an advantage by lowering transportation costs or by freeing up agricultural land to grow crops that would yield higher returns, such as properties located close to Kyoto. The benefit to coastal estates, which reduced the risks of seafood spoilage by selling locally rather than shipping to proprietors, is obvious. In each instance, lowered transaction costs coincided with opportunities for greater local control and for more wealth to stay within the provincial community.

These cases reveal the frustrating complexity of studying commutation. Depending on the individual circumstances, either side or both sides might gain from the switch to tax payments in cash. In the end I must concur with Nagahara Keiji, who concluded that it is impossible to attribute the push for commutation solely to one side of the center-periphery equation or the other.[21] What stands out, however, is that with the spread of an emerging money economy, and with the advan-

---

20. Sasaki Gin'ya, *Chūsei shōhin ryūtsūshi no kenkyū.*
21. Nagahara, *Shōen,* 210.

tage of influence over local markets, provincial players were able to exert greater control over their economic ties to the center than at any time earlier in Japanese history.[22] For central elites to dictate the means of payment was nothing new; they had been doing so for hundreds of years. But only in the medieval economy were provincials able to effect such change.

Why Switch to Cash?

In Chapter 2, we explored the incentives that merchants, warriors, religious institutions, and peasants had to favor using cash in marketplace transactions. Tax commutation, however, involved changing the means of payment for the most fundamental part of the economy: the *nengu* system. In order for elite proprietors to accept coins, either they had to be convinced that coins were advantageous or rural economic agents had to have the strength to force changes in elite attitudes. Why did their push to commute tax and tribute payments succeed, and why did they start during the thirteenth century? To fully answer these questions, we must look to two types of explanations: the first highlighting economic factors that stem from the general advantages of using cash, and the second focusing on historical factors specific to the thirteenth century that offer insight into why commutation became popular at that time.

As Chapter 1 explained, with regard to the importation of coins, there are a number of advantages inherent in using metal currency rather than barter or other forms of commodity money. Those advantages include uniform size and weight, no risk of spoilage, and easier transportability, among others. Although early medieval Japanese did not speak of money

---

22. An alternative hypothesis is that in earlier periods we only have the view from the center since documents that reflect Heian-period provincial economic power do not survive. This is not as convincing an argument, though, for earlier elites kept records of petitions they received from their estates. There is a noticeable difference in the quantity and types of petitions between the tenth and the fifteenth centuries.

using such terms, contemporary documents reveal that they favored using cash in order to realize those very advantages. Consider the judicial pronouncement that the *bakufu* issued in 1298 to resolve a dispute between the manager and the *jitō* of Akanabe estate in Mino province:

Although there should be an inspection of the cloth, there have been continuous arguments over its quality. Therefore from this point forward, in keeping with the agreement reached by the disputing parties in the 12th month of 1280 . . . let payments be made in cash at a rate of 5,500 coins for every 1 *tan* 10 *ryō* of cloth.[23]

In this case, the disputing parties turned to cash because they believed its relative uniformity would minimize arguments that were otherwise bound to arise over the quality of the good being paid. Notably, the provincial disputants made the decision to switch to cash on their own. The *bakufu* neither proposed nor enforced this agreement, but merely lent its stamp of approval. People using cash in the provinces recognized its advantages and took steps to use it in their tribute payments.

Another benefit from switching to coins was lower transportation costs. The benefits of using cash were obvious in some cases. One straightforward example comes from 1341, when a boat carrying tax rice to Tōdaiji from one of its estates in Chikuzen province encountered storms, waves, and pirates before it finally reached port, at which point it was discovered that the rice had been soaked through.[24] Since coins retained their value even when wet, incidents such as this one may have convinced some proprietors to favor selling taxes locally and then shipping cash rather than rice or other goods. But aside from avoiding the risk of crops lost to bad weather in transit, was it actually less expensive to transport coins rather than other products?

---

23. *KI*, doc. 19709, Einin 6 (1298) 6th month 12th day.
24. *Tōdaiji monjo*, series 3, vol. 5, Ryaku'ō 4 (1341) 5th month 24th day.

Fig. 5 One *kan* of coins, divided into two strings
of 500 coins each, unearthed in Yamanashi prefecture.
Used by permission of the Kitamori City Board of Education.

Logic suggests that the compact size and convenient "stringability" of coins would make them more affordable to transport than bulkier produce, but it is surprisingly difficult to substantiate this position with concrete evidence.[25] Sasaki Gin'ya examined transportation fees paid by a number of estates on Kyushu that switched from rice to coin payments. He found that whereas earlier rice payments required spending up to 50 percent or more of the total amount being shipped on transportation costs, cash payments only required around 30 percent: a substantial savings. The numbers must be used with caution, since they compare estates over time. In other words, earlier payments were made in rice and later payments in coin. Other factors, such as improvements in the transportation network, might account for the reductions in costs, a point that Sasaki readily concedes. But the research at least suggests that coins may have helped to reduce transportation expenses.[26]

25. As described in Chapter 1, Song and Ming copper coins were round with a square hole in the middle through which a string was run to bundle coins in units of hundreds and thousands. One "string" of cash contained approximately 1,000 coins.

26. Sasaki, *Chūsei shōhin ryūtsūshi no kenkyū*, 292–97. Of course, Sasaki acknowledges the problems inherent in comparing estates over time. There is no way to control for factors other than the switch from rice to cash that might account for the lowered transportation costs associated with the later cases. Still, although far from conclusive, there is evidence that suggests monetization helped reduce transportation costs.

Yet these economic benefits do not explain why *daisennō* became a common practice only in the late thirteenth century. The advantages of using metal currency had not been enough to prevent the imperial twelve coins from dying out in the tenth century. Therefore we must also look for causal factors unique to Japan's early medieval period. Several have already been described in the preceding chapters, including changes to the market system and the growing volume of Chinese coins that became available for cheap importation from the Asian mainland after the fall of the Northern Song. Traveling merchants and local markets also made it possible for estates to explore alternative means of fulfilling their obligations to central elites. Inasmuch as local markets emerged in large part due to the agricultural surplus that resulted from double cropping and new rice strains, the surplus was another significant factor that had not existed earlier.

The growth in regional trade made possible by this agricultural surplus and monetary exchange was an additional, crucial element in facilitating the substitution of cash for use in tax payments. Underlying the classical proprietor economy had been the principle that the periphery supplied goods to the center. As far as elites in Nara and the Heian capital were concerned, the estates and public lands of the provinces were self-sufficient. Of course, there must have been some degree of regional exchange even in Nara and Heian times to allow inland and coastal communities to acquire goods that they could not produce themselves.[27] Documentary evidence from the twelfth and thirteenth centuries, however, reveals that such exchange became much more common during the early medieval period.

Consider the plan of the residential manager of Noke estate in Chikuzen province to fulfill his tribute obligations in 1181, a year after the outbreak of the Genpei civil war.[28] The annual payment deadline was upon him, but the manager wrote that

---

27. Farris, "Trade, Money, and Merchants in Nara Japan," 309–12.
28. *Heian ibun supplement*, doc. 6405, Yōwa 1 (1181) 11th month 23rd day.

he had only been able to collect 470 of the 709 *koku* of rice due that month. With rumors of war afoot and the people unsettled, he did not think that he would be able to raise the remaining balance in rice, the official means of estate payments. Instead, the manager planned to sell salt made on the estate to traveling merchants, who usually visited Noke by ship in the second or third month. The manager would then send the profits from the salt sales to the proprietor. There is much that the manager's letter does not reveal, such as whether he would trade the salt for rice or cash, but the fact that merchants made regular stops at the estate shows that Noke was tied into a network of regularized commerce in northern Kyushu.

Merchant ships such as these, known as *kaisen*, became important links connecting different coastal areas in regional exchange. For example, some of the communities in Wakasa province operated merchant ships that ran up and down the Sea of Japan coast from Wakasa (modern Fukui prefecture) to Izumo (modern Shimane prefecture), trading in salt, rice, and cash.[29] Similar regular routes existed in the Inland Sea and on the sea lanes connecting Kii and Ise provinces with eastern Japan.[30] Bruce Batten refers to these merchant vessels as using "hop, skip, and jump" routes to connect small regional ports with each other.[31] At the same time, artisans, smiths, and other provincial estate residents who did not engage in farming pushed for greater regional exchange in order to create markets for their goods.[32]

---

29. Usami, *Nihon chūsei no ryūtsū to shōgyō*, 199–202.

30. On the sea trade in eastern Japan, see Minegishi and Murai, eds., *Chūsei tōgoku no butsuryū to toshi,* and Nagahara, "Kumano, Ise shōnin to chūsei no tōgoku."

31. Batten, *To the Ends of Japan*, 170–72. These trade networks appear to have gradually expanded; by the fifteenth century, they formed a Japan-wide trade network that centered on the port of Hyōgo, with records revealing that ships came to Hyōgo from 104 different ports scattered around fourteen provinces.

32. Nagahara, *Shōen*, 147–50.

These and other steps toward expanded regional exchange were important for two reasons. First, regional exchange networks fostered trade that was not mediated by the center or elites. In other words, they were periphery-periphery interactions. This was in sharp distinction to the tribute system of earlier ages, in which the center-periphery relationship dominated economic exchange. During the medieval period, such regional trade was not nearly so difficult. Individual estates could trade with each other through local markets and traveling merchants without involving their proprietors. Second, the growth of this regional commerce created demand for estate goods outside of the capital, and thereby made it possible for managers and peasants to sell goods for cash and commute their taxes. In short, there were factors unique to the thirteenth century that made commutation possible. Without provincial demand, *daisennō* never could have taken place.

Commutation and Bakufu *Economic Policy*

The basic philosophy of the Kamakura *bakufu* was to permit taxes on commercial goods but leave untaxed the *nengu* that provincial estates owed to their patrons and proprietors.[33] It should be noted that Kamakura did not directly tax *nengu* itself; rather, it granted others the authority to do so. A similar philosophy was adopted by the Muromachi *bakufu*, the warrior government that succeeded Kamakura in 1336 after Go-Daigo's brief imperial interregnum. Transport fees were levied at ports and toll stations, most of which were maintained by major temples and shrines, as commercial goods moved around the country. Unlike its predecessor, though, the Muromachi warrior government took a much more active role in promoting and taxing commerce. In some cases it attempted

---

33. Aida Nirō first observed this division between commercial and *nengu* items for taxation purposes; other scholars have concurred. See Aida, *Chūsei no sekisho*; Toyoda, *Zōho chūsei Nihon shōgyōshi no kenkyū*; Amino, "Bun'ei igo shinseki chōjirei ni tsuite"; Ihara, "*Bakufu*, Kamakura-fu no ryūtsū keizai seisaku to nengu unsō."

to directly control toll stations and their income. Following the Ōnin War, for example, Hino Tomiko laid claim to income from toll stations built around the seven entrances to Kyoto.[34] The commutation of *nengu*, however, presented problems for *bakufu* economic policy, as even those toll operators who tried to follow the *bakufu*'s guidelines became unable to distinguish taxable from non-taxable items.

In 1339, for example, the head of the Muromachi *bakufu*'s regional headquarters in Kamakura wrote to Engakuji temple that "in accordance with precedent, temple holdings are exempt from the rice levies usually taken at Mutsura and other toll stations."[35] The fact that the *bakufu* office refers to precedent suggests that the exemption was originally a Kamakura-period policy.[36] Although the *bakufu* had just confirmed Engakuji's tax-free status, later that year a dispute arose when warriors at the Iijima toll station levied taxes on an Engakuji shipment. According to the temple, the shipment contained only *nengu* from its holdings in Owari province. Due to worries over safety following the recent war, temple agents had decided to sell the entire shipment in a local market and ship the profits to the temple rather than the *nengu* itself.[37] Engakuji claimed that the shipment was still temple *nengu* – it was merely in a different form, and therefore it should have been exempt from taxation. The toll station, though, saw a boat full of commercial items that had been purchased at a market and insisted upon taking a portion as tax.

Disputes such as this one became increasingly common as tax commutation spread in the fourteenth century. Temples turned to merchants to handle their *nengu* shipments and often found it advantageous to sell *nengu* before it arrived at its final

---

34. Gay, *Moneylenders of Late Medieval Kyoto*, 164–65.

35. *Kanagawa kenshi shiryōhen*, doc. 3463, Ryakuō 2 (1339) 8th month 22nd day. Mutsura was one of Kamakura city's port districts.

36. Ihara, "*Bakufu*, Kamakura-fu no ryūtsū keizai seisaku to nengu unsō," 152.

37. *Kanagawa kenshi shiryōhen*, doc. 3471, Ryakuō 2 (1339) 12th month 9th day.

destination. This was true not only of Kamakura-based temples such as Engakuji, but appears to have been a countrywide phenomenon. The testimony of a merchant in 1396, involved in a dispute over some missing funds, reflects this trend.[38] The man claimed to have been asked by Yano estate officials to help them because of his business connections. The estate officials did not want the residents to know what they sent to their temple proprietor, so the officials asked the merchant, who traveled regularly between the capital and the countryside, to transport cash for them to Kyoto. Although the document does not specify from where the money had come, given that the estate was forwarding it to the proprietor, it seems reasonable to conclude that the cash came from tax goods that had been sold. As these examples illustrate, estate proprietors were quite willing to use the new commercial economy and loopholes in *bakufu* economic policy to protect their income.

In the fourteenth century, merchants and moneylenders became indispensable to the transport of *nengu*. It is also around this time that we see the appearance of *toimaru*, professional shippers who specialized in the storage, movement, and sale of goods. There are some scattered references to *toi* in Heian documents. The earliest reference comes from the *Chōshūki*, which makes mention of *toi* (戸居) living at ports.[39] They appear much more frequently in Kamakura-period materials, often in conjunction with the movement of *nengu* from the provinces to the capital along waterways. There are references to *toi* (問い) around Osaka Bay at places including Hyōgo port, the Yodo River, and Amagasaki, as well as on Lake Biwa at Ōtsu and Sakamoto.[40] Thus, early *toi* appear to have performed functions that ranged from dockworkers to shippers and cargo transport specialists. They developed relationships with particular estates, as evidenced by a will from the year 1220 in which a father bequeathed to his sons the *toi shiki* to specific *shōen* or

---

38. *Aioi shishi*, doc. 574, Ōei 2 (1395) 11th month 11th day.
39. *Chōshūki*, Hōen 1 (1135) 8th month 14th day.
40. Sakurai, "Chūsei no shōhin ichiba," 207–9.

suppliers.[41] By the late Kamakura period, however, *toimaru* were branching out into other areas of operation and becoming more specialized. Urban proprietors who wished to convert some of their estate *nengu* into cash turned to *toimaru* for assistance. Although some *toimaru* remained actively involved in shipping, others worked more as merchants or brokers to change goods into cash. This became possible, of course, with the preference for *daisennō*, which dates to the end of the thirteenth century. By the late fourteenth and early fifteenth centuries, some *toimaru* had branched into finance and were offering bills of exchange to estate proprietors and/or managers.[42]

Bills of Exchange

Daisennō was a significant change to the established tribute payment system, but an even greater institutional innovation followed shortly thereafter: the bill of exchange, known variously in Japanese as *kaezeni*, *saifu*, or *kawase*.[43] These were paper certificates that the holder could redeem for cash at a specified location. *Kawase* made it possible to transfer taxes from estates to urban proprietors without the risks that accompanied moving large quantities of goods or coins. For even with the switch from paying in kind to paying in cash, challenges to the smooth movement of goods remained.

As already established, one incentive to commute payments was that coins were easier—and therefore cheaper—to ship to the capital. Even so, transportation costs were a significant expense for local estate managers and/or central proprietors. As discussed above, Sasaki Gin'ya found that some Kyushu estates had to spend around 30 percent of the cash total being

---

41. *KI*, doc. 2670, Jōkyū 2 (1220) 11th month 13th day.

42. Sakurai, "Chūsei no shōhin ichiba," 208.

43. Other names include *kaesen*, *warifu*, and possibly *kirizeni*. The last term is commonly thought to represent a different phenomena, that of damaged coins, but Hotate Michihisa makes a strong case in arguing that Kamakura-period references to *kirizeni* may have been to paper certificates along the lines of *kawase*. Hotate, "Kirimono to kirizeni," 15–22.

shipped for transportation costs.[44] Other cases documenting shipping expenses in different regions of Japan reflect even higher percentages. For example, in 1304 officials Uma no Jō Sanetoki and Keijitsu forwarded *nengu* from Noda estate in Bizen province to the estate's proprietor, Tōdaiji. Altogether, they sent 62 *kanmon* in cash to the temple, money that they obtained by converting over 53 *koku* in tax rice that the officials had collected from the estate. The document explaining this transaction provides a detailed breakdown of how estate officials spent all of that year's *nengu*, including the cost of having it transported to the capital.[45] On this occasion, the Noda officials paid 24 *kanmon* in cash as a porter's fee (*kyūbutsu*)—close to 40 percent of the value of the cash being forwarded. Such fees varied a great deal with location, season, and other conditions, but with transportation costs consuming such a large amount of income, it is obvious why officials—even those practicing *daisennō*—would seek any means to further lower those fees.[46]

Switching from goods to coins also did little to eliminate the dangers of robbery. Consider the case of Tara estate, located in Wakasa province along the Sea of Japan. There was no market on the estate itself, but neighboring Onyū market provided plenty of opportunities for trade. It was situated to take advantage of a number of nearby institutions: it was close to a major Buddhist temple (Kokubunji) and an important provincial shrine (Wakasahime jinja) as well as several estates, and it was just upriver from Obama port on the coast. This prosperous market attracted more than just traders, however. In 1334, peasants bringing goods home from the market were robbed in broad daylight. They lost cash, rice, silk, clothing, swords, and a bow to "evil bands" (*akutō*) whom the peasants

---

44. Sasaki, *Chūsei shōhin ryūtsūshi no kenkyū* (see the discussion above).

45. *Okayama kenshi*, vol. 19, doc. 1248, Kagen 2 (1304) 12th month.

46. For more on the costs of transporting goods during this period, see Nagamatsu, "Chūsei zenki no kyōbun to shūnō kankō," 19–45. Also, her "Kamakura jidai no nengu fukazei," 57–74.

claimed had connections to local warriors.[47] Goods and cash in transit from the provinces to the cities were just as vulnerable to bandits and pirates.[48] In theory, *bakufu*-affiliated warriors were supposed to stop such highway theft, but as seen in the case from Onyū market, bandits knew to strike deals with local warriors. Whether by sea or over land, estate managers had to be concerned when they shipped large quantities of goods or cash.

A solution to these problems came in the form of paper certificates (*kawase*) that paid a specified amount of cash to the holder. Traveling merchants often dealt in these certificates, giving them to provincial land managers in exchange for all or some of the yearly rice crop or other estate products. The manager forwarded the certificate to his estate's proprietor, who could then present it at a designated location—usually a moneylender's stall—and receive cash or other goods. Thus, *kawase* were a means of forwarding large sums of money from the provinces at a fraction of the cost required to transport actual goods. Bills of exchange were far less bulky, weighed a fraction of the equivalent amount of coins, and could be much more easily hidden in the event of a robbery. In effect, the manager shifted the risk of transporting bulk goods or cash to the merchants.

Although the economic advantages of *kawase* are obvious, there are many things that remain unknown about the workings of bills of exchange. For example, traveling merchants acquired goods in exchange for the *kawase* that they provided to estate managers, but little is known of how they transported those goods to the capital. Although wandering merchants are depicted in a number of medieval illustrated materials, such as the *Tōhokuin shokunin uta awase*, they are always pictured

---

47. *Dai Nihon shiryō*, series 6, volume 2, Kenmu 1 (1334) 11th month 24th day.

48. There are many other examples of early medieval documents citing pirate attacks on boats carrying *nengu*; see, for example, *KI*, doc. 19147, Einin 4 (1296) 9th month 21st day. For more on piracy, *nengu*, and the medieval economy, see Sakurai, *Nihon chūsei no keizai kōzō*, 275–93.

alone. Surely these cannot be the same merchants who handled *daisennō* or *kawase* for provincial estates, since they would have faced the same dangers of weather and robbery that estate managers faced when confronted with the challenge of delivering goods to the city. Traveling merchants must have had men (or pack animals) to carry goods for them and others to act as security guards to protect against bandits and pirates, but evidence of those entourages has not survived.[49]

The origins of *kawase* are equally obscure, though medieval Japanese were certainly not the first to create such a system of monetary remittance. Similar instruments existed in thirteenth-century Europe and in the Islamic world. In Europe, bills of exchange originated in conjunction with medieval trade fairs, and students used paper certificates of credit to avoid carrying large sums of money over great distances. Unlike Asian bills of exchange, however, European bills were also used as a means of settling international payments. Letters of credit known as *suftajah* also circulated widely in the Islamic world, moving between Spain, Egypt, Baghdad, and the Sudan in some cases.[50]

Of greater direct relevance to the Japanese case was the money remittance system used for centuries in China known as "flying cash" (*feiqian*) or "convenient exchange" (*bianhuan*). During the Tang dynasty, the government of each circuit had an office in Chang'an, the capital. Merchants who sold their wares in the markets of the capital could give the cash they earned to the office of their home circuit and receive in exchange half of a credit certificate. The other half of the certificate was sent via government channels to the circuit office back in the provinces. When the merchants returned home,

---

49. The sole reference that I have found is the story of the wealthy mercury merchant traveling with pack horses in the *Konjaku* tales; see Chapter 2.

50. On European bills of exchange, see Usher, "Origin of the Bill of Exchange"; de Roover, "Money, Banking, and Credit in Medieval Bruges"; and Lopez, *Commercial Revolution of the Middle Ages*, 103–5. Islamic conveyances are described in Labib, "Capitalism in Medieval Islam," 79–96; and Abu-Lughod, *Before European Hegemony*, 222–24.

they could go to the office, match their half of the certificate with the half held by the government, and redeem it for the original amount of cash that they had deposited in the capital.[51]

One of the Japanese names for their system of money remittance was *warifu* or *saifu* (meaning "divided tally"), suggesting a connection with Chinese "flying cash," though there is no evidence that medieval Japanese certificates involved the matching of divided halves for authentication. In addition, medieval Japanese merchants, unlike their Tang counterparts, did not involve government authorities—neither the imperial government nor the *bakufu*—in their long-distance transactions. Nor did the Japanese have provincial offices located in the capital that paralleled the Tang circuit office system. Although it is possible that Chinese merchants operating in Japan or Japanese travelers to China may have imported the idea of bills of exchange, exactly what influence, if any, the Chinese example had on Japanese *kawase* remains unclear.

The earliest forms of money conveyance in Japan did not involve cash at all. These were paper certificates that temples used to convey large amounts of rice (*kaemai*). Rice certificates were most common in the late Heian period, but references to *kaemai* can be found in documents from as late as the first half of the thirteenth century. For example, in a letter believed to have been written in 1224, Gyōji, a priest with the Jingoji temple, instructs a provincial officer in Bitchū province to forward seven *koku* of rice to the temple via a bill of exchange.[52] In this instance, the rice appears to have been a loan, for Gyōji specifies that another priest named Higuchi will pay it back at a later date. That priests like Gyōji were still using certificates to transmit rice in the thirteenth century confirms that non-metallic forms of money such as cloth and rice disappeared only gradually as media of exchange during the Kamakura period.

---

51. Peng, *A Monetary History of China*, vol. I, 329–31.

52. *Okayama kenshi*, vol. 19, doc. 1063, Jōō 4 (1224) 9th month 29th day. The document is inscribed with the month and day; the editors have attributed it to the year 1224.

By the second half of the thirteenth century, bills of exchange began to appear that specifically indicated that they were to be redeemed for cash. They were issued most frequently by temples to convey money to Kamakura for their representatives to use in lawsuits brought before the *bakufu*. In one of the earliest examples, the Kōyasan monastery sent cash via *kawase* in 1278 to one of its monks in Kamakura so that he could represent the monastery in court; unfortunately, the document does not specify the amount being sent.[53] In another example, Tōji sent money to its Kamakura agent to use for legal fees in a 1293 lawsuit. The *kawase* specified where the cash was to be redeemed and that the payment was to be made within five days of presenting the document.[54] Whether this five-day waiting period was to allow the merchant time to verify the document or gather funds together is unstated, though such stipulations were not uncommon.[55]

These money transfers did provide considerable savings over shipping money directly. For example, in another case involving Tōji, the temple conveyed 23 *kanmon* to its representative in Kamakura by means of three *kawase* in the year 1291. The first certificate, valued at 10 *kanmon*, required a fee of 1 *kan* 500 *mon* (15 percent) to the moneylender, a merchant located on the street that sold needles.[56] Later cases also seem to confirm a fee rate of around 15 percent, which was much less than the 30 pecent to 50 percent figures required to ship coins or goods mentioned above.[57]

---

53. *KI*, doc. 13246, Kōan 1 (1278) 11th month 3rd day.

54. *KI*, doc. 18418, Einin 1 (1293) 12th month 2nd day.

55. Bills of exchange in medieval Europe had similar verification methods, such as a waiting period or specified date for redemption. De Roover, "Money, Banking, and Credit in Medieval Bruges," 55.

56. *Tōji hyakugo monjo* document, published in Toyoda, *Chūsei Nihon no shōgyō*, 272. Unfortunately, the fees for the other two *kawase* are not listed.

57. For example, see document 140 in the *Aioi shishi*, Jōwa 2 (1346) 3rd month 27th day, in which a fee of 1 *kan* 200 *mon* is assessed on a 10-*kanmon kaezeni*. See also the discussion of Sasaki's research earlier in this chapter.

Most of these thirteenth-century cases of money remittance involved major religious houses forwarding money to their representatives in distant locations. With very few exceptions, bills of exchange were not commonly used for transporting *nengu* from estates until the Muromachi period (1336–1573).[58] By the fourteenth century, merchant moneylenders had the resources to issue and back these certificates. As with most other aspects of the commercial economy, gender was no barrier to participation; the merchants issuing bills of exchange included both men and women. For example, a letter from someone affiliated with the shrine Itsukushima jinja explains to the recipient that he or she should redeem a certain bill of exchange at the stall of a widow nun in the Fukatsu marketplace.[59] Unlike the women portrayed in the Fukuoka market scene of Ippen's picture scroll (described in Chapter 2), whose status is unclear, the widow nun in the Fukatsu market must have been a merchant of some means, for she owned her own stall and could finance bills of exchange.

How did bills of exchange work? In the simplest type of transactions, traveling merchants might take bills of exchange with them on their rounds of the countryside. An estate manager, looking for a safe way to ship goods to his proprietor in the capital, would sell his produce to the merchant in exchange for the paper certificate. He would then forward the certificate to the proprietor, who would redeem it for cash at the specified location. But transactions were rarely this simple, as Fig. 6 illustrates. There might be a redemption date

---

58. Toyoda, "Chūsei no kawase," 73. However, a reference to cash being forwarded from Noda Estate as "kawashi yōtō" appears in the letter of acknowledgement written by the moneylender Hōren in 1298; see *Okayama kenshi*, vol. 19, doc. 1216.

59. This excerpt from an undated letter attributed to the late Kamakura period can be found in the primary-source collection *Nihonshi shiryō [2] chūsei*, doc. 187, pp. 206–07. I have followed Hotate Michihisa's annotation in that volume in interpreting this document fragment.

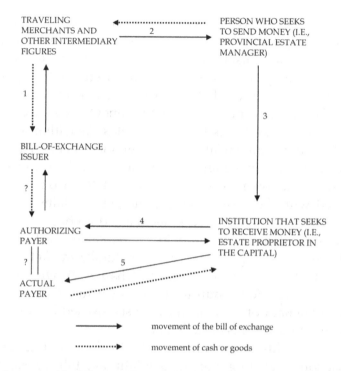

—————————▶   movement of the bill of exchange

·············▶   movement of cash or goods

1. Issuer provides bill to traveling merchant in exchange for goods or on credit.
2. Traveling merchants and other intermediary figures may exchange the bill multiple times. At some point, it is used to purchase estate produce.
3. The estate manager forwards the bill to his proprietor.
4. The proprietor brings the bill to the designated payer, who verifies the bill and returns it to the proprietor for actual payment elsewhere.
5. The proprietor brings the bill to the designated place for actual payment.

Fig. 6 Steps in the circulation of a bill of exchange

specified on the bill, or the location might be far away from the proprietor; both conditions were true of a *kawase* sent by Niimi estate to Tōji in 1468, which required someone to travel from Tōji to the port of Sakai (a two-day journey, though still much closer than Niimi itself).[60] Furthermore, the bill of exchange might change hands many times before finally being sold to the estate manager. Sakurai Eiji, starting from that

———

60. *Okayama kenshi*, vol. 20, doc. 427, Ōnin 2 (1468) 1st month 10th day. This document is also discussed in Usami, *Nihon chūsei no ryūtsū to shōgyō*, 225.

observation, contends that these bills actually circulated as a form of paper money.[61]

In support of his position, Sakurai notes an additional important fact: merchants did not write out bills of exchange for individual estates. In other words, a merchant did not arrive at Niimi Estate and create a bill of exchange for a cash amount corresponding to the value of the goods he was receiving. To the contrary, almost all Muromachi bills of exchange were fixed at a value of 10 *kanmon*. They were created by urban money-lenders and merchants with no foreknowledge of who would later redeem them. Thus, to use modern analogies, bills of exchange did not resemble an American checkbook, which allows the check writer to issue a paper certificate to a specific party for any required amount, to be paid later by the writer's bank. Instead, Muromachi-period bills of exchange were like hundred-dollar bills that change hands many times in exchange for various goods and services. Although the final end user, usually an estate proprietor, would in fact turn in the bill for hard currency, to all of the intermediate users, the bill of exchange functioned as paper money.

Sakurai's contention is provocative. It suggests an extremely sophisticated set of economic institutions for medieval Japan. Paper money is generally a form of fiat currency, with the guarantees of a strong state government lending credibility to the bills. Certainly government involvement was key to the success of the "flying cash" of Tang China. Medieval Japan, however, had no such state authority backing up its bills of exchange. Transactions were between parties that often did not know each other well, and involved long distances that made it potentially difficult to resolve problems should they arise. Furthermore, the merchant had an incentive to cheat if the proprietor was not likely to be a repeat customer. With no strong third-party such as a state government to enforce

---

61. Sakurai, *Nihon chūsei no keizai kōzō*, 235–73. For an analysis of the European bill of exchange and its relationship to paper money, see Rowlinson, "The Scotch Hate Gold," 47–67.

agreements and punish "cheaters," the merchant had only minimal fear of repercussions. How could estate managers and proprietors trust that certificates would be honored?

This was a difficult problem, and one that surely kept many from using bills of exchange despite the benefits of lowered transaction costs. Others found that the benefits outweighed the risks, and so they devised means of minimizing their exposure to bad bills of exchange. Consider the case of Niimi estate and Tōji. Once a merchant was known to sell good certificates, estate managers were likely to trust that individual with repeat business. But when using the services of a merchant for the first time, the Niimi estate manager would send only a small portion of the taxes as *saifu*, either holding on to the rest or sending it as cash. Correspondence between the estate and the temple, in which the manager asks for information, reveals this to have been the case: "We sent two *saifu* to you but have not yet heard whether or not they were honored. If they worked, and you agree, then we will send more of the same type next spring."[62] One can only assume that the high costs of shipping cash directly, or the dangers of robbery, outweighed the risks of receiving a bad *saifu* for the Tōji.

Figure 6 is a diagram that illustrates the more complicated paths taken by many fourteenth- and fifteenth-century bills of exchange. According to this model, a *saifu* was drawn up by an urban moneylending house and then given to a traveling merchant in exchange for cash or goods. The certificate might then pass through several different hands, as merchants purchased goods, paid off debts, and so on. At some point, a merchant would use the *saifu* to acquire an estate's tax produce. The estate manager would then forward the *saifu* to the proprietor, and the proprietor would dispatch someone to the office of the moneylender who wrote the bill of exchange in the first place. After verification, the moneylender might instruct the proprietor to go to a different location to receive

---

62. *Okayama kenshi*, vol. 20, doc. 916, Ōnin 1 (1467) 12th month 18th day.

payment, sometimes on a specified day. Bills of exchange surely saw more of medieval Japan than did most people.

This careful clarification of the complex path taken by certificates suggests additional insights into the status of merchants in medieval Japanese society. For example, the model shows that a *saifu*'s path began with the traveling merchant obtaining the certificate from a moneylending house. Consider this proposition for a moment. In order to obtain the certificate, either the merchant must already have rice or money to sell to the moneylender or else the merchant had to borrow from the moneylender, placing himself in debt. Once the merchant obtained the *saifu*, he had to immediately try to find someone to take it off of his hands so that he could either get more goods to sell or pay off his debts. The bill of exchange itself must have been like a hot potato that the merchant did not want to get caught holding for too long. As the merchant was likely to be in debt much of the time, his position was not as strong as it might otherwise appear.

By the same token, if a merchant knew the needs of the different estates in the area, his advantage in information would allow him to facilitate the exchange of goods much more efficiently than ordinary exchanges between uninformed parties. The most successful merchants, such as Dōsho, who ran ships along the Tōkaidō coastline in the 1330s, and Suzuki Dōin, who managed much of the trade between Shinagawa and Kumano in the 1430s, stationed representatives in different regions so as to determine where they could obtain the best prices for different goods.[63] They accumulated large fortunes in part through the sale and transportation of *nengu*, signifying the complete commodification of provincial goods that had in earlier centuries been thought of as distinct from commercial products.

---

63. Nagahara, *Shōen*, 265–69; Satō, "Utokunin Suzuki Dōin ni tsuite no oboegaki," 112–28.

Conclusion

As the medieval economy attained maturity in the late fourteenth and fifteenth centuries, patterns of trade and commerce
began to look quite different from what was seen in earlier
times. Sweeping economic forces led to changes in the ways
that the center tried to rule as well as changes in the ways that
the provinces asserted themselves. At the center, elites had
traditionally relied on goods paid as taxes from the provinces
for their income. Those that continued to rely on such sources
of income found themselves in increasingly dire straits in the
Muromachi period. But other medieval groups adapted to the
evolving economy, agreeing to receive commuted payments
in cash. Those that were particularly tuned in to the changes
taking place opted to create toll stations so that they could
tax commercial goods, sponsor medieval guilds (*za*) that paid
them in exchange for assistance in maintaining monopoly
rights, or get involved in pawn brokering and moneylending.
They used the cash that they acquired to purchase goods in
urban markets that bore little resemblance to the original eastern and western markets of the capital. Warrior institutions
also changed as the economy matured. Whereas the Kamakura
bakufu did not directly tax commercial establishments and
mainly got involved in economic matters to preserve peace
and order, the Muromachi *bakufu* took a radically different
approach. As will be described further in the next chapter, it
taxed commercial establishments in the city of Kyoto, accepted
cash "contributions" in exchange for assisting with debt relief
(or debt collection), and sent diplomatic missions to China in
hopes of obtaining large quantities of copper currency.

Things looked quite different on the periphery as well. In
earlier times, provincial officials and estate managers had little
say in what they paid to their superiors. As discussed at the
start of this chapter, in some instances provinces were required
to pay in goods that they did not produce! But the spread of
coins and markets meant that they had alternatives. They could
sell agricultural surplus and use the earnings to bolster their
own bargaining power vis-à-vis central proprietors. Or, if al-

lowed to pay their taxes in coins rather than in goods, they could choose to grow whatever combination of products would fetch the highest amount at the marketplace. Central proprietors often took the lead in promoting *daisennō*, and as this chapter shows, they had good reason. They benefited from being able to use money in urban markets to acquire the combination of goods that they desired. But in other instances, provincial estate managers, warriors, and agricultural communities pushed for tax commutation, a development that seems somewhat remarkable. After all, central proprietors had been determining the means of payment for centuries, but for provincials to also play an active role in *daisennō* signals how far things had changed from the top-down tribute economy of the Heian period.

In between were the merchants, who bridged the spaces between the countryside and the urban centers. They were quite different from the merchants of the Nara period, many of whom were in fact lower government officials who used their connections and their access to government transportation networks to facilitate the movement of goods. Medieval merchants did not hold government office (at least as far as can be determined from the surviving sources). Many instead turned to religious institutions because the backing of a temple or shrine could help them cross political boundaries and avoid certain tolls and taxes. Nor did medieval merchants rely on government transportation networks. They apparently had their own connections, perhaps with the *toimaru*, that allowed them to move goods to the cities more safely than others. Alternatively, they may have sold goods throughout a region, never bringing goods to the capital. Such exchanges among people on the periphery had surely taken place since earliest times, but the spread of money and markets in the medieval period made it far easier for provincial people to trade with each other than ever before.

All of these changes proved to be quite a challenge for warrior institutions to handle. The economic policies of the Kamakura and Muromachi *bakufu* were based on outdated notions of a clear distinction between *nengu* and commercial goods. Consequently, the policies led to conflicts among elites as they debated what could and could not be taxed. These disputes, as well as the income that was lost when goods were exempted from taxation, contributed to a transformation of political authority during Japan's medieval age. The Muromachi *bakufu* remained one of the country's most important political and economic institutions, but it did so by crafting new policies and seeking new sources of income that bore little resemblance to the economic role of earlier governments in Japan.

Another significant change was the development of bills of exchange to deliver *nengu* from the provinces to the center. Bills of exchange were the culmination of several different improvements to the traditional tribute payment system. The first began in the twelfth century, as demand for an improved medium of exchange led to the importation of cash despite the opposition of the nobles. Then, in the thirteenth century, monetization led to the commodification of goods. With the value of most goods assessed in coin by the fourteenth century, the substitution of one commodity for another became easy. In short, once people started using money, and goods became commodities that could be sold locally, the need to ship them directly to the capital was reduced.

This process went one step further with *kawase*, as it no longer became necessary to transport cash to the capital either. *Kawase* stand out as having circulated in a manner similar to paper money but without government backing. Merchants could cheat, as estates such as Niimi discovered when the *kawase* they purchased proved unredeemable. But these cases were the exception rather than the rule. Only merchants with no interest in repeat customers had an incentive to sell bad bills. For most, building trust by selling valid bills of exchange was key to their long-term prosperity. They sought to convince estate managers to trust them so that they could take advantage of superior information and thereby realize a profit from the sale of rural produce.

In fact, the distinction between *kawase* and other types of exchange is not as significant as it might seem. The trust placed in bills of exchange should also be recognized as stemming from earlier economic developments. After all, Chinese coins had no effective state backing when they were brought to Japan, yet they circulated far and wide with few problems, at least until the late fifteenth century. Viewed in this light, the difference between *kawase* and metal currency might be seen merely as one of scale, for a single bill of exchange was usually worth 10,000 coins. That medieval Japanese were able to create a system of exchange in which *kawase* could be used without a strong third-party guarantor speaks volumes about how creatively merchants and provincial estate managers could circumvent the problems of divided central government in the fifteenth century.

FIVE

Late Medieval and Beyond

This study is expressly designed to call attention to the economic roles of non-elites at the periphery. As the preceding chapters have shown, individuals in their capacities as provincial warriors, estate managers, itinerant merchants, and money-lending priests all played active roles in the emerging economy of the thirteenth and fourteenth centuries.

But of course they were not the only people involved. These sweeping social and economic changes involved people from all levels of society, including the traditional powerbrokers. Elites and urban residents made important contributions to the spread of money and markets as well. Some, such as the traditional estate proprietors Shōmyōji and Tōji, chose to join in the commercial economy by having certain of their estates switch to making cash payments of *nengu*. Others, notably Enryakuji and Emperor Go-Daigo, chose to tax the monetary holdings of urban businesses such as sake brewers and pawnshops. The Ashikaga shoguns were undoubtedly the most active in promoting monetization. Beginning with the third shogun, Yoshimitsu, they embraced the new cash economy much more fully than their Kamakura predecessors. Among other tactics, the Ashikaga devised ways to charge fees for *tokuseirei* and became major importers of Chinese coins in the fifteenth century. All three "branches" of the *kenmon* elite — the noble, religious, and military houses — became heavyweight players in the economy as the medieval period progressed.

Yet the trend toward greater economic participation from those in the provinces did not end because of increased elite interest in money and markets after the thirteenth century. Non-elites continued to play important roles in the growing economy. Pirates and merchants helped import and circulate coins and mobilize against barriers that impeded trade. Peasants rioted and attacked the city of Kyoto numerous times as they fought for debt relief. Villages sold their surplus produce and cash crops in local markets and pooled the monies they earned to challenge the authority of civil landlords and local warriors. In short, medieval non-elites on the periphery were able to utilize the evolving economy to realize greater agency than in earlier times. Some scholars have seemingly dismissed their actions as merely taking advantage of political elites' preoccupation with other matters.[1] But closer examination reveals that their actions were not merely responses to the disintegration of effective central government; rather, they actively contributed to it. Only the most successful *sengoku* daimyo were able to develop new ways of bringing economic matters back under their control.

This chapter explores issues in monetary history from the fourteenth century to the end of the medieval period. These were times of tremendous political change, including the destruction of the Kamakura *bakufu*, the brief imperial restoration of the 1330s, and the establishment of the Muromachi *bakufu*. War also became much more common. There was frequent violence during the period of the Northern and Southern Courts (1336–92) as well as during the last century of Muromachi rule, known as the *sengoku* or "Warring States" period (1467–1573). Yet even in the midst of these political and social upheavals, there are still signs of economic growth from this period. Faced with uncertain political leadership and unable

---

1. Toyoda and Sugiyama, "The Growth of Commerce and the Trades," 129; Hall, *Government and Local Power*, 179–83, 191–92.

to rely on income from landed estates, elites and non-elites alike turned to new ways of securing revenue, protecting their interests, and understanding the world.

From Kamakura to Kenmu

As explained earlier, the Kamakura *bakufu* had rather under-developed commercial policies. Its primary interest was in land and the ability of its retainers to render service to the *bakufu* when called upon. The few actions that the *bakufu* took toward the commercial economy were all attempts to regu-late: the size of merchant districts, the number of ocean-going boats, the prices of various commodities, and so on. Another way the *bakufu* asserted its regulatory role was to authorize dispute settlements such as the agreement between the civilian manager and the *jitō* of Akanabe estate, discussed in the pre-vious chapter. Kamakura officially endorsed the use of copper cash with its 1226 decree, but it must have grown increasingly wary of monetization, since debts from gambling and the loss of lands due to unpaid loans were such a source of trouble for the *gokenin*. Its attempts to regulate moneylenders proved quite ineffective, as seen in the response to the provisions of the 1297 *tokuseirei* (discussed in Chapter 3). In one part of the *tokuseirei*, the *bakufu* forbade moneylenders and other creditors from appealing to the Kamakura courts. In another section, the *bakufu* promulgated a blanket amnesty, allowing retain-ers to reclaim lands without repaying debts. Both provisions proved more disruptive than beneficial and had to be repealed soon after they were issued. Although the *bakufu* eventually began to explore alternative sources of income such as author-izing toll stations (*seki*), these never became important revenue streams for the warrior government. Instead, they were left to the management of the imperial court and major temples.

The court and temples took the lead in developing new ways to tap into the expanding economy of the thirteenth and early fourteenth centuries. One of the first was Enryakuji, which had already developed patron-client relationships with Kyoto moneylenders by the start of the thirteenth century. These moneylenders, many of whom were monks, paid a certain percentage of their income to Enryakuji in exchange for support and protection.[2] Various government ministries also began seeking to tax commercial enterprises in Kyoto. For example, the Distillery Office (Zōshushi) spent decades trying to win the right to tax malt producers. Originally a purveyor of *sake* for ceremonial use by the court, the office had come to rely on an annual tax paid by provincial governors for its income by the second half of the Heian period. Yet as Kamakura's warriors began to interfere with the collection of provincial taxes, governors became less willing — or perhaps simply less able — to pay the Distillery Office. The office appealed to the retired emperor for permission to directly tax the brewers of Kyoto, which it eventually secured.[3]

Along with taxing businesses, elites searched for new sources of income on Japan's roads and waterways by establishing toll barriers that took advantage of the increased movement of people and goods. These stations could tax travelers, merchants, shippers, and potentially anyone else who did not possess an exemption. Tōdaiji, concerned because it was receiving less from its landed estates, turned to such tolls to help compensate for lost income. In 1308, the court granted Tōdaiji the right to institute tolls at Hyōgo, one of medieval Japan's busiest ports. Collections from this and other stations were a major source of income for the temple in the fourteenth century.[4] It was not unique — other powerful institutions, from temples such as Tōfukuji to *bakufu* figures such as Hino Tomiko, turned to toll stations as new sources of revenue. As all of these examples illustrate, the court and religious houses

---

2. Suzanne Gay discusses a case from 1213 in which moneylenders had to appeal to the Enryakuji to protect them from the aggressive actions of warriors who owed money. Gay, *Moneylenders of Late Medieval Kyoto*, 71.

3. Ibid., 74. The office first petitioned for this tax in 1240 and did not secure it until 1302, presumably because the court did not want to risk confrontation with Enryakuji. The Hie jinja, part of the Enryakuji network, already levied a tax on brewers.

4. Joan Piggott, "Hierarchy and Economics," 76.

were driven to find new ways of securing income by warriors who obstructed more traditional revenue streams.

The individual who most aggressively tried to tap into these resources was Emperor Go-Daigo, whose Kenmu Restoration brought about the destruction of the Kamakura *bakufu*. Go-Daigo clearly recognized the importance of secure revenue and took steps to improve the imperial coffers long before he succeeded in overthrowing the *bakufu*. As early as 1322, more than ten years before the restoration, he was exploring new ways of taxing cash and commerce. First, Go-Daigo announced his intention to liberate *jinin* and *kugonin* from their obligations to the imperial house and the various temples and shrines. Some of these purveyors, it seems, were profiting handsomely in the emerging economy. The spread of markets not only presented more opportunities for them to acquire goods, but it also facilitated their ability to sell any surplus they collected for cash. If Go-Daigo had successfully enacted this plan, it would have greatly increased the number of merchants and moneylenders subject to imperial taxation. But he bowed to strong resistance from temple patrons, who threatened to send their armed monks in protest against any moves that would deprive them of income. The purveyors themselves, who were anxious about the increased competition that they would face if their existing affiliations were nullified, also mobilized against a change in their status. As a result, Go-Daigo refrained from implementing this policy.[5]

His second measure met with greater, if limited, success. Go-Daigo reclaimed taxing authority over lands that had been awarded to Tōji by his father, Go-Uda (now a retired emperor). Again, there was resistance: the temple appealed to both Go-Daigo and his father that it needed the extra income. But the emperor succeeded in collecting tax revenue from those properties on at least two occasions before agreeing to restore the exemption. Although Go-Daigo did not secure this as a long-term source of revenue, in fact it was a victory for his authority,

---

5. Goble, *Kenmu*, 48.

since the temple was forced to acknowledge Go-Daigo's power to grant or deny the exemption. Go-Daigo's third and most successful measure was his assertion of the court's right to tax *sake* brewers. He declared in 1322 that all brewers were henceforth considered imperial purveyors, regardless of other affiliations that they might have held. Those who failed to pay taxes in accordance with the decree were jailed for noncompliance. This became an important source of income for the court in the days leading up to Kenmu.[6] Go-Daigo was not the first emperor to recognize the value of the commercial economy, but as these examples illustrate, his varied policy initiatives showed how bold he was in attempting to secure income from it.

Go-Daigo had a much freer hand in 1333 and 1334, after the *bakufu* had been destroyed and he directly ruled the country. Full of confidence, he abolished most toll stations, especially those that held authorization from the old warrior regime. This was important because many merchants and shippers had been blocked from reaching Kyoto by such stations while the fighting was underway. Others were able to reclaim goods that had been confiscated by forces from one side or the other during the conflict. Another innovative move by the emperor was his announcement of plans to cast new domestic currency (described in the Introduction). Given that there was a great deal of currency already in circulation, it might strike some readers that new coinage need not have been a priority. There were, however, ideological as well as economic reasons for Go-Daigo to move so quickly. On the ideological side, the emperor was well educated in Chinese ideas of governance and shared the belief that the production of coins was an imperial privilege and a mark of sovereignty. This is evident in his proclamation from 1334, which declared, "To seek [coinage] from overseas and willfully circulate it in the world, as has been done . . . until the recent past, is . . . contrary to the proper way and warps the laws of government."[7] His proclamation recalls the mind-

---

6. Ibid., 49–52.
7. Ibid., 205–7.

set of the late twelfth-century Japanese nobles who opposed imported coins. Go-Daigo was eager to mint in part because he believed that issuing domestic currency would bolster his legitimacy.

Economic concerns were surely just as important, though. Go-Daigo's ambitious plans to rebuild the imperial palace (among other projects) meant that he needed to increase revenues. The production of new money was just such an opportunity. One of the advantages of a minting agency is that it can capture the difference between the costs of making coins and the value at which they circulate. Go-Daigo hoped to benefit from just such profits through the minting of his new coin of the realm. It was to bear the inscription *Kenkon tsūhō*, an inscription that signaled the beginning of a new era through its combination of the characters for the first and last trigrams of the *Book of Changes*.[8] Presumably the coins would have been round, square-holed, and otherwise similar in design to the imperial twelve coins of the Nara and early Heian periods. The plan appears to have been well conceived, for new coinage might have helped the Kenmu regime politically as well as economically. But some of Go-Daigo's other initiatives were not as well received. For example, his decision to levy a 5 percent income tax on the *jitō* only earned him their enmity. And his decision to pass over his leading warriors and instead name his own son as shogun offended his generals. In 1335, Ashikaga Takauji, one of his most powerful generals, rebelled against the fledgling regime. By the following year he had taken Kyoto and forced Go-Daigo to flee the capital for the hills of Yoshino, bringing the short-lived imperial restoration to an end.

Economic Policies of the Muromachi Bakufu

Takauji went on to found the second of Japan's three warrior governments, known as the Muromachi (or Ashikaga) *bakufu*, which lasted from 1336 to 1573. Unlike the previous shogunate,

---

8. Ibid., 206.

which rejected Kyoto as the location of its headquarters in favor of the distant city of Kamakura, the Ashikaga chose to base their new government in the Muromachi district of Kyoto. There were several reasons for this move. One was the unstable political situation, as warriors who professed loyalty to Go-Daigo and his so-called Southern Court threatened to retake the city and install their own emperor. Takauji's decision to headquarter his administration in Kyoto was surely made in part to better defend the city. But another important reason was to take advantage of Kyoto's commercial development. By the 1330s, Kyoto had started to become a commercial city. Unlike the leaders of the Kamakura *bakufu*, who relied primarily on landed estates for their income, the Ashikaga shoguns fully embraced monetization and urban taxation as sources of revenue.

Despite Takauji's antipathy toward Go-Daigo, the Muromachi *bakufu* built on many of his policies, including his efforts to reassert elite control over the economy. This new warrior concern for fiscal matters is made evident in the founding document of the regime, the *Kenmu shikimoku*, issued by Takauji in 1336.[9] It consists of an introduction and seventeen provisions that call for everything from an end to violent crimes and the return of abandoned property to its rightful owners to an appeal to listen carefully to the lawsuits of the poor. Article 6 addresses the pawnshops and storehouses that functioned as Kyoto's moneylenders. Noting that some had been hit with enormous taxes while others had been broken into, the provision called for such behavior to cease and desist so that the financial institutions could operate safely.[10] The government

---

9. Although Go-Daigo fled the capital in the eighth month of Kenmu 3 (1336) and was replaced on the throne by Emperor Kōmyō of the Northern Court, the government continued to use the era name Kenmu until the eighth month of Kenmu 5 (1338). Hence, although the era name Kenmu is most closely associated with Go-Daigo, the *Kenmu shikimoku* is actually the founding document of the Ashikaga who deposed him.

10. *Kenmu shikimoku*, Kenmu 3 (1336), 11th month 7th day, in *Chūsei hōsei shiryōshū*, vol. 2, 5.

needed to have the moneylending houses, which suffered during the upheaval of Go-Daigo's and then Takauji's attacks on the city, open for business again, both to restore normalcy to the capital and because they were potential sources of revenue. This was a marked difference in approach from the Kamakura *bakufu*, which had viewed moneylenders as causing problems (i.e., the loss of retainers' lands) and compared them to thieves. In contrast, the Muromachi *bakufu* embraced the cash economy and saw moneylenders as part of the solution to its own financial needs.

Of course, the moneylenders had no particular desire to help underwrite the expenses of the new warrior government. They had their own networks to manage and obligations to meet. Many were affiliated with Enryakuji, a major political (as well as religious) institution that protected moneylenders in exchange for payment. Nonetheless, the *bakufu* would eventually turn to them as a source of additional revenue. In a series of decrees issued in 1393, Ashikaga Yoshimitsu asserted the *bakufu*'s right to tax moneylenders, demanding a yearly levy of 6,000 *kanmon*.[11] Yoshimitsu's edicts did not deny or dissolve the relationship between the moneylenders and Enryakuji, and they expressly confirmed the right of the Distillery Office to continue its malt tax, so neither the temple nor the court had much reason to protest vociferously.[12] But for the moneylenders, who already paid taxes to Mt. Hiei and the Distillery Office, this newly-added burden must have been particularly heavy. Nonetheless, Yoshimitsu's successors continued this policy and went further, imposing special cash levies (*kurayaku*) to raise additional income. The eighth shogun, Yoshimasa, reportedly instituted various types of special levies multiple times per month, much to the consternation of Kyoto's wealthier residents.[13] His profligate spending on architectural

11. *Kenmu irai tsuika*, Meiō 4 (1393), 11th month, 26th day, in *Chūsei hōsei shiryōshū*, vol. 2, 59–60.

12. Gay, *Moneylenders of Late Medieval Kyoto*, 81–85.

13. Hayashiya, "Kyoto in the Muromachi Age," 27.

projects such as the Silver Pavilion and his indulgent support for the arts (including Noh) drained the *bakufu* treasury and forced his administrators to constantly seek more cash.

The Ashikaga shoguns did not merely levy taxes in copper coins—they also imported cash, sending diplomatic missions to China in order to obtain coins from the source. This marked a major foreign policy shift. The Japanese had not sent diplomatic missions to China since the ninth century, and in the late thirteenth century, the Yuan Mongols twice tried to conquer Japan. But conditions had changed by the second half of the fourteenth century. The first Ming emperor, Hongwu (r. 1368–1398), was eager to symbolically confirm his legitimacy as the ruler of a new dynasty. One way to do that was to reestablish China's prominence by accepting tribute from neighboring states. In 1368, his first year on the throne, he sent envoys announcing the start of his reign to Champa, Annam, Korea, and Japan.[14] The Ming emperor's diplomatic letters reveal that he had an additional reason for pursuing diplomacy with Japan: he sought the government's cooperation in suppressing pirates (*wakō*) from Japan who frequently attacked China and Korea. The Ming envoys traveled to Kyushu, the closest of Japan's major islands, but it was under the control of the Southern Court whose general, Prince Kanenaga, was unwilling or unable to engage in diplomacy.[15] The Ming sent another envoy in 1370, but Kanenaga was in no position to stop the pirate raids. Meanwhile, Yoshimitsu was eager to open diplomatic relations with the Ming, but it was only after he unified the Northern and Southern Courts that he was able to convince the Chinese to deal with him. In 1401, he sent a mission to China led by a Buddhist priest and a merchant from Hakata that successfully negotiated the reopening of official relations between the two countries.

For the Japanese, those relations came at a price, for the Ming would only agree to diplomacy with other states if they ac-

---

14. Wang, *Official Relations between China and Japan*, 10.
15. Tanaka, "Japan's Relations," 163–64.

knowledged China's superiority by sending tribute missions. Yoshimitsu agreed to meet those conditions, sending a diplomatic letter with his envoys in which he referred to himself as the "king of Japan," a subject of the Ming emperor. Many Japanese criticized Yoshimitsu for humbling himself in this way, and scholars have long debated what led Yoshimitsu to make such a move.[16] Surely one of the factors was Yoshimitsu's interest in acquiring Chinese goods, especially coins, through diplomatic trade. His counterpart, Emperor Yongle (r. 1403–1424), had come to power through a civil war rather than through an orderly transfer of power. As a result, some questioned his legitimacy. Yongle was eager to cement his position as China's ruler and therefore quite generous in rewarding missions that brought tribute. He presented 1,500 *min* of coins to the Japanese in 1403, 15,000 *min* in 1407, and a further sum of 5,000 *min* the following year. He also bestowed additional gifts of cash to individual envoys. The mission from the fifth Ming emperor, Xuande (r. 1426–1435), reportedly gave the Japanese 300,000 *kan*, though scholars have noted that this figure seems too high to be regarded as reliable.[17] Even if the last figure is somewhat exaggerated, the *bakufu*'s engagement in such diplomacy gave it access to huge amounts of coins and enabled it to become the major importer of cash for more than half of a century.

Finally, the *bakufu* supported its *shugo* and major temples in their efforts to acquire cash income. With *bakufu* endorsement, the *shugo* converted the land tax known as *tansen* from a periodic, public levy used to fund special ceremonies or temple-rebuilding projects into a regular tax that the *shugo* could use for his own private ends.[18] Of even greater significance was the *bakufu*'s decision to legalize *hanzei*, the right of the *shugo* to claim half of a given estate's output. First issued in

---

16. Imatani, "Not for Lack of Will or Wile," 45–46.

17. Wang, *Official Relations between China and Japan*, 102. The counter *min* was used for strings of cash and contained approximately 1,000 coins, the same as the *kan*.

18. Hall, "The Muromachi *Bakufu*," 200.

1352 as a temporary move to support warriors fighting for the Northern Court, *hanzei* became permanent in 1368.[19] As the estates themselves were increasingly paying their taxes in cash, the *shugo* were able to obtain cash by exercising this right. In earlier times, when Kamakura *jitō* appropriated more than their designated share of *nengu*, civilian proprietors could sue them in court and perhaps win back what they had lost. But *hanzei* offered no such opportunity for redress. As Regent Konoe Michitsugu noted with despair some years thereafter, "*Hanzei* is no illegal act, but is authorized by the [Muromachi] *bakufu*. It is difficult for court nobles to pass judgment on it. There are no precedents to go by. All we can do is complain directly to the *bakufu*."[20] By supporting warriors' designs on landed estate income in this way, the *bakufu*'s policies were a further blow to the income streams of many traditional elites.

The *bakufu* also helped temples that it favored to thrive in the medieval economy. Zen temples in particular benefited from *bakufu* support. Tenryūji recorded an income of over 8,000 *kanmon* in cash and rice in 1387, and Nanzenji enjoyed regular income of over 4,000 *koku* from estates in at least six provinces.[21] Ashikaga patronage meant that these temples could expect exemptions from *shugo* levies, freedom from toll-barrier charges, favorable treatment in court, and other benefits such as the right to levy commercial taxes of their own. Thus, Nanzenji was given permission to charge fees for passage through toll barriers that it erected in mid-fourteenth-century Kyoto, and Tōfukuji taxed a merchant community that developed at the temple's gates. In the cases of both the *shugo* and Zen temples, the *bakufu* asserted its control over the economy by functioning as the authorizing power behind their actions.

----

19. Imatani, "Muromachi Local Government: Shugo and Kokujin," 242–43.
20. As cited in and translated by Wintersteen in "The Muromachi Shugo and Hanzei," 217.
21. Collcutt, "Zen and the Gozan," 637–38.

Instability and Other Weaknesses of the Muromachi System

The image conveyed by the preceding section is one of the Muromachi *bakufu* having successfully taken on the role of effective central government. It demonstrated its active interest in the economy by attempting to set rates of taxation, import and issue currency, and confirm property rights (at least the rights of those that it favored). Yet closer examination reveals that the Ashikaga had much greater difficulty in managing their economic affairs than this picture seems to suggest. For much of its existence, the Muromachi *bakufu* was politically weak and divided. Eastern Japan was often administered by a semi-independent deputy, the *Kantō kubō*, and the *bakufu* itself was only as strong as the coalition of *shugo* daimyo who supported it. From 1336 to 1392, its principal figures were preoccupied by the war between the Northern and Southern Courts. Fighting was common during those years as major *shugo* and even the leading members of the Ashikaga family at times turned against the *bakufu*. Yoshimitsu brought an end to the violence, and he and his immediate successors presided over several decades of stability. But the assassination in 1441 of the sixth shogun, Yoshinori, led to a further weakening of *bakufu* influence. Finally, from the start of the Ōnin War in 1467 to the end of the regime in 1573, the *bakufu* was only able to wield minimal power outside of central Japan. Of course, all of these political and military problems hindered the *bakufu*'s efforts at promoting and managing economic matters.

One reason why the *bakufu* had such difficulty in exerting coercive political power was that it could not rely on a regular revenue stream. It enjoyed little income from traditional sources such as landed estates. According to one estimate, the Ashikaga directly controlled only 300,000 *koku* of land, far less than the Tokugawa shoguns who eventually succeeded them (and who controlled some 4 million *koku* of land).[22] Ashikaga

---

22. Since land values were generally not calculated in *koku* during the Muromachi period, these figures can only be approximate, but they clearly

family members exercised personal control over only a few provinces, and although they awarded many other provinces to warrior families such as the Yamana and the Hosokawa (who were their relatives), blood ties did little to ensure stability. In fact, those two families were the leading antagonists in the Ōnin War. Precisely because the *bakufu* could not rely on income from landed estates, it aggressively pursued cash from domestic urban sources such as toll stations and moneylenders. On the one hand, the Muromachi *bakufu* must be recognized for fully embracing the medieval economy and devising new ways to garner revenue and secure cash (including importing coins from the Ming). On the other hand, only some of its moves were innovative or unique. As already mentioned, traditional elites, such as the major temples and the bureaucratic offices of the imperial court, took similar steps in levying tolls and taxes. Furthermore, while the various policies of the major temple complexes, imperial court offices, and the *bakufu* may have earned them additional income in the short term, they also (depending on the policy) interfered with exchange and thereby hindered continued economic expansion.

The erection of toll barriers, for instance, impeded trade and, in some cases, led to violence. Enryakuji established a series of seven toll stations along Lake Biwa that proved extremely profitable: in one year, a single station could collect as much as 1,200 *kanmon*.[23] But those who sought to use Lake Biwa to transport goods or conduct other transactions were forced to pay a fee at each station, raising the costs of doing business. Nanzenji provides another example. As mentioned above, the temple set up toll stations with *bakufu* approval to fund the reconstruction of its main gate. In 1367, an Onjōji monk tried to force his way through one of Nanzenji's barriers in Ōmi province. Violence erupted, and the Nanzenji agents

---

show that the Ashikaga directly ruled over only a fraction of the realm. Hisamitsu, *Nihon kahei monogatari*, 59.
23. Tonomura, *Community and Commerce*, 98–99.

killed the Onjōji monk.[24] Onjōji retaliated by destroying the barrier, with more deaths on each side. At the heart of the conflict was not the original monk's murder but rather Onjōji's perception that the *bakufu*'s support gave an unfair economic edge to Nanzenji.

The *bakufu* tried a different approach with its involvement in debt collection and relief. Starting in 1454, the shogun began issuing variants of *tokusei* debt-relief decrees known as conditional debt amnesties (*buichi tokuseirei*),[25] which adopted the language of good governance. The initial decree purported to be an effort to restore order in response to rumors that indebted commoners threatened to attack their creditors: warehouses (*dosō*) and daily money traders (*hizeniya*, lenders who extended very short-term loans at high interest).[26] In reality, however, *buichi tokuseirei* were anything but virtuous. The *bakufu* promulgated them for profit. Groups requesting relief had to pay 10 percent or 20 percent of the amount that they owed to the *bakufu*. When some groups failed to pay, the *bakufu* invented a variant under which *creditors* paid the *bakufu* a portion of the debt owed to them so that the government would sanction their efforts at collection.[27] In either case, the *bakufu* served only to help itself by raising some funds. These debt amnesties did little to aid the people or the overall economy.

Finally, we must consider the role of the Ashikaga as importers of Chinese cash. There is no question that this trade proved quite lucrative, hence the *bakufu*'s eagerness to continue it. Some modern scholars have even suggested that because the *bakufu* monopolized this right to import currency,

---

24. This summary of events draws on Adolphson, "Enryakuji: An Old Power in a New Era," 250.

25. I have followed Suzanne Gay in adopting this translation of the term *buichi tokuseirei*. Gay, *Moneylenders of Late Medieval Kyoto*, 142.

26. *Kenmu irai tsuika*, Juntoku 3 (1254), 10th month (probably), 29th day, in *Chūsei hōsei shiryōshū*, vol. 2, 84–85.

27. Gomi, *Chūsei no shakai to genzai*, 59; Gay, *Moneylenders of Late Medieval Kyoto*, 142–44.

it was effectively as if the *bakufu* had minted the coins itself.[28] If this were true, then one might convincingly claim that the *bakufu* had established control over the money supply. Closer examination of Japanese trade with the Ming, however, reveals three reasons why it is a problematic contention.

To begin with, the *bakufu* only participated in exclusive diplomatic trade with the Ming for the first decade of the fifteenth century. Yoshimitsu successfully reopened relations with the Chinese in 1401, but his son and successor, Ashikaga Yoshimochi, refused to participate in such exchanges after 1410. When the sixth shogun, Yoshinori, resumed relations with the Ming in the 1430s, he was but one sponsor of the Japanese mission that was sent to China. Temples including Shōkokuji and Sanjūsangendō, and daimyo such as the Yamana, sponsored their own boats that accompanied the diplomatic mission. For the remainder of the fifteenth century, daimyo, temples, and shrines joined the *bakufu* in sending ships to China for trade. By the early sixteenth century, the *bakufu* did not have the resources to participate at all: the final five missions, from 1511 to 1549, consisted of vessels sponsored by the Ōuchi and Hosokawa.[29] Therefore, the importation of cash was spread among a large number of elite families and institutions.

Second, the Ming rarely provided the Japanese with the amounts of coins that they requested. As the figures noted above illustrate, the Japanese received very generous amounts of cash from the Ming in the 1400s and 1430s. But after the passing of Emperor Xuande in 1435, the Chinese interest in foreign policy waned and the high costs of the tribute trade became increasingly objectionable. When Yoshimasa sent a mission to China in 1453, it was the largest Japanese mission so far: nine boats carrying over 1,200 people and huge amounts of copper ore, sapan wood, sulphur, swords, and other goods for sale. The Japanese expected to bring home a handsome

---

28. Toyoda and Sugiyama, "The Growth of Commerce and the Trades," 132; Takizawa, "Early Currency Policies of the Tokugawa," 24.

29. Tanaka, "Japan's Relations with Overseas Countries," 169.

profit, but the Chinese did not offer the high prices that they had twenty years ago. After months of negotiation, they compromised — the Japanese returned home with copper cash, but not as much as they had expected.[30] Subsequent Japanese missions encountered similar difficulties, and their appeals to the Ming court for more Chinese coins became a routine feature of the tally trade in the second half of the fifteenth century. This certainly suggests that the Ashikaga were rather limited in their ability to operate as if they were minting the coins themselves.

Third and perhaps most importantly, even when the Muromachi *bakufu* was acquiring large quantities of Chinese cash through diplomatic trade missions, unofficial trade by non-elite figures remained another significant way for coins to reach Japan. It is difficult to quantify their contributions, for unlike official trade missions, these importers left behind no receipts or records. But archaeologists have been able to uncover clues that shed light on such trade. Kuroda Akinobu, citing the findings of Suzuki Kimio, notes that coins found in some medieval buried hoards are not consistent with the types of coins given by the Chinese government; instead, they are privately minted Chinese coins that he believes were brought to Japan by *wakō* pirates.[31] We know that the Japanese had the sailing vessels and the motivation to bring coins to Japan in the Muromachi period and that *wakō* raids were frequent during these years, so his contention is quite plausible. Although there is no question that the *bakufu* played an important role in bringing copper currency to Japan, it seems very unlikely that it truly monopolized the importation of cash or could act as though it had cast the coins itself.

---

30. This account follows Wang, *Official Relations*, 64–73.
31. Kuroda, "Copper Coins Chosen," 79–80.

The Role of Non-Elites in the Muromachi Economy

As this last point reveals, non-elites played an important part in later medieval Japan's economic expansion. There is additional evidence of trade between Japan and its neighbors during this period, much of it involving non-*bakufu* figures. Chinese officials record that Japanese merchant ships visited them regularly in the mid-fourteenth century, decades before the official tribute trade had resumed. Charlotte von Verschauer posits that provincial leaders or estate managers in southern Japan may have sponsored these ships. In one instance, a Kyoto physician proposed to the government that it tax the city's residents at the rate of ten coins per household to fund construction of a ship that would take the physician to China. His plan was to sell Japanese goods in China and use the profits to underwrite construction of a hospital in Kyoto.[32] The Japanese also enjoyed a lively trade relationship with the Koreans, from whom they imported cotton among other goods. And there were occasionally visitors from farther away: the Japanese port of Obama, along the Sea of Japan coast, received several ships from Palembang in the early fifteenth century.[33] These examples illustrate quite effectively that foreign trade and exchange could flourish outside of diplomatic channels.

Non-elites took steps to safeguard their goods and facilitate the easy shipment of money, such as their development of *kawase* bills of exchange independent of government involvement (discussed in the Chapter 4). They were also willing to fight for their economic livelihoods. When the *bakufu* erected toll barriers in the mid-1450s, people mobilized and staged protests, forcing the government to remove the stations.[34] Even more dangerous were the peasant-led *doikki* (or *tsuchiikki*) that periodically descended upon the city, usually in demand of

---

32. Von Verschauer, *Across the Perilous Sea*, 97.
33. Ibid., 122, 132–33.
34. Nagahara, *Gekokujo no jidai*, 80.

debt relief.[35] The first such major protest erupted in 1428. Although it started with protests in Ōmi and Yamashiro provinces, the culmination of the movement was a half-month-long attack on Kyoto, during which the protesters raided several moneylending establishments and caused a great deal of destruction. More than twenty such attacks befell Kyoto over the next hundred years. Violent protests like these left no doubt in anyone's mind that commoners were a force with which to be reckoned.

In the provinces, tax commutation, changing patterns of trade, and the withering of effective *shōen* management led to the rise of new village communities. Organized communities became increasingly able to assert control over water resources, forests, and other lands that had formerly been under the authority of absentee proprietors or local samurai landholders (*kokujin*). In earlier times, proprietors' representatives frequently mobilized their peasants to help win disputes over water resources with neighboring estates, but by the fifteenth century, peasants were organizing themselves.[36] They pooled their resources to acquire common agricultural lands (*sōyūden*). Villagers often jointly worked those fields, selling the crops and using the money to acquire water rights, pursue litigation, or assist needy members of the community.[37] Economic growth was key to these developments as villages required financial capital in order to purchase the rights to common lands. In some instances, peasant communities were powerful enough that *kokujin* had to band together or become the vassals of stronger *kokujin* in order to resist them.[38]

There is both archaeological and documentary evidence to confirm that copper cash was widely used in the Muromachi period. Archaeological evidence includes large buried caches

---

35. The classic work on this topic remains Nakamura, *Tokusei to doikki*. A thorough English-language description appears in Gay, *Moneylenders of Late Medieval Kyoto*, 128–48.

36. Hōgetsu, *Chūsei kangaishi no kenkyū*, 336–37.

37. Nagahara, "Village Communities and Daimyō Power," 112–13.

38. Miyagawa, "From Shōen to Chigyō," 100.

of medieval coins that have been unearthed in every region of Japan. These finds are sometimes referred to as *bichikusen* because it is presumed that the owner buried the coins in order to save or stockpile them, but the exact circumstances remain unknown. Often the coins were placed inside a ceramic jar or wooden box before being buried and are discovered having fused into the shape of the container. Most finds contain a mix of imported Chinese cash, with Northern Song currency the most prevalent. However, other types of Chinese coins (Ming, Tang, and Southern Song) as well as coins from Korea, Ryukyu, and / or Annam have been discovered in some hoards. The types of coins clearly indicate medieval collections, though it is sometimes difficult to date the caches more precisely. One crude measure is to look at the "newest" coin in a given collection, since the collection must have been interred after the date of that coin. Using such evidence, Suzuki Kimio has determined that the peak of coin-burial activity was between the end of the fourteenth century and the first half of the sixteenth.[39] Of course, that does not necessarily correspond to the peak period of coin use, since people may have used coins for decades or more before conditions drove them to bury their wealth.

Written materials that make mention of copper currency range from land-sale deeds to village self-governing covenants. A peasant petition sent to Tōji in 1407, for example, refers to taxes (*tansen* and *kajishi*) being collected in coin as well as a cash bribe of 3 *kan* 500 *mon* that the peasants were paying to the *shugo*.[40] Some of the best evidence that merchants and other non-elite figures were transacting in cash comes from the laws against coin shroffing, known as *erizenirei*. These were proclamations issued by regional daimyo or the *bakufu* that stipulated acceptable mixes of coins for use in all kinds of transactions. By the fifteenth century, the high demand for copper cash had led to the domestic production of counterfeit

---

39. Suzuki, *Shutsudō senka*, 63–78.
40. *Tōji hyakugō monjo*, "ni" box, Ōei 14 (1407) 12th month 15th day, in Kodama, ed., *Shiryō ni yoru Nihon no ayumi*, 351–52.

coins, many of them bearing no inscription (and therefore known as *mumonsen*).[41] Because these coins were of inferior quality, some people refused to accept them or only accepted them at a discount. In addition, concerns were raised about the value of certain Ming coins, probably because the Ming stopped producing copper coinage in the fifteenth century. In short, people had started distinguishing between different kinds of metal currency, valuing some coins more than others. When they insisted upon only certain types of coins for payments, disputes could result and the economy slowed down. Therefore, political elites (the daimyo and the *bakufu*) promulgated *erizenirei* with the intent of minimizing such problems. The *erizenirei* declared which coins could or could not be used in specific territories, or in some cases what percentage of different coin types was acceptable.

The Ōuchi daimyo's anti-shroffing proclamation of 1485 is the oldest surviving example of this type of legislation.[42] It contains two clauses. The first addresses specific types of Ming coins: those bearing the inscriptions Yongle (Jp. Eiraku) and Xuande (Jp. Sentoku). It specifies that these types of Ming coins should not exceed 20 percent of the total amount of cash used for tax payments, though all other Chinese coins are acceptable. The second clause addresses money used for interest payments and general transactions, stating that mixes containing 30 percent Ming coins are to be permitted. The fact that the acceptable percentage of Ming coins for use in paying taxes was lower than the rate for general transactions reveals that the Ōuchi did not favor Ming coins. The provision also proclaims that cut, misshapen, or otherwise altered currency should not be used. This further confirms that the Ōuchi did not care for Ming currency, as it links those coins (which were apparently *worth less* than the coins of other dynasties) with damaged currency (which they declared unfit for use and therefore *worthless*).

---

41. Honda, "Copper Coinage, Ruling Power, and Local Society," 228.
42. *Dai Nihon shiryō* entry for Bunmei 17 (1485) 4th month 15th day.

If all *erizenirei* limited or banned the use of the same types of coins, then it would be easy to determine which kinds of currency were devalued in late fifteenth- and sixteenth-century Japan. However, not all daimyo stipulated against Ming coins. The acceptable mix varied by region and issuing authority. For example, in eastern Japan, the Hōjō (and later the Tokugawa) favored Eiraku coins over other types of currency.[43] The first example of a *bakufu erizenirei* dates to 1500. It opens by stating:

Recently [we hear that] people have been selfishly shroffing coins. This should not be. Henceforth, coins newly cast in Japan should be strictly picked out (i.e., not used). Coins from China — Eiraku [Yongle], Kōbu [Hongwu], and Sentoku [Xuande] coins — these should be used now and in the future."[44]

These types of decrees, which favored all legitimate Ming coins and disallowed the use of coins produced in Japan, would be repeated by the *bakufu* over the next several decades.

Scholars have interpreted these laws in various ways. All recognize that the daimyo wanted to promote business and ensure smooth transactions, since that would attract merchants and a wider variety of goods as well as increase the taxable base. Therefore *erizenirei* that ban shroffing altogether are easily understood. But for those laws that stipulate percentages, the motives of the daimyo are not as clear. Kozo Yamamura proposes that daimyo issued *erizenirei* to ensure that they would receive the types of coins in highest demand, or that changing the acceptable mix of coins used for tax payments was a covert way of raising the effective rate of taxation.[45] From a monetary perspective, if this is correct then anti-shroffing laws should be seen as a key step in the gradual process of reasserting central control over the economy. Other scholars contend that

---

43. Takizawa, "Early Currency Policies," 26–29.

44. *Chūsei hōsei shiryōshū*, vol. 2, 105–6.

45. For the first view, see Yamamura, "From Coins to Rice," 341–67; for the second interpretation, see Yamamura, "The Growth of Commerce," 386–87.

the daimyo were primarily concerned with political and ideological matters. Proponents of this view hold that asserting authority over domain money was merely part of defining its sovereignty, like fixing weights and measures.[46] But while these interpretations may reveal something about the intentions of the daimyo, they miss the most important point: the values of coins were being determined in the marketplace.

In order to compensate for the mixture of coins in use, buyers and sellers in local markets assigned different values to different coins. In other words, they negotiated and settled upon exchange ratios: 100 Tang and Song dynasty coins might be worth 200 Ming dynasty coins or 400 privately minted Japanese coins. Although documentary evidence of such practices is limited, historian Honda Hiroyuki has identified several examples that illustrate this point quite clearly. One is a receipt from Ōuchi territories dated 1550 that distinguishes between "new" (*shinsen*) and "inferior" (*nankin* / *nankinsen*) money. Another is an invoice and accompanying receipt from the Usa Hachimangū shrine, dated 1514, that equates 2 *kanmon* of "ordinary money" (*namisen*) with 500 *mon* of "pure money" (*seisen*). A third example, from Buzen province, shows that a stipulated payment of 40 *mon* in "pure money" was actually made with 100 *mon* of "ordinary money."[47] In just these three examples, we see that the terms for different kinds of money varied from market to market and the discount rates for less favored coins changed over time: note that in the second example, the rate of ordinary to pure money was 4:1, whereas in the third example, the rate was 2.5:1. Documents like these illustrate how difficult it must have been to enforce *erizenirei* because it was already common practice in local markets to assign different values to different coins.

Actions such as shroffing coins, demanding certain kinds of payments, and acquiring land and water rights cut into the

---

46. Katsumata and Collcutt, "Development of Sengoku Law," 113.

47. Honda, "Coppper Coinage, Ruling Power, and Local Society," 232–37. See also his *Sengoku shokuhōki no kahei*.

ability of traditional elites to command economic resources. In that sense, they contributed to the political dissolution of late medieval Japan as much as they benefited from it. But even as the fifteenth and sixteenth centuries represented the height of economic empowerment for those in the provinces, authority figures were devising new means of taming the commercial economy. Warriors abandoned the capital to reside in their territories and directly administer their lands. The leaders among these warriors, known as *sengoku* daimyo, became actively involved in economic affairs in ways that their predecessors had never attempted. They gave up the scattered land holdings of earlier periods in favor of single contiguous domains that were more easily defended. They restricted domain exports so as to prevent potential enemies from receiving valuable goods in trade, using embargoes as a rudimentary form of economic warfare.[48] Some of the most successful *sengoku* daimyo, such as the (Later) Hōjō of eastern Japan, carried out regular cadastral surveys to ensure that they received as much as possible in annual land taxes.

The scale of warfare had changed by the sixteenth century, and daimyo could only hope to succeed if they had enough revenue and capital to pay for troops, supplies, weapons, and more. They tried a variety of means to bolster economic activity within their domains. The Date, for example, promulgated legal codes that specifically included provisions for the protection of merchants in hopes of attracting more to their territory. Others, such as the Imagawa and the Takeda, appointed well-connected merchants as trade managers to attract more business.[49] Oda Nobunaga used similar policies in his domain as well as famously eliminating toll barriers and abolishing market and guild fees (*raku-ichi raku-za*). These types of actions were crucial to Nobunaga's success, as well as for Hideyoshi and Tokugawa Ieyasu after him. The steps they took to unify

48. Toyoda, *Zōtei chūsei Nihon shōgyōshi*, 340–47.
49. Sasaki with Hauser, "Sengoku Daimyō Rule and Commerce," 130.

the country and restore effective central government necessarily led to the end of Japan's medieval age.

Medieval Money in the Early Modern Economy

Japanese society underwent major transformations in the late sixteenth and early seventeenth centuries. Daimyo created castle towns all over the country, and the Tokugawa *bakufu* brought peace after more than a century of warfare. Although it did not directly rule the entire country, it was a central government strong enough to promote stability and enforce property rights. The extended peace, creation of improved infrastructure, and increases in population and urbanization all helped fuel economic growth that far surpassed what medieval Japanese had known. By the end of the seventeenth century, Edo and Osaka were major cities that rivaled some of the largest in the world at that time. Japanese merchants developed banking and credit institutions to facilitate trade between the two cities, and their commoner residents were prosperous enough to form an urban consumer class that paid money to shop at stores, eat at restaurants, and attend the theater. The prosperity of urban commoners seemed to contrast sharply with the increasingly grim financial straits of many samurai, whose incomes were tied to rice stipends. This problem forced some of the period's brightest minds to reflect on money and the economy.

Curiously, many of them wrote as though they had no knowledge of the fact that their medieval ancestors had been using coins for centuries. Kusama Naokata (1753–1831), the Osaka merchant-scholar, argued in his *Sanka zui* (Illustrated Collection of Three Currencies) that the real history of currency in Japan only began with the large-scale mintings of the Keichō era (1596–1615).[50] Dazai Shundai (1680–1747), at least as reflected in his *Keizairoku shūi* (Addendum to *On the Political Economy*), seems to have regarded the copper money produced

---

50. As cited in Najita, *Visions of Virtue*, 234.

in ancient Japan as having been insignificant. He held that "from about 1636 the minting of cash coins increased," leading people to use them for small transactions. Dazai linked the growth in coin use to urbanization, as people used cash to pay for their expenses in the cities.[51] Ogyū Sorai (1666–1728) saw the use of money as an even more recent phenomenon, noting, "In olden days, the countryside had hardly any money and all the purchases were made with rice or barley . . . however, I have heard that from the Genroku period [1688–1703] on, money economy has spread to the countryside."[52] The idea was widespread enough that popular poets including Matsuo Bashō (1644–94) referenced it in their *haikai*. In the famous linked-verse sequence "The Summer Moon," he wrote:

> *kono suji wa* Here in the boonies
> *kane mo mishirazu* they don't even know what coins are,
> *fujiyusa yo* damned inconvenient![53]

These writers clearly imply that the rise of a money economy was a relatively recent, urban development of the Tokugawa period.[54]

Although writers frequently failed to acknowledge the widespread use of coins in earlier times, medieval money had a significant impact on the formation of Tokugawa monetary practices. Most importantly, it helped lay the groundwork for the much more widespread monetization and commercialization of the seventeenth century. The early Tokugawa shoguns are correctly credited with having produced Japan's first official domestic currency since the mid-Heian period. As is well

---

51. Dazai, *Keizairoku Shūi*, as translated in Najita, *Tokugawa Political Writings*, 143.

52. Ogyū, *Seidan*, as translated in Lu, *Japan: A Documentary History*, 229.

53. As translated in Arntzen, "Haiku, Haikai and Renga."

54. In fact, Kusama Naokata knew that the imperial court had produced its own coins in the Nara and early Heian periods, as well as that medieval Japanese had used imported Chinese coins. He discussed this in his *Sanka zui*. But these writers' rhetoric emphasized the significance of copper coins as an Edo-period phenomenon.

known, they devised a tri-metallic currency system that used gold and silver for larger transactions and copper cash for smaller ones. But perhaps less well known is that for most of the first century of Tokugawa rule, people continued to use imported Chinese cash, especially Ming Eiraku coins, and privately minted medieval counterfeit coins (*bitasen*) in their daily business dealings.

The Tokugawa *bakufu* took numerous steps to assert its authority and legitimacy in the early seventeenth century, including half-hearted attempts at producing domestic currency. In 1606, it produced small numbers of a new copper coin, the *Keichō tsūhō*, and issued proclamations banning the use of Eiraku coins and coin shroffing. But the *bakufu*'s plans did not find acceptance in the marketplace, and use of the older coins continued. The Tokugawa were forced to recognize this just two years later, when they issued a new directive that decreed one *ryō* of gold to be exchangeable for one *kan* of Eiraku coins or four *kan* of medieval counterfeit coins.[55] The *bakufu* issued another new coin, the *Genna tsūhō*, in 1619, but if this was another attempt to unify currency, it also met with failure.

In 1636, the third shogun, Iemitsu, made the boldest attempt yet to introduce new currency with large-scale production of the *Kan'ei tsūhō*. To facilitate a smooth transition to the new coinage, the *bakufu* declared that same year that the *Kan'ei tsūhō* should be treated as having exactly the same value as older coins already in circulation.[56] Production of the *Kan'ei tsūhō* was sporadic over the next few decades, and it was not until 1670 that the *bakufu* finally proscribed the use of Eiraku coins. Archaeological evidence confirms that both new and old coins were used until the 1670s. One source of such information is burial practices. In the seventeenth century, it was common to inter the bodies of the dead with six coins known as *rokudō-sen* (in southern Kyushu, seven coins were more common).

---

55. Yoshihara, *Edo no zeni*, 24–25.
56. Ibid., 34–35.

Figs. 7a and 7b Ming *Eiraku tsūhō* (*left*) and Tokugawa *Kan'ei tsūhō* (*right*) coins. Used by permission of the Bank of Japan Currency Museum.

The deceased's spirit was supposed to use the coins to pay the ferry fee for transportation across the River Sanzu to the world of the dead. In the twentieth century, Japan's construction boom has led to the unearthing of many of these Edo-period coffins, often with the coins still inside. They reveal that some bodies were buried with Chinese coins, some with Tokugawa coins, and some with a mix of the two.[57] Thus, during the crucial decades when the *bakufu* was establishing its institutions, medieval money continued to be a currency of choice.

The legacy of Chinese currency lived on even after the use of Eiraku and other medieval coins was discontinued, for the Kan'ei coins had, in more than one way, inherited the legacies of medieval money. They contained copper that had been collected by melting down old Chinese coins, so in a very literal sense, they were made of the same materials. And their shape and design were in the tradition of medieval imported cash: round, with square holes, bearing a four-character inscription on one face, and approximately the same size (around 2.4 centimeters in diameter). Surely their familiar shape and feel was as important as the gradual shift from Eiraku to Kan'ei coins in facilitating the Tokugawa's move from old to new currency.

57. Suzuki, *Zeni no kōkogaku*, 22–35.

Conclusion

It was not only the physical form of copper cash that owed something to the earlier medieval economy. The medieval connection between appeals to virtuous rule and debt amnesty carried into the Edo period as well. Peasants engaged in *ikki* protests, appealing for *tokusei* even as they marched against—and sometimes attacked—their creditors. The eighth shogun, Yoshimune (r. 1716–1745), attempted debt amnesty as part of his reforms to help the financial positions of samurai. But like the Kamakura *bakufu* and its famous *tokuseirei* of 1297, the result of such policies was that moneylenders were afraid to lend. In 1729, the Tokugawa shogunate had to reopen *bakufu* courts to moneylenders and their lawsuits in order to make it easier for samurai to continue borrowing.[58] In addition, the early modern policy of tax contracting with villages—that is, placing the burden on an entire village and allowing the village community to work out how payments would be divided— was a practice that originated as a *sengoku* daimyo response to the economically empowered villages of the late medieval era.[59] These topics are beyond the scope of this book but are mentioned here simply to hint at other areas where we might look for connections between the economic thought and practice of medieval and early modern Japan. Eighteenth-century *ikki* were not identical to their fifteenth-century predecessors, nor were Tokugawa-period debt absolutions exactly the same as the Einin *tokuseirei*. Yet it is no coincidence that they referenced some of the same language and ideas.

For much of the twentieth century, scholars saw the Warring States period as a divide that separated premodern Japan from the Tokugawa era. Its long decades of warfare led to the destruction of traditional forms of political governance, economic institutions such as the *shōen*, and even most of the city of Kyoto itself. In the minds of some historians, it seemed

---

58. Totman, *Early Modern Japan*, 296–307.
59. Nagahara, "Village Communities and Daimyo Power," 118.

that nothing prior to the Ōnin War was relevant to the development of later society.[60] Yet few scholars today see the Warring States period as marking so clear a division. Many of the artistic practices that we associate with "traditional Japan," from Noh theatre to tea ceremony, were created in the Muromachi period. And key political institutions, such as the *sankin kōtai* system, originated in the control policies of the Ashikaga shoguns. Susan Hanley's research into material culture has shown that elements of everyday life such as housing, bedding, and clothing were Muromachi-period innovations that only became commonplace in the Tokugawa era. More recently, William Wayne Farris has argued that population growth, previously thought to have taken off only in the seventeenth century, actually began its rise in medieval times.[61] This chapter has suggested ways in which the early modern use of money owed something to earlier medieval practice as well. I do not dispute that there were many new factors favoring seventeenth-century growth that resulted in far higher levels of monetization than were seen in earlier times. Yet to suggest that the Tokugawa invented their monetary institutions as if from whole cloth is to ignore the real threads (however slender) of continuity that carried over from the medieval period.

---

60. Hall, *Japan in the Muromachi Age*, 2.

61. Hanley, *Everyday Things in Premodern Japan*, 84–85; Farris, *Japan's Medieval Population*, 262–66.

CONCLUSION

Money and Japanese History

The Heian-period *setsuwa* collection *Nihon ryōiki* includes spectacular tales of Buddhist wonders and karmic retribution. Among them is the story of Homuchi no Makihito, who encountered a ghost while on his way to the market.[1] According to the tale, which is set in the late eighth century, Makihito set out for the Fukatsu market from his home in Bingo province late in the twelfth month to buy things for the New Year. The market was too far away to reach in one day, so he stopped for the night in a bamboo field called Ashida no Takehara. There he encountered the skull of a man who had been murdered. Makihito knew this because the skull spoke, telling how his uncle had murdered him for his horse and the goods that he carried to trade. It convinced Makihito to visit the dead man's grieving parents and tell them what had befallen their son. The parents then confronted the uncle, who confessed that he had murdered his nephew, sold the horse to a man from Sanuki province, and kept the other goods (silk, cloth, and salt) for his own use.

The moral of this gruesome tale of talking skulls and murder appears to have been that good deeds are rewarded: Maki-

---

1. *Nihon ryōiki*, 397–401. In English, see Nakamura, *Miraculous Stories*, 259–61.

hito, who helped the skull, was rewarded with good fortune.[2] However, the story also reveals a great deal about markets in the Nara and early Heian periods. Fukatsu presumably was the market nearest to Makihito's home, yet still far enough away that he needed to camp for the night in order to reach it. Markets were rare enough that people traveled to them from all over Bingo province as well as from neighboring provinces like Sanuki, as evidenced by the man who purchased the horse. Clearly this was not the kind of market that one could visit on a daily or weekly basis. In addition, it is interesting that the story makes no mention of coins, even though this was the period when the imperial government was producing and circulating copper currency. Rather than cash, the murdered man carried silk, cloth, and salt to use in trading for desired goods at the market. The tale gives the impression that regional markets in the Nara period were few in number, inconvenient to use, and the journey to reach them could be dangerous.

Things had changed dramatically by the thirteenth and fourteenth centuries. Markets were now much more common and much easier to use. This was certainly true for urban centers such as medieval Kyoto. In looking at the illustrations of working people that are included in medieval *shokunin uta awase*, Barbara Ruch writes as though she can feel the "lively street action" and hear the echoing calls of "fishmongers, herb sellers, incense and medicine vendors, and peddlers of firewood, charcoal, brooms, footgear, salt, oil, and fresh greens."[3] Provincial markets were much smaller in scale but appear to have been just as busy. As described in Chapter 2 of this book, materials from the *Ippen shōnin eden* to the travelogue *Tōkan kikō* suggest that early medieval markets were bustling places full of people, animals, goods, and, most of all, activity. Some of those illustrated materials also confirm what documents such as land-sale deeds and tax receipts convey to us through writing:

---

2. This is the lesson that the tale's compiler, Keikai, appended to the story at its conclusion. Nakamura, *Miraculous Stories*, 261.

3. Ruch, "The Other Side of Culture," 513.

the people of medieval Japan increasingly used copper cash in their transactions.

How quickly did imported coins come to find acceptance in Japan? The timing of medieval monetization has been difficult to pinpoint due to the scattered nature of the evidence. Scholars have proposed several different interpretations, each for good reasons. The move toward temple fundraising campaigns as new sources of revenue in the late Heian and early Kamakura periods led Janet Goodwin to argue for an "economic revolution" that came from rising agricultural productivity and the use of money.[4] Kozo Yamamura saw economic expansion as happening more slowly, however. The limited evidence of regular market days and the fact that most cultivators still paid their dues in kind led him to claim that "even in the second half of the Kamakura period, market activities, monetization, and commutation affected the lives of cultivators to only a limited extent."[5] William Wayne Farris, drawing upon his study of daily life and population trends, falls closer to Yamamura but in between, concluding that "commerce was on the upswing by the second half of the Kamakura era."[6] Part of the problem, of course, is that the extant evidence is limited in what it can tell us. What does this study of monetary history reveal about the spread of money and markets during Japan's medieval period?

I think it is important to first highlight the fact that money and markets began to appear in the early to mid-twelfth century. Goodwin's *kanjin* campaigns, which recorded donations in cash, cannot be ignored. Temples such as Hōrakuji could not have collected monetary donations in 1151 unless at least *some* people were using copper currency, nor would the nobles have written of "cash fever" in 1179 if imported coins were still exceedingly rare. However, if we seek to identify when money and markets started to become truly commonplace, then we must look to the late thirteenth century. There is a substantial

---

4. Goodwin, *Alms and Vagabonds*, 40–41.
5. Yamamura, "The Growth of Commerce," 372.
6. Farris, *Japan's Medieval Population*, 85.

amount of evidence to support such a view. Consider Sasaki Gin'ya's research into tax commutation, a topic of Chapter 4 in this book. Although there were only six cases of *daisennō* prior to 1250, there were 38 cases in the second half of the thirteenth century and 126 cases in the first half of the fourteenth.[7] Land sales recorded as *baiken* reflect the same trend: Tamaizumi Tairyō found only 29 documented transactions in cash from 1186 to 1219, but the number jumps to 232 transactions for the period from 1220 to 1283, and even higher, to 257, between the years 1284 and 1333.[8] Money was not just used in and around the capital but also began to spread throughout the country. Tamaizumi noted cash land sales in his middle period from the Kinai region, eastern Japan, the San'in, and Shikoku, while for the late Kamakura period he found evidence of transactions in coin for every region of the country. In addition, money was reaching provincial communities, as can be seen in correspondence between Kōyasan and three of its Kii province estates. In 1275, the temple instructed its estate managers to levy cash fines as punishments for offenses ranging from unauthorized hunting to the failure to report suspected criminals.[9] The same document also forbade warriors and administrators from taxing the peasants for trips to the capital or robbing their collective funds, provisions that would only have been necessary if peasants had cash in the first place.

This proposed theory of a late thirteenth-century increase in the spread of money and markets is strengthened if one considers developments on the continent. First, as explained in Chapter 1, the Northern Song dynasty produced extremely large amounts of coins in the late eleventh and early twelfth centuries. After the dynasty fell in 1127, the Southern Song was unable to continue producing coins at such rates and had to turn to alternative forms of currency such as paper money. Northern Song coins were not as valued, so some Chinese chose to export

---

7. Suzuki, *Shutsudo senka*, 60–61.
8. Tamaizumi, *Muromachi jidai no densō*, 143.
9. *KI*, doc. 12184, Kenji 1 (1275) 12th month.

their cash. Presumably some of those coins arrived in Japan and became the coins used in late Heian-period land sales and temple fundraising donations. Next, as Ōta Yukio has shown, the Mongols banned copper cash in 1270 and instead began issuing paper money. This meant that coins in the areas under Mongol control were not worth as much as they had been previously, so people were even more willing to export them. Although the lack of shipping records means that there is no "smoking gun" to conclusively prove that more coins entered Japan in the late thirteenth century, the assumption seems plausible based on the limited evidence. It also helps place Japan in a broader East Asian context by linking events on the continent with domestic developments. By the end of the thirteenth century, shipbuilding technology had improved enough to allow Japanese to sail their own vessels to Asia in search of coin. Whether with the government-endorsed Tenryūji ships and diplomatic missions of the Ashikaga *bakufu* or by means of the unauthorized raids of the *wakō*, Japanese would continue to import Chinese coins over the rest of the medieval period.

The story of the gradual transition away from rice, silk, and other forms of commodity money is one worth telling, for it reveals much about attitudes toward trade, the importance of reliable media of exchange, and the workings of the market. The move to copper currency, however, signified much more than just a change in the form of payment. It was also a sign of economic growth that tentatively began in the mid-twelfth century. For the first one hundred years or more, this growth was slow. It was clearly not substantial enough to prevent periodic famines from devastating the population in the Kangi and Shōka eras.[10] But by the late thirteenth century, increased agricultural output helped lessen the dangers of famine. So did the spread of markets, which aided in the distribution of food and other commodities. And, of course, tax commutation allowed estates to grow a wider range of goods. These are not the statistical measures of growth that economists prefer, but

---

10. Farris, *Japan's Medieval Population*, 33–57.

the data from early medieval Japan do not permit such cal- culations. They do, however, suggest that the economy was expanding and that it was moving in some very different di- rections than it had in earlier times. After all, economic growth did not just happen—there were real people and institutions that brought it about. Some were traditional elites who rose to the challenge of finding new sources of income. Others were the provincial figures who are the primary object of this study, from estate managers and *jitō* to merchants and priests.

As this book has tried to show, monetization accompanied noteworthy changes in the relationship between center and pe- riphery. In earlier times, people living on lands administered by the imperial government had to pay taxes in certain kinds of goods (such as rice or silk) and services (human labor). Some provincial land owners avoided public taxation by having their territory converted into *shōen*, but they still had to pay stipu- lated goods to central elites in exchange for protection against government officials. Monetization and markets allowed the commutation of such payments, with potential benefits for both sides: estates could grow the products best suited to their lands, while proprietors could use the cash they received to purchase what they wanted in urban markets. Individuals in the provinces, as well as urban landlords, had incentives to switch to cash as local and regional markets became more available. Both played important roles in the sweeping changes that accompanied economic expansion in Japan's medieval pe- riod. Even more interesting, however, is that figures on the periphery were able, in some cases, to negotiate or even in- sist upon the form of their payments. This was something new.

The use of money also led to important changes in the ways that people thought about the world. As explained in Chapter 2, *jitō* began punishing thieves differently depending on the value of the goods they had stolen. This meant, of course, that people had to develop a sense of the monetary value of their belongings. Tax commutation also promoted new ways of thinking. Goods such as silk came to be measured by their worth in coins rather than by determinations of quality. In other words, people started evaluating things in terms of numbers. Joel Kaye observed something similar in his study of medieval Europe after it underwent a period of rapid monetization. As he explains, "The accelerated use of money had ever-expanding social, economic, and intellectual consequences."[11] Commerce and markets in medieval university towns produced a heightened awareness of money and numbers, which in turn inspired fourteenth-century European scholars to seek to quantify, measure, and compare things in ways that they had not attempted in earlier times. Medieval Japanese, experiencing similar changes that accompanied monetization, must have also come to think about the world in new ways. Perhaps we can see this best in the evolving ambitions of commoners as portrayed in the theater. As Barbara Ruch has argued, characters in classical fiction frequently sought upward social mobility, but characters in medieval fiction most often sought wealth. Medieval Japanese came to worry about riches and success in business, which led to the newfound popularity of the gods of good fortune: Ebisu, Bishamon, and Daikoku with his magical coin-producing mallet.[12]

As with so much research into the distant past, this study may have raised more questions than it has answered. There are still many aspects of the medieval economy that remain unexplained. Who were the merchants who brought Chinese cash to Japan in the twelfth and thirteenth centuries? And how did currency come to circulate evenly throughout society? Since there were no banks, what prevented coins from accumulating at the major markets and never reaching the more rural ones? Unfortunately, the surviving documents are unable to shed much light on these and many other puzzles. What did the influx of coins in the early medieval period do to prices? Some have suggested that coin importation increased the money supply and therefore caused inflation.[13] The limited

11. Kaye, *Economy and Nature*, 14.
12. Ruch, "The Other Side of Culture," 517–20.
13. Yamamura, "The Growth of Commerce," 359.

supply of coins in the thirteenth century, however, as well as the effects of famine on the population may have caused deflationary pressures. Even with the sparse data that we have on prices, this question may yet be answerable with additional research.

Finally, how did the economy grow when, for much of the medieval period, political authority was splintered and neither the imperial court nor the *bakufu* was able to issue currency? What led people to lend and invest if they could not count on a strong central government to enforce contracts and protect property? One possible answer is that less government was a positive development for the Japanese economy. Economic historian Avner Greif, in detailed studies of medieval Europe, has drawn distinctions between "contract-enforcing" institutions that aided economic growth and "coercive" institutions that inhibited it.[14] Applying this same framework to medieval Japan helps us recognize that although medieval Japan may have suffered from a lack of contract-enforcing institutions provided by the state, it appears to have benefitted even more from the gradual disappearance of government structures that contained coercive institutions. The Muromachi *bakufu* provided an important service by importing coins, but some of its other policies—such as selling *tokuseirei* to debtors or creditors, depending on whoever would pay—must have created greater insecurity, discouraged borrowing and lending, and dampened growth. In the absence of unified central government, figures in the center and on the periphery devised new ways of minimizing risk and lowering the costs of doing business. Although the institutions that they created did not survive unaltered into the seventeenth century, the patterns of economic behavior that they invented—from monetization to bills of exchange—helped to lay the groundwork for the even greater economic growth of the early Tokugawa period.

---

14. See, for example, Greif, "Commitment, Coercion, and Markets," 727–30.

Reference Matter

Works Cited

Note: *The place of publication for Japanese-language sources is Tokyo, unless otherwise specified.*

Primary Sources

Aioi shishi. 8 vols. Aioishi kyōiku iinkai, 1984–95.

Azuma kagami. Vols. 53–56 of *Kokushi taikei*. Yoshikawa kōbunkan, 1979–81.

Chibaken no rekishi: shiryōhen chūsei 2. Chiba: Chiba-ken shiryō kenkyū zaidan, 1987.

Chōshūki. Vol. 17 of *Zōho shiryō taisei*. Kyoto: Rinsen shoten, 1965.

Chūsei hōsei shiryōshū. Compiled by Satō Shin'ichi, Ikeuchi Yoshisuke, Maki Kenji, and Momose Kesao. 6 volumes. Iwanami shoten, 1955–2005.

Chūsei seiji shakai shisō. Ed. Satō Shin'ichi et al. 2 vols. Iwanami shoten, 1972.

Dai Nihon shiryō series 4–8. Ed. Shiryō hensan kakari. Tōkyō Daigaku shuppansha, 1901.

Engishiki. Ed. Torao Toshiya. Shūeisha, 2000.

Fusō ryakki (Kōen). Vol. 12 of *Shintei zōho kokushi taikei*. Yoshikawa kōbunkan, 1965.

Gonki (Fujiwara Yukinari). Vols. 15–16 of *Zoku shiryō taisei*. Naigai shoseki, 1938.

Gyokuyō (Kujō Kanezane). *Shintei zōho kokushi taikei bon*. Ed. Fukuda Toyohiko. Yoshikawa kōbunkan, 1999.

Heian ibun. Ed. Takeuchi Rizō. 15 vols. Tōkyōdō, 1963–74.

Hōjōki (Kamo no Chōmei). Vol. 30 of *Nihon koten bungaku taikei*. Iwanami shoten, 1977.

Honchō seiki (Fujiwara Michinori). Kokushi taikei kankōkai, 1933.

Honchō zoku monzui (Fujiwara Akihira). *Shintei zōho kokushi taikei bon*. Ed. Kokushi taikei henshūkai. Yoshikawa kōbunkan, 1999.

Hossō shiyōshō. Vol. 4 of *Gunsho ruijū*. Ed. Hanawa Hokinoichi. Keizai zasshisha, 1893–94.

Hyakurenshō. Vols. 10–11 of *Kokushi taikei*. Ed. Kokushi taikei henshūkai. Yoshikawa kōbunkan, 1965.

Ippen shōnin eden. Vol. 27 of *Nihon emaki taisei*. Chūō kōronsha, 1978.

Jianyan yilai xinian yaolu. Ser. 2, vol. 3, no. 8. Taipei: Wenhai, 1968.

Kaidōki. In *Chūsei nikki kikōshū*. Vol. 48 of *Shinpen Nihon koten bungaku zenshū*. Shōgakukan, 1994.

Kamakura bakufu saikyōjōshū. Ed. Seno Seiichirō. 2 vols. Yoshikawa kōbunkan, 1970.

Kamakura bakufu tsuikahō. Vol. 1 of *Chūsei hōsei shiryōshū*. Ed. Satō Shin'ichi and Ikeuchi Yoshisuke. Iwanami shoten, 1955.

Kamakura ibun. Ed. Takeuchi Rizō. 51 vols. Tōkyōdō, 1971–.

Kanagawa kenshi. 21 vols. Kanagawa-ken kikaku chōsabu kenshi henshūshitsu, 1970–82.

Kanchūki (Hirohashi Kanenaka). Vol. 35 of *Zōho shiryō taisei*. Kyoto: Rinsen shoten, 1965.

Kokon chomonjū. Vol. 19 of *Shintei zōho kokushi taikei*. Yoshikawa kōbunkan, 1964.

Kōyasan monjo. Kōyasan monjo kankōkai. 7 vols. 1936–41.

Kugyō bunin. Vols. 13–14 of *Shintei zōho kokushi taikei*. Yoshikawa kōbunkan, 1937.

Lunyu yizhu. Beijing: Zhonghua shuju, 1980.

Meigetsuki (Fujiwara Teika). Kokusho kankōkai, 1977.

Midō kanpakuki (Fujiwara Michinaga). Vol. 1 of *Dai Nihon kokiroku*. Iwanami shoten, 1952.

Minkeiki (Hirohashi Tsunemitsu). *Dai Nihon kokiroku*. 8 vols. Iwanami shoten, 1975–2001.

Nihon kiryaku. *Kokushi taikei*, vols. 10–11. Ed. Kokushi taikei henshūkai. Yoshikawa kōbunkan, 1965.

Nihon kōki. *Kokushi taikei*, vol. 3. Keizai zasshisha, 1914–18.

Nihon ryōiki (Keikai). Ed. Endō Yoshimoto and Kasuga Kazuo. *Nihon koten bungaku taikei*, vol. 70. Iwanami shoen, 1967.

Nihonshi shiryō [2] chūsei. Ed. Rekishigaku kenkyūkai. Iwanami shoten, 1998.

Nihon shoki. Vol. 4 of *Nihon koten bungaku zenshū*. Shōgakukan, 1994.

Okayama kenshi. Vol. 19: *hennen shiryō*; vol. 20: *iewake shiryō*. Okayama kenshi hensan iinkai. 1981, 1985.

Ryō no gige. Kokushi taikei, vols. 12–15. Yoshikawa kōbunkan, 1961.

Shin sarugakuki. In *Tōyō bunko* 424. Ed. Kawaguchi Hisao. Heibonsha, 1983.

Shiryō ni yoru Nihon no ayumi. Ed. Kodama Kōta, Yasuda Motohisa, and Ōno Tatsunosuke. Yoshikawa kōbunkan, 1958.

Shoku Nihongi. Vol. 2 of *Kokushi taikei*. Keizai zasshisha, 1914–18.

Shōyūki (Fujiwara Sanesuke). *Dai Nihon kokiroku*. 11 vols. Iwanami shoten, 1959–86.

Song shi. Taipei: Dingwen, 1975–81.

Tōdaiji monjo. Vol. 18 of *Dai Nihon komonjo iewake*. Tōkyō Daigaku shiryō hensanjo, 1999.

Tōji hyakugō monjo. Vol. 10 of *Dai Nihon komonjo iewake*. Tōkyō Teikoku Daigaku, 1925.

Tōkan kikō. Nihon koten zenshū, vol. 106. Asahi shinbunsha, 1958.

Secondary Sources

Adachi Keiji. "Chugoku kara mita Nihon kaheishi no ni, san no mondai." *Atarashii rekishigaku no tame ni* 203 (May 1991): 1–11.

Adolphson, Mikael. "Enryakuji: An Old Power in a New Era." In *The Origins of Japan's Medieval World: Courtiers, Clerics, Warriors, and Peasants in the Fourteenth Century*, ed. Jeffrey P. Mass. Stanford, CA: Stanford University Press, 1997: 237–60.

——. *The Gates of Power: Monks, Courtiers, and Warriors in Premodern Japan*. Honolulu: University of Hawai'i Press, 2000.

Aida Nirō. *Chūsei no sekisho*. Yoshikawa kōbunkan, 1983 [1942].

——. *Mōko shūrai no kenkyū*. Yoshikawa kōbunkan, 1958.

Allmand, Christopher, ed. *The New Cambridge Medieval History, Vol. 7: c. 1415–c. 1500*. Cambridge, UK: Cambridge University Press, 1998.

Amino Yoshihiko. "Bun'ei igo shinseki chōjirei ni tsuite." *Nenpō chūseishi kenkyū* 9 (1984): 50–61.

——. *Chūsei saikō*. Nihon editā sukūru, 1986.

——. "Commerce and Finance in the Middle Ages: The Beginnings of 'Capitalism.'" *Acta Asiatica* 81 (2001): 1–19.

——. "Kyōkai ryōiki to kokka." In *Nihon no shakaishi*, vol. 2. Iwanami shoten, 1987: 325–71.

——. *Mōko shūrai*. Vol. 10 of *Nihon no rekishi*. Shōgakukan, 1974.

——. *Muen, kugai, raku*. Heibonsha, 1978.

———. *Nihon shakai saikō.* Shōgakukan, 1994.

———. *Rethinking Japanese History.* Trans. Alan Christy. Ann Arbor: Center for Japanese Studies, University of Michigan, forthcoming.

"Ancient Coins Alter Japan's Cash History." *Japan Times,* January 20, 1999.

Anderlini, Luca, and Hamid Sabourian. "Some Notes on the Economics of Barter, Money and Credit." In *Barter, Exchange and Value: An Anthropological Approach,* ed. Caroline Humphrey and Stephen Hugh-Jones. Cambridge, UK: Cambridge University Press, 1992: 75–106.

Aoki, Masahiko. *Toward a Comparative Institutional Analysis.* Cambridge, MA: MIT Press, 2001.

Arntzen, Sonja. "Haiku, Haikai and Renga: Communal Poetry Practice." *Simply Haiku: A Quarterly Journal of Japanese Short Form Poetry* 5, no. 1 (Spring 2007).

Aston, W. G., trans. *Nihongi: Chronicles of Japan from the Earliest Times.* London: George Allen & Unwin, 1956 [1896].

Batten, Bruce L. *Gateway to Japan: Hakata in War and Peace, 500–1300.* Honolulu: University of Hawai'i Press, 2006.

———. "An Open and Shut Case? Thoughts on Late Heian Overseas Trade." In *Currents in Medieval Japanese History: Essays in Honor of Jeffrey P. Mass,* ed. Gordon M. Berger, Andrew Edmund Goble, Lorraine F. Harrington, and G. Cameron Hurst III. Los Angeles, CA: Figueroa Press, 2009: 301–30.

———. "State and Frontier in Early Japan: The Imperial Court and Northern Kyushu, 645–1185." PhD diss., Stanford University, 1989.

———. *To the Ends of Japan: Premodern Frontiers, Boundaries, and Interactions.* Honolulu: University of Hawai'i Press, 2003.

Berry, Mary Elizabeth. *The Culture of Civil War in Kyoto.* Berkeley, CA: University of California Press, 1994.

Borgen, Robert. "Jōjin's Travels from Center to Center (with Some Periphery in between)." In *Heian Japan: Centers and Peripheries,* ed. Mikael Adolphson, Edward Kamens, and Stacie Matsumoto. Honolulu: University of Hawai'i Press, 2007: 384–413.

———. *Sugawara no Michizane and the Early Heian Court.* Cambridge, MA: Council on East Asian Studies, Harvard University, 1986.

Brown, Delmer. "The Japanese *Tokusei* of 1297." *Harvard Journal of Asiatic Studies* 12, no. 1/2 (June 1949): 188–206.

———. *Money Economy in Medieval Japan: A Study in the Use of Coins.* New Haven, CT: Far Eastern Association, Yale University, 1951.

Brownlee, John. "Crisis as Reinforcement of the Imperial Institution. The Case of the Jōkyū Incident, 1221." *Monumenta Nipponica* 30:2 (1975): 193–201.

Cavanaugh, Carole. "Text and Textile: Unweaving the Female Subject in Heian Writing." *Positions* 4.3 (Winter 1996): 595–636.

Conlan, Thomas Donald. *In Little Need of Divine Intervention: Takezaki Suenaga's Scrolls of the Mongol Invasions of Japan.* Ithaca, NY: Cornell East Asia Series, 2001.

———. *State of War: The Violent Order of Fourteenth-Century Japan.* Ann Arbor: Center for Japanese Studies, University of Michigan, 2003.

Cooper, Michael, ed. *They Came to Japan: An Anthology of European Reports on Japan, 1543–1640.* London: Thames and Hudson, 1965.

De Roover, Raymond. "Money, Banking, and Credit in Medieval Bruges." *Journal of Economic History*, vol. 2 suppl. (December 1942): 52–65.

Duby, Georges. *Early Growth of the European Economy.* Translated by Howard Clarke. Ithaca, NY: Cornell University Press, 1974.

Ebersole, Gary. *Ritual Poetry and the Politics of Death in Early Japan.* Princeton, NJ: Princeton University Press, 1989.

Elvin, Mark. *The Pattern of the Chinese Past.* Stanford, CA: Stanford University Press, 1973.

Farris, William Wayne. *Japan's Medieval Population: Famine, Fertility, and Warfare in a Transformative Age.* Honolulu: University of Hawai'i Press, 2006.

———. *Sacred Texts and Buried Treasures: Issues in the Historical Archaeology of Ancient Japan.* Honolulu: University of Hawai'i Press, 1998.

———. "Shipbuilding and Nautical Technology in Japanese Maritime History: Origins to 1600." *The Mariner's Mirror* 95, no. 3 (August 2009): 260–84.

———. "Trade, Money, and Merchants in Nara Japan." *Monumenta Nipponica*, 53:3 (Autumn 1998): 303–34.

Friday, Karl. *Hired Swords: The Rise of Private Warrior Power in Early Japan.* Stanford, CA: Stanford University Press, 1992.

———. "Lordship Interdicted: Taira no Tadatsune and the Limited Horizon of Warrior Ambitions." In *Heian Japan: Centers and Peripheries,* ed. Mikael Adolphson, Edward Kamens, and Stacie Matsumoto. Honolulu: University of Hawai'i Press, 2007: 329–54.

Gay, Suzanne. *The Moneylenders of Late Medieval Kyoto.* Honolulu: University of Hawai'i Press, 2001.

Geary, Patrick. "Gift Exchange and Social Science Modeling: The Limitations of a Construct." In *Negotiating the Gift*, ed. Valentin Groebner and Bernhard Jussen. Göttingen: Vandenhoeck & Ruprecht, 2003: 129–40.

Gernet, Jacques. *A History of Chinese Civilization*. Trans. J. R. Foster and Charles Hartman. Cambridge, UK: Cambridge University Press, 1982 [1972].

Goble, Andrew. *Kenmu: Go-Daigo's Revolution*. Cambridge, MA: Council on East Asian Studies, Harvard University, 1996.

Godelier, Maurice. *The Enigma of the Gift*. Trans. Nora Scott. Chicago, IL: University of Chicago Press, 1999 [1950].

Gomi Fumihiko. *Inseiki shakai no kenkyū*. Yamakawa shuppansha, 1984.

———. *Chūsei shakai to gendai*. Yamakawa shuppansha, 2004.

Goodwin, Janet. *Alms and Vagabonds: Buddhist Temples and Popular Patronage in Medieval Japan*. Honolulu: University of Hawai'i Press, 1994.

Grapard, Allan. "Religious Practices." In *The Cambridge History of Japan, Vol. 2: Heian Japan*, ed. Donald Shively and William H. McCullough. Cambridge, UK: Cambridge University Press, 1999: 517–75.

Greif, Avner. "Commitment, Coercion, and Markets: The Nature and Dynamics of Institutions Supporting Exchange." In *The Handbook of New Institutional Economics*, ed. C. Ménard and M. Shirley. Dordrecht: Springer, 2005: 727–86.

———. "Cultural Beliefs and the Organization of Society: A Historical and Theoretical Reflection on Collectivist and Individualist Societies." *Journal of Political Economy* 102 (1994): 912–50.

Haber, Stephen, Armando Razo, and Noel Maurer. *The Politics of Property Rights: Political Instability, Credible Commitments, and Economic Growth in Mexico, 1876–1929*. Cambridge, UK: Cambridge University Press, 2003.

Hall, John Carey. "The Hojo Code of Judicature." *Transactions of the Asiatic Society of Japan* 34.1 (August 1906): 17–44.

Hall, John W. *Government and Local Power in Japan, 500 to 1700*. Princeton, NJ: Princeton University Press, 1966.

———. *Japan from Prehistory to Modern Times*. Ann Arbor: Center for Japanese Studies, University of Michigan, 1991 [1968].

Hall, John W., and Jeffrey P. Mass, eds. *Medieval Japan: Essays in Institutional History*. Stanford, CA: Stanford University Press, 1988 [1974].

Hall, John W., Nagahara Keiji, and Kozo Yamamura, eds. *Japan before Tokugawa: Political Consolidation and Economic Growth, 1500 to 1650*. Princeton, NJ: Princeton University Press, 1981.

Hane, Mikiso. *Premodern Japan: A Historical Survey*. Boulder, CO: Westview Press, 1991.

Harrington, Lorraine. "Social Control and the Significance of the Akutō." In *Court and Bakufu in Japan: Essays in Kamakura History*, ed. Jeffrey P. Mass. Stanford, CA: Stanford University Press, 1988: 221–50.

Hashimoto Yoshihiko. "In no hyōjōsei ni tsuite." *Nihon rekishi* 261 (1970): 1–18.

Hayashiya Tatsusaburō. "Kyoto in the Muromachi Age." In *Japan in the Muromachi Age*, ed. John W. Hall and Toyoda Takeshi. Berkeley, CA: University of California Press, 1977: 15–36.

Hisamitsu Jūhei. *Nihon kahei monogatari*. Mainichi shinbunsha, 1976.

Hōgetsu Keigo. *Chūsei kangaishi no kenkyū*. Yoshikawa kōbunkan, 1983 [1943].

Honda Hiroyuki. "Copper Coinage, Ruling Power, and Local Society in Medieval Japan." *International Journal of Asian Studies* 4:2 (2007): 225–40.

———. *Sengoku shokuhōki no kahei to kokudakasei*. Yoshikawa kōbunkan, 2006.

Hongō Kazuto. "Kamakura jidai chōtei soshō no ichizokumen." In *Hō to soshō*, ed. Kasamatsu Hiroshi. Yoshikawa kōbunkan, 1992: 111–43.

———. *Chūsei chōtei soshō no kenkyū*. Tōkyō Daigaku shuppankai, 1995.

Hongō Keiko. *Chūseijin no keizai kankaku: "okaimono" kara saguru*. Nihon hōsō shuppan kyōkai, 2004.

Hori, Kyotsu. "The Economic and Political Effects of the Mongol Wars." In *Medieval Japan: Essays in Institutional History*, ed. John W. Hall and Jeffrey P. Mass. Stanford, CA: Stanford University Press, 1988 [1974]: 184–98.

Horiike Shunpō. *Todaiji shi e no izanai*. Kyoto: Shōwadō, 2004.

Hotate Michihisa. "Chūsei zenki no shinsei to kokahō: toshi ōken no hō, ichiba, kahei, zaisei." *Rekishigaku kenkyū* 687 (August 1996): 1–17.

———. "Kirimono to kirizeni." *Miura kobunka* 53 (December 1993): 15–22.

———. *Monogatari no chūsei: shinwa, setsuwa, minwa no rekishigaku*. Tōkyō Daigaku shuppankai, 1998.

Hurst, Cameron G. III. "Insei." In *The Cambridge History of Japan, Vol. 2: Heian Japan*, ed. Donald Shively and William H. McCullough. Cambridge, UK: Cambridge University Press, 1999: 576–643.

——. "*Kugyō* and *Zuryō*: Center and Periphery in the Era of Fujiwara no Michinaga." In *Heian Japan: Centers and Peripheries*, ed. Mikael Adolphson, Edward Kamens, and Stacie Matsumoto. Honolulu: University of Hawai'i Press, 2007: 66–101.

Ichisawa Tetsu. "Kuge tokusei no seiritsu to tenkai." *Hisutoria* 109 (1985): 112–28.

Ihara Hiroshi. "Sōdai shakai to zeni: bonmin no shisanryoku o megutte." *Ajia yūgaku tokushū: Sōsen no sekai*. Bensei shuppan (2000): 4–18.

Ihara Kesao. "Bakufu, Kamakura-fu no ryūtsū keizai seisaku to nengu unsō." In *Chūsei no hakken*, ed. Nagahara Keiji. Yoshikawa kōbunkan, 1993.

——. *Chūsei no ikusa, matsuri, totsukuni to kawari: nōson seikatsushi no danmen*. Kōsō shobō, 1999.

——. "Sōsen yunyū no rekishiteki ishiki." In *Senka: zenkindai Nihon no kahei to kokka*, ed. Ike Susumu. Aoki shoten, 2001.

Ike Susumu, ed. *Senka: zenkindai Nihon no kahei to kokka*. Aoki shoten, 2001.

Imatani Akira. "Muromachi Local Government: Shugo and Kokujin." In *The Cambridge History of Japan, Vol. 3: Medieval Japan*, ed. Kozo Yamamura. Cambridge, UK: Cambridge University Press, 1990: 231–59.

Imatani Akira with Kozo Yamamura. "Not for Lack of Will or Wile: Yoshimitsu's Failure to Supplant the Imperial Lineage." *Journal of Japanese Studies* 18, no. 1 (Winter 1992): 45–78.

Inoue Masao. "Kokusai tsūka to shite no sōsen." *Ajia yūgaku tokushū: Sōsen no sekai*. Bensei shuppan (2000): 19–29.

Ishii Susumu. "12, 13 seiki no Nihon: kodai kara chūsei e." *Iwanami kōza Nihon tsūshi 7 chūsei 1*, ed. Asao Naohiro. Iwanami shoten, 1993: 1–71.

——. "Chūsei no kyokanshi to kasen." *Chikuma* 15 (1977).

——. *Chūsei no mura o aruku*. Asahi sensho, 2000.

——. "The Decline of the Kamakura Bakufu." In *The Cambridge History of Japan, Vol. 3: Medieval Japan*, ed. Kozo Yamamura. Cambridge, UK: Cambridge University Press, 1990: 128–74.

Iwanami Nihonshi jiten, ed. Nagahara Keiji. Iwanami shoten, 1999.

Jones, A. H. M. *The Later Roman Empire, 284–602: A Social, Economic, and Administrative Survey*. 2 vols. Oxford, UK: Blackwell, 1986 [1964].

Kaizu Ichirō. *Chūsei no henkaku to tokusei*. Yoshikawa kōbunkan, 1994.

——. *Mōko shūrai: taigai sensō no shakaishi*. Yoshikawa kōbunkan, 1998.

Kamo no Chōmei. "Hōjōki." In *Nihon koten bungaku taikei*, vol. 30. Iwanami shoten, 1977.

Kapleau, Phillip. *The Three Pillars of Zen: Teaching, Practice, and Enlightenment*. Garden City, NY: Anchor Press, 1980.

Kasamatsu Hiroshi. "Nusumi." In *Chūsei no tsumi to batsu*, ed. Amino Yoshihiko, Ishii Susumu, Kasamatsu Hiroshi, and Katsumata Shizuo. Tōkyō Daigaku shuppankai, 1983: 71–88.

——. *Tokuseirei: chūsei no hō to kanshū*. Iwanami shoten, 1983.

Katsumata Shizuo and Martin Collcutt. "The Development of Sengoku Law." In *Japan Before Tokugawa: Political Consolidation and Economic Growth, 1500 to 1650*, ed. John W. Hall, Nagahara Keiji, and Kozo Yamamura. Princeton, NJ: Princeton University Press, 1981: 101–24.

Katsuyama Seiji. *Chūsei nengusei seiritsushi no kenkyū*. Hanawa shobō, 1995.

Kiley, Cornelius J. "Estate and Property in the Late Heian Period." In *Medieval Japan: Essays in Institutional History*, ed. John W. Hall and Jeffrey P. Mass. Stanford, CA: Stanford University Press, 1988 [1974]: 109–24.

——. "Provincial Administration and Land Tenure in Early Heian." In *The Cambridge History of Japan, Vol. 2: Heian Japan*, ed. Donald H. Shively and William H. McCullough. Cambridge, UK: Cambridge University Press, 1999: 236–340.

Kira Kunimitsu. "Kii no kuni Yuasashi no ryōshusei to soma." In *Nihon chūseishi ronkō*, ed. Kawazoe Shōji sensei kanreki kinenkai. Bunken shuppan, 1987: 203–37.

Kiyotaki, Nobuhiro, and Randall Wright. "On Money as a Medium of Exchange." *Journal of Political Economy* 97:4 (August 1989): 927–54.

Kobata Atsushi. *Kōzan no rekishi*. Shibundō, 1957.

——. *Nihon kahei ryūtsūshi*. Tōkō shoin, 1969.

——. *Nihon no kahei*. Shibundō, 1958.

Kokushi daijiten. 17 vols. Yoshikawa kōbunkan, 1989.

Kondō Shigekazu. "1247 as a Turning Point for the Kamakura Bakufu." Trans. Ethan Segal. In *Turning Points in Japanese History*, ed. Bert Edström. London: Japan Library, 2002: 25–33.

Kuroda Akinobu. "Copper Coins Chosen and Silver Differentiated: Another Aspect of the Silver Century in East Asia." *Acta Asiatica* 88 (2005): 65–86.

Kuroda Hiroko. *Mimi o kiri hana o sogi*. Yoshikawa kōbunkan, 1995.

Kuroda Toshio. "Chūsei josetsu." *Iwanami kōza Nihon rekishi 5 chūsei 1.*
Iwanami, 1974: 1–34.
——. *Nihon chūsei no kokka to shūkyō.* Iwanami shoten, 1976.
Labib, Subhi Y. "Capitalism in Medieval Islam." *Journal of Economic History* 29.1 (March 1969): 79–96.
Lévi-Strauss, Claude. *Introduction to the Work of Marcel Mauss.* Trans. Felicity Baker. London: Routledge and Kegan Paul, 1987.
Little, Lester. "Pride Goes before Avarice: Social Change and the Vices in Latin Christendom." *American Historical Review* 76, no. 1 (February 1971): 16–49.
——. *Religious Poverty and the Profit Economy in Medieval Europe.* Ithaca, NY: Cornell University Press, 1978.
Loewe, Michael. "The Religious and Intellectual Background." In *The Cambridge History of China, Vol. 1: The Ch'in and Han Empires, 221 B.C.–220 A.D,* ed. Denis Twitchett and Michael Loewe. Cambridge, UK: Cambridge University Press, 1986: 649–725.
Lopez, Robert. *The Commercial Revolution of the Middle Ages, 950–1350.* Cambridge, UK: Cambridge University Press, 1976.
Lughod, Janet Abu. *Before European Hegemony: The World System A.D. 1250–1350.* New York: Oxford University Press, 1989.
Mass, Jeffrey P. "Black Holes in Japanese History: The Case of Kamakura." In *Antiquity and Anachronism in Japanese History.* Stanford, CA: Stanford University Press, 1992: 157–77.
——. *The Development of Kamakura Rule.* Stanford, CA: Stanford University Press, 1979.
——. "Of Hierarchy and Authority at the End of Kamakura." In *The Origins of Japan's Medieval World: Courtiers, Clerics, Warriors, and Peasants in the Fourteenth Century,* ed. Jeffrey P. Mass. Stanford, CA: Stanford University Press, 1997: 17–38.
——. "Jitō Land Possession in the Thirteenth Century: The Case of Shitaji Chūbun." In *Medieval Japan: Essays in Institutional History,* ed. John W. Hall and Jeffrey P. Mass. Stanford, CA: Stanford University Press, 1988 [1974]: 157–83.
——. "The Kamakura Bakufu." In *The Cambridge History of Japan, Vol. 3: Medieval Japan,* ed. Kozo Yamamura. Cambridge, UK: Cambridge University Press, 1990: 46–88.
——. *The Kamakura Bakufu: A Study in Documents.* Stanford, CA: Stanford University Press, 1976.

──── . *The Origins of Japan's Medieval World: Courtiers, Clerics, Warriors, and Peasants in the Fourteenth Century.* Stanford, CA: Stanford University Press, 1997.

──── . *Warrior Government in Early Medieval Japan: A Study of the Kamakura Bakufu, Shugo, and Jito.* New Haven, CT: Yale University Press, 1972.

──── . *Yoritomo and the Founding of the First Bakufu.* Stanford, CA: Stanford University Press, 1999.

Mauss, Marcel. *The Gift: The Form and Reason for Exchange in Archaic Societies.* Trans. W. D. Halls. New York: W. W. Norton, 1990 [1950].

McCullough, William. "Azuma Kagami Account of the Shokyu War." *Monumenta Nipponica* 23, no. 1/2 (1968): 102–55.

──── . "The Capital and Its Society." In *The Cambridge History of Japan, Vol. 2: Heian Japan,* ed. Donald H. Shively and William H. McCullough. Cambridge, UK: Cambridge University Press, 1999: 97–182.

Mikami Yoshitaka. "Kōchōsen no shūen to toraizeni no hajimari." *Shutsudo senka* 12. Shutsudo senka kenkyūkai (December 1999): 43–52.

Minegishi Sumio and Murai Shōsuke, eds. *Chūsei tōgoku no butsuryū to toshi.* Yamakawa shuppansha, 1995.

Miura Hiroyuki. *Hōseishi no kenkyū.* 2 vols. Iwanami shoten, 1944.

Miura Keiichi. "Villages and Trade in Medieval Japan." *Acta Asiatica* 44 (1983): 53–76.

Miyagawa Mitsuru. "From Shōen to Chigyō: Proprietary Lordship and the Structure of Local Power." In *Japan in the Muromachi Age,* ed. John W. Hall and Toyoda Takeshi. Berkeley, CA: University of California Press, 1977: 89–106.

Miyahara Takeo et al. *Kōkō Nihonshi B Shinteiban.* Jikkyō shuppan, 1988.

Mori Katsumi. "The Beginning of Overseas Advance of Japanese Merchant Ships." *Acta Asiatica* 23 (1972): 1–24.

──── . "Sōdōsen no wagakuni ryūnyū no tansho." In *Zoku zoku Nissō bōeki no kenkyū.* Kokusho kankōkai, 1975: 177–201.

──── . "Sōdōsen ryūtsū e no kiban." *Nihon rekishi* 300 (May 1973): 109–39.

Morrell, Robert. *Sand and Pebbles: The Tales of Mujū Ichien, a Voice for Pluralism in Kamakura Buddhism.* Albany, NY: State University of New York Press, 1984.

Nagahara Keiji. "The Decline of the Shōen System." In *The Cambridge History of Japan, Vol. 3: Medieval Japan,* ed. Kozo Yamamura. Cambridge, UK: Cambridge University Press, 1990: 260–300.

——. *Gekokujo no jidai*. Chūō kōronsha, 1965.

——. "Kumano, Ise shōnin to chūsei no tōgoku." In *Muromachi sengoku no shakai*. Yoshikawa kōbunkan, 1992: 88–116.

——. "The Medieval Peasant." In *The Cambridge History of Japan, vol. 3: Medieval Japan*, ed. Kozo Yamamura. Cambridge, UK: Cambridge University Press, 1990: 301–43.

——. *Nihon chūsei shakai kōzō no kenkyū*. Iwanami shoten, 1973.

——. *Shōen*. Yoshikawa kōbunkan, 1998.

——. "Villages Communities and Daimyo Power." In *Japan in the Muromachi Age*, ed. John W. Hall and Toyoda Takeshi. Berkeley, CA: University of California Press, 1977: 107–23.

Nagamatsu Keiko. "Chūsei zenki no kyōbun to shūnō kankō." *Hisutoria* 151 (June 1996): 19–45.

——. "Kamakura jidai no nengu fukazei." *Nihonshi kenkyū* 370 (June 1993): 57–74.

Najita, Tetsuo. *Visions of Virtue in Tokugawa Japan: The Kaitokudō Merchant Academy of Osaka*. Chicago, IL: University of Chicago Press, 1987.

Nakai Nobuhiko. *Shōnin*. Nihon no rekishi, vol. 21. Shōgakukan, 1975.

Nakajima Keiichi. "Nihon no chūsei senka to kokka." In *Ekkyō suru kahei*, ed. Rekishigaku kenkyūkai. Aoki shoten, 1999: 109–39.

Nakamura Kichiji. *Tokusei to doikki*. Shibundō, 1959.

Nakamura Kyoko Motomichi. *Miraculous Stories from the Japanese Buddhist Tradition: The Nihon ryōiki of the Monk Kyōkai*. Cambridge, MA: Harvard University Press, 1973.

Nara kokuritsu bunkazai kenkyūjo, *Heijōkyū hakkutsu chōsa hōkoku VI* (1975).

North, Douglass. *Institutions, Institutional Change, and Economic Performance*. New York: Cambridge University Press, 1990.

Ōba Yasutoki. "Hakata ni okeru toraizeni no hajimari." *Shutsudō senka* 12 (1999), 52–54.

Ono Masatoshi, ed. *Zukai Nihon no chūsei iseki*. Tōkyō Daigaku shuppankai, 2001.

Ono Takeo. *Nihon shōenseishi ron*. Yūhikaku, 1943.

Ōta Yukio. "12–15 seiki shotō higashi ajia ni okeru dōsen no rufu." *Shakai keizai shigaku* 61.2 (June/July 1995): 20–48.

Ōyama Kyōhei. *Kamakura Bakufu*. Nihon no rekishi, vol. 9. Shōgakukan, 1974.

——. *Nihon chūsei nōsonshi no kenkyū*. Iwanami shoten, 1978.

Parry, J., and Bloch, M. "Introduction." *Money and the Morality of Exchange*. Cambridge, UK: Cambridge University Press, 1989: 1–32.

Peng Xinwei. *A Monetary History of China*. 2 vols. Trans. Edward Kaplan. Bellingham, WA: Western Washington University Press, 1994.

Piggott, Joan. *The Emergence of Japanese Kingship*. Stanford, CA: Stanford University Press, 1997.

——. "Hierarchy and Economics in Early Medieval Todaiji." In *Court and Bakufu in Japan: Essays in Kamakura History*, ed. Jeffrey P. Mass. Stanford, CA: Stanford University Press, 1988: 45–91.

Pryor, Frederic. "The Origins of Money." *Journal of Money, Credit, and Banking* 9:3 (August 1977): 391–409.

Redish, Angela. "Anchors Aweigh: The Transition from Commodity Money to Fiat Money in Western Economies." *Canadian Journal of Economics* 26:4 (November 1993): 777–95.

Rosenwein, Barbara. *To Be the Neighbor of Saint Peter: The Social Meaning of Cluny's Property, 909–1049*. Ithaca, NY: Cornell University Press, 1989.

Rossabi, Morris, ed. *China Among Equals: The Middle Kingdom and Its Neighbors, 10th to 14th Centuries*. Berkeley, CA: University of California Press, 1983.

Rowlinson, Matthew. "'The Scotch Hate Gold': British Identity and Paper Money." In *Nation-States and Money: The Past, Present, and Future of National Currencies*, ed. Emily Gilbert and Eric Helleiner. London: Routledge, 1999: 47–67.

Saeki Kōji. *Mongoru shūrai no shōgeki*. Chūō kōron shinsha, 2003.

Saitō Tsutomu, Takahashi Teruhiko, and Nishikawa Yuichi. "Kodai senka ni kan suru rikagakuteki kenkyū." Discussion paper 2002-J-30, Institute for Monetary and Economic Studies, Bank of Japan (2002): 1–45.

Sakaehara Towao. "Coinage in the Nara and Heian Periods." *Acta Asiatica* 39 (1980): 1–20.

——. "Nihon kodai kokka no senka hakkō." In *Senka: zenkindai Nihon no kahei to kokka*, ed. Ike Susumu. Aoki shoten, 2001: 43–61.

——. *Nihon kodai senka ryūtsūshi no kenkyū*. Hanawa shobo, 1993.

Sakudō Yōtarō, ed. *Nihon kaheishi gairon*. DaiNihon kaheishi kankōkai, 1970.

Sakurai Eiji. "Chūsei no shōhin ichiba." In *Ryūtsū keizai shi*, ed. Sakurai Eiji and Nakanishi Satoru. Yamakawa shuppansha, 2002: 199–234.

———. "Nihon chūsei ni okeru kahei to shin'yō ni tsuite." *Rekishigaku kenkyū* 703 (October 1997): 68–78.

———. *Nihon chūsei no keizai kōzō.* Iwanami shoten, 1996.

Sansom, George. *A History of Japan to 1334.* Stanford, CA: Stanford University Press, 1958.

Sasaki Gin'ya. *Chūsei shōhin ryūtsūshi no kenkyū.* Hōsei Daigaku shuppankyoku, 1972.

———. *Shōen no shōgyō.* Yoshikawa kōbunkan, 1964.

Sasaki Gin'ya with William B. Hauser. "Sengoku Daimyō Rule and Commerce." In *Japan Before Tokugawa: Political Consolidation and Economic Growth, 1500 to 1650,* ed. John W. Hall, Nagahara Keiji, and Kozo Yamamura. Princeton, NJ: Princeton University Press, 1981: 125–48.

Satō Hironobu. "Utokunin Suzuki Dōin ni tsuite no oboegaki." In *Chūsei tōgoku no butsuryū to toshi,* ed. Minegishi Sumio and Murai Shōsuke. Yamakawa shuppansha, 1995: 112–28.

Schopen, Gregory. *Bones, Stones, and Buddhist Monks: Collected Papers on the Archaeology, Epigraphy, and Texts of Monastic Buddhism in India.* Honolulu: University of Hawai'i Press, 1997.

Segal, Ethan. "Awash in Coins: The Spread of Money in Early Medieval Japan." In *Currents in Medieval Japanese History: Essays in Honor of Jeffrey P. Mass,* ed. Gordon M. Berger, Andrew Edmund Goble, Lorraine F. Harrington, and G. Cameron Hurst III. Los Angeles, CA: Figueroa Press, 2009: 331–61.

Sekiguchi Tsuneo. "Shōen kōryōsei keizai no hen'yō to kaitai." In *Nihon keizaishi o manabu: kodai chūsei hen,* ed. Nagahara Keiji et al. Yūhikaku, 1982: 134–69.

Smith, Thomas C. "The Growth of the Market." In *The Agrarian Origins of Modern Japan.* Stanford, CA: Stanford University Press, 1959: 67–86.

Sone Hiromi. "Prostitution and Public Authority in Early Modern Japan." In *Women and Class in Japanese History,* ed. Hitomi Tonomura, Anne Walthall, and Wakita Haruko. Ann Arbor: Center for Japanese Studies, University of Michigan, 1999: 169–86.

Sørensen, Henrik H. "A Study of the 'Ox-Herding Theme' as Sculptures at Mt. Baoding in Dazu County, Sichuan." *Artibus Asiae* Vol. 51, No. 3/4 (1991): 207–33.

Steenstrup, Carl. *Hōjō Shigetoki and His Role in the History of Political and Ethical Ideas in Japan.* London: Curzon Press, 1979.

Suzuki Kimio. *Shutsudo senka no kenkyū*. Tōkyō Daigaku shuppankai, 1999.

——. *Zeni no kōkogaku*. Yoshikawa kōbunkan, 2002.

Tabata Yasuko. "Women's Work and Status in the Changing Medieval Economy." Trans. Hitomi Tonomura. In *Women and Class in Japanese History*, ed. Hitomi Tonomura, Anne Walthall, and Wakita Haruko. Ann Arbor: Center for Japanese Studies, University of Michigan, 1999: 99–118.

Takahashi Hisako. *Goseibai shikimoku*. Kasama shōin, 1995.

Takizawa, Matsuyo. *The Penetration of Money Economy in Japan and Its Effects upon Social and Political Institutions*. New York: Columbia University Press, 1927.

Takizawa Takeo. "Early Currency Policies of the Tokugawa, 1563–1608." *Acta Asiatica* 39 (1980): 21–41.

——. "Heian kōki no kahei ni tsuite." *Shikan* 82 (1970): 2–16..

——. "Kamakura jidai zenki no kahei." *Zoku shōensei to buke shakai*. Yoshikawa kōbunkan, 1978.

Takizawa Takeo and Nishiwaki Yasushi, ed. *Kahei*. Tōkyōdō, 1999.

Tamaizumi Tairyō. *Muromachi jidai no denso*. Yoshikawa kōbunkan, 1969.

Tanaka Takeo, trans. *Kaitō shokokuki: Chōsenjin no mita chūsei no Nihon to Ryūkyū*. Iwanami shoten, 1991.

Tanaka Takeo with Robert Sakai. "Japan's Relations with Overseas Countries." In *Japan in the Muromachi Age*, ed. John W. Hall and Toyoda Takeshi. Berkeley, CA: University of California Press, 1977: 159–78.

Tōno Haruyuki. *Kahei no Nihonshi*. Asahi shinbunsha, 1997.

Tonomura, Hitomi. *Community and Commerce in Late Medieval Japan: The Corporate Villages of Tokuchin-ho*. Stanford, CA: Stanford University Press, 1992.

Totman, Conrad. *Early Modern Japan*. Berkeley, CA: University of California Press, 1993.

——. *A History of Japan*. Malden, MA: Blackwell Publishers, 2000.

Toyoda Takeshi. *Chūsei Nihon no shōgyō*. Yoshikawa kōbunkan, 1982.

——. *Chūsei Nihon shōgyōshi no kenkyū*. Iwanami shoten, 1952.

——. "Chūsei no kawase." *Shakai keizai shigaku* 6.10 (February 1937): 1267–91.

——. *Chūsei no shōnin to kōtsū*. Yoshikawa kōbunkan, 1982.

Toyoda Takeshi and Sugiyama Hiroshi with V. Dixon Morris. "The Growth of Commerce and the Trades." In *Japan in the Muromachi*

Age, ed. John Whitney Hall and Toyoda Takeshi. Berkeley, CA: University of California Press, 1977: 129–144.

Troost, Kristina Kade. "Common Property and Community Formation: Self-Governing Villages in Late Medieval Japan, 1300–1600." PhD diss., Harvard University, 1990.

———. "Peasants, Elites, and Villages in the Fourteenth Century." In *The Origins of Japan's Medieval World: Courtiers, Clerics, Warriors, and Peasants in the Fourteenth Century,* ed. Jeffrey P. Mass. Stanford, CA: Stanford University Press, 1997: 91–109.

Ury, Marian. *Tales of Times Now Past.* Berkeley, CA: University of California Press, 1979.

Usami Takayuki. *Nihon chūsei no ryūtsū to shōgyō.* Yoshikawa kōbunkan, 1999.

Usher, Abbott Payson. "The Origin of the Bill of Exchange." *Journal of Political Economy* 22:6 (June 1914): 566–76.

Vilar, Pierre. *A History of Gold and Money, 1450–1920.* Trans. Judith White. Atlantic Heights, NJ: Humanities Press, 1976.

Vivier, Brian Thomas. "Chinese Foreign Trade, 960–1276." PhD diss., Yale University, 2008.

Von Glahn, Richard. *Fountain of Fortune: Money and Monetary Policy in China, 1000–1700.* Berkeley, CA: University of California Press, 1996.

Von Verschauer, Charlotte. *Across the Perilous Sea: Japanese Trade with China and Korea from the Seventh to the Sixteenth Centuries.* Trans. Kristen Lee. Ithaca, NY: Cornell East Asia Series, 2006.

———. "Life of Commoners in the Provinces: The *Owari no gebumi* of 988." In *Heian Japan: Centers and Peripheries,* ed. Mikael Adolphson, Edward Kamens, and Stacie Matsumoto. Honolulu: University of Hawai'i Press, 2007: 305–28.

Wakita Haruko. "Bukka yori mita Nichi-Min bōeki no seikaku." In *Nihonshi ni okeru kokka to shakai,* ed. Miyakawa Shūichi. Shibunkaku shuppan, 1992: 253–72.

———. "Chūsei josei no yakuwari buntan to joseikan." *Rekishigaku kenkyū* 542 (June 1985): 16–30.

———. "The Medieval Household and Gender Roles within the Imperial Family, Nobility, Merchants, and Commoners." Trans. Gary Leupp. In *Women and Class in Japanese History,* ed. Hitomi Tonomura, Anne Walthall, and Wakita Haruko. Ann Arbor: Center for Japanese Studies, University of Michigan, 1999: 81–98.

Watson, Michael. "Warriors Rewarded: *Kimi no go-on* in Gunki Mono-gatari." Unpublished paper presented at the Asian Studies Conference Japan, Sophia University, Tokyo, June 26, 1999.

Wintersteen, Prescott. "The Muromachi Shugo and Hanzei." In *Medieval Japan: Essays in Institutional History*, ed. John W. Hall and Jeffrey P. Mass. Stanford, CA: Stanford University Press, 1988 [1974]: 210–20.

Xiong, Victor Cunrui. *Sui-Tang Chang'an: A Study in the Urban History of Medieval China*. Ann Arbor: Center for Chinese Studies, University of Michigan, 2000.

Yamamura, Kozo. "From Coins to Rice: Hypotheses on the Kandaka and Kokudaka Systems." *Journal of Japanese Studies* 14.2 (Summer 1988): 341–67.

———. "The Growth of Commerce in Medieval Japan." In *The Cambridge History of Japan, Vol. 3: Medieval Japan*, ed. Kozo Yamamura. Cambridge, UK: Cambridge University Press, 1990: 344–95.

———. "Introduction." In *The Cambridge History of Japan, Vol. 3: Medieval Japan*, ed. Kozo Yamamura. Cambridge, UK: Cambridge University Press, 1990: 1–45.

Yamamura, Kozo, and Tetsuo Kamiki. "Silver Mines and Sung Coins: A Monetary History of Medieval and Modern Japan in International Perspective." In *Precious Metals in the Later Medieval and Early Modern Worlds*, ed. J. F. Richards. Durham, NC: Carolina Academic Press, 1983: 329–62.

Yokota Fuyuhiko. "Imagining Working Women in Early Modern Japan." In *Women and Class in Japanese History*, ed. Hitomi Tonomura, Anne Walthall, and Wakita Haruko. Ann Arbor: Center for Japanese Studies, University of Michigan, 1999: 153–68.

Yoshihara Ken'ichirō. *Edo no zeni to shomin no kurashi*. Dōseisha, 2003.

Character List

dosō 土倉

Ebisu　恵比寿
Echigo province　越後国
Echizen province　越前国
Edo　江戸
Eiraku　永樂
Engakuji　円覚寺
Engishiki　延喜式
Engi tsūhō　延喜通宝
Enkyū　延久
Enryakuji　延暦寺
erizenirei　選銭令
Etchū province　越中国

feiqian　飛銭
fuhō junpu　不法准布
fuhonsen　富本銭
Fujiwara no Arikuni　藤原有国
Fujiwara no Atsumitsu
　　藤原敦光
Fujiwara no Kimitsugu
　　藤原公継
Fujiwara no Michinaga
　　藤原道長
Fujiwara no Otsugu　藤原緒嗣
Fujiwara no Sadanaga
　　藤原定長
Fujiwara no Takaie　藤原隆家
Fujiwara no Yoshimune
　　藤原能宗
Fujiwara no Yukinari　藤原行成
Fukatsu　深津
Fukuhara　福原
Fukuoka market　福岡市

gaibyō　咳病

genin　下人
genkurabe　験比べ
Genna tsūhō　元和通宝
Genpei　源平
Genroku　元禄
gesu　下司
Go-Daigo　後醍醐
Go-Fukakusa　後深草
Go-Horikawa　後堀河
Go-Saga　後嵯峨
Go-Uda　後宇多
gokenin　御家人
Guoan Shiyuan　廓庵師遠
Gyōji　行慈
Gyokuyō　玉葉

hanzei　半済
Harima province　播磨国
Heian　平安
Heian ibun　平安遺文
Heiji　平治
Heijō　平城
Heike monogatari　平家物語
Hie jinja　日枝神社
hinin　非人
Hino Tomiko　日野富子
Hiraga Tomomasa　平賀朝雅
Hizen province　肥前国
hizeniya　日銭屋
Hōgen　保元
Hōjō Tokimune　北条時宗
Hōjō Tokiyori　北条時頼
Hōjō Yasutoki　北条泰時
Homuchi no Makihito
　　品治牧人
Hongwu　洪武
honke　本家

honke shiki 本家職
Hōrakuji 法楽寺
Hōshōgon'in 宝荘厳院
Hosokawa 細川
Hossō shiyōshō 法曹至要抄
hyakushō 百姓

ichien shōen 一円荘園
Ichijō 一条
Iga province 伊賀国
Iki 壱岐
ikoku gassen 異国合戦
Imatomi estate 今富庄
Inaba province 因幡国
Insai 印西
Ippen 一遍
Ippen hijiri-e 一遍聖絵
Iriki estate 入来院
Ishiguro estate 石黒庄
Izumo fudoki 出雲風土記

Jakuren hosshishū 寂蓮法師集
Ji (sect) 時
Jianyan yilai xinian yaolu
  建炎以來繫年要錄
Jingoji 神護寺
Jingū kaihō 神功開宝
jinin/jinnin 神人
jitō 地頭
Jōei 貞永
Jōen 定宴
Jōjin 成尋
Jōkyū 承久
jūka 重科

kaemai 替米
kagura 神楽

Kaidōki 海道記
Kaiki shōhō 開基勝宝
Kaiyuan tongbao 開元通宝
kajishi 加地子
Kamakura 鎌倉
Kamakura kaidō 鎌倉街道
Kameyama 亀山
Kamikuze estate 上久世庄
Kamimura 上村
Kan'ei tsūhō 寛永通宝
Kanenaga 懐良
Kangi 寛喜
kanjin 勧進
kanmon 貫文
Kanna 寛和
kanpaku 関白
Kanpyō taihō 寛平大宝
Kantō kubō 関東公方
kariya 仮屋
kashiage 借上
kawase 為替
Kayatsu no shuku 萱津宿
Kazan-in Tadatsune
  花山院忠経
Kazusa province 上総国
Kebiishichō 検非違使庁
Keichō 慶長
Keichō tsūhō 慶長通宝
Keigen 慶元
Keikai 景戒
Keizairoku shūi 経済録拾遺
Kengen taihō 乾元大宝
Kenkon tsūhō 乾坤通宝
kenmon 権門
Kenmu 建武
Kenmu shikimoku 建武式目
Kii province 紀伊国

Kinai　機内
kinsen　今銭
kishinjō　寄進状
Kiso Yoshinaka　木曽義仲
Kiyohara no Yorinari　清原頼業
Kōan　弘安
Kōbu　洪武
kōchō jūnisen　皇朝十二銭
kōden　公田
Kōfukuji　興福寺
kokahō　沽価法
Kokon chomonjū　古今著聞集
koku　石
kokufu　国府
kokujin　国人
komo　薦
Konjaku monogatarishū
　　今昔物語集
Kōno estate　神野庄
Konoe Michitsugu　近衛道嗣
kōnohai　紺灰
Kōrokan　鴻臚館
kosen　古銭
kōsen　功銭
koshibukuro　腰袋
Kōyasan　高野山
kudashibumi　下文
kugonin　供御人
Kujō Kanezane　九条兼実
Kujō Michiie　九条道家
Kujō Yoshitsune　九条良経
Kuni-kyō　恭仁京
Kunitomi estate　国富庄
kurayaku　倉役
Kuroda estate　黒田庄
Kurōdodokoro　蔵人所
Kusado sengen　草戸千軒

Kusama Naokata　草間直方
kyūsen　旧銭

Makuni estate　真国庄
Mannen tsūhō　万年通宝
Matsuo Bashō　松尾芭蕉
Miiri estate　三入庄
Minamoto no Mitsuyuki
　　源光行
Minamoto no Yoritomo　源頼朝
Minkeiki　民経記
Mino province　美濃国
miuchibito　御内人
Miura　三浦
Miyagawa estate　宮川庄
mokkan　木簡
Mōko gassen　蒙古合戦
mon　文
monzen ichi　門前市
muen　無縁
Mujū Ichien　無住一円
mumonsen　無文銭
munabechisen　棟別銭
Muromachi　室町
Musashi province　武蔵国
Mutsu province　陸奥国
myōshū　名主

Nagaoka-kyō　長岡京
Nagato province　長門国
Nakahara Motohiro　中原基広
namisen　並銭
nankin/nankinsen　難金/南京銭
Nanzenji　南禅寺
Nara　奈良
nengō　年号
nengu　年貢

Nihon kiryaku 日本紀略
Nihon ryōiki 日本霊異記
Nihon shoki 日本書紀
Niimi estate 新見庄
Ningbo 寧波
Nintoku 仁徳
Noke estate 野介庄

Obama bay 小浜湾
ōban'yaku 大番役
Oda Nobunaga 織田信長
Ōe Kiyosada 大江清定
Ogyū Sorai 荻生徂徠
Okuyama estate 奥山庄
Ōmi province 近江国
ōniwa onmaki 大庭御まき
Onjōji 園城寺
onritsugan 御立願
Onyū market 遠敷市
Ōshū 奥州
Ōtsu 大津
Ōuchi 大内
Ōwa 応和
Owari province 尾張国
Ōyama estate 大山庄

qianhuang 錢荒

raku-ichi raku-za 楽市楽座
Rishō 利正
ritsuryō 律令
rizeni 利銭
rokudōsen 六道銭
rokusai-ichi 六斎市
Ruiju sandai kyaku 類聚三代格
ryō 両
ryōke 領家

Ryō no gige 令義解
ryūtsū 流通

saifu 割符
Saionji Kintsune 西園寺公経
Sanka zui 三貨図彙
sankin kōtai 参勤交代
Sanjūsangendō 三十三間堂
sansai-ichi 三斎市
sansō 山僧
Sanuki province 讃岐国
Sarukawa estate 猿川庄
Sasakibe estate 雀部庄
Satsuma province 薩摩国
Seiken 清賢
seisen 清銭
seki 関
sengi 僉議
sengoku 戦国
Sentoku 宣徳
sesshō 摂政
setsuwa 説話
Settsu province 摂津国
shashika 奢侈化
Shibuya Jōshin 渋谷定心
shichihan 七半
shiki 職
Shimazu estate 島津庄
Shimomura 下村
Shimōsa province 下総国
Shinano province 信濃国
Shin sarugakuki 新猿楽記
shinsei 新制
shinsen 新銭
shitaji chūbun 下地中分
shōen 荘園
Shōka 正嘉

shōkan 庄官
Shōkokuji 相国寺
shokunin uta awase 職人歌合
Shōmu 聖武
Shōmyōji 称名寺
shugo 守護
Sōchō no zeni 宋朝の銭
sōyūden 総有田
Sōma mikuriya 相馬御厨
Sugano no Mamichi
　菅野真道
Suō province 周防国

Taihei genpō 大平元宝
Taira no Kiyomori 平清盛
Taira no Narimasa 平生昌
Taira no Tadamori 平忠盛
Taira no Tadatsune 平忠常
Takezaki Suenaga 竹崎季長
Tamaki estate 玉置庄
tan 段
Tanba 丹波
tanomoshi 憑支/頼母子
tansen 段銭
Tara estate 太良庄
Tendai 天台
Tenryaku 天暦
Tenryūji 天竜寺
to 斗
Tōdaiji 東大寺
Tōdo yori wataruru no zeni
　唐土より渡るる之銭
Tōfukuji 東福寺
Tōji 東寺
Tōkan kikō 東関紀行
Tokugawa Iemitsu 徳川家光
Tokugawa Ieyasu 徳川家康

Tokugawa Yoshimune
　徳川吉宗
tokusei 徳政
tokuseirei 徳政令
tokusei tanpo mongon
　徳政担保文言
Tomono 伴野
Tosa province 土佐国
Tosa nikki 土佐日記
Tōsen 唐船
Tōshōdaiji 唐招提寺
Toyotomi Hideyoshi
　豊臣秀吉
Tsuchimikado 土御門
Tsushima 対馬

ukesho 請所
Usa Hachimangū 宇佐八幡宮
Utsuho monogatari 宇津保物語

Wagae 和賀江
Wakasa province 若狭国
Wakasahime jinja 若狭姫神社
Wakasa Tadakiyo 若狭忠清
Wadō kaichin 和同開珎
wakō 倭寇
warifu 割符
wayo 和与

Xuande 宣徳

Yamana 山名
Yamashiro province 山城国
Yamato province 大和国
Yano estate 矢野庄
yokka-ichi 四日市
Yongle 永樂

yoriudo 寄人
Yoshima estate 好島庄
yōto 用途
Yuasa 湯浅
Yugenoshima estate
　弓削島庄

Yuigahama 由比ケ浜

zeni no yamai 銭病
Zōshushi 造酒司
Zuo Qiuming 左丘明
zuryō 受領

Index

Harvard East Asian Monographs
(*out-of-print)

Harvard East Asian Monographs

170. Denise Potrzeba Lett, *In Pursuit of Status: The Making of South Korea's "New" Urban Middle Class*
171. Mimi Hall Yiengpruksawan, *Hiraizumi: Buddhist Art and Regional Politics in Twelfth-Century Japan*
172. Charles Shirō Inouye, *The Similitude of Blossoms: A Critical Biography of Izumi Kyōka (1873–1939), Japanese Novelist and Playwright*
173. Aviad E. Raz, *Riding the Black Ship: Japan and Tokyo Disneyland*
174. Deborah J. Milly, *Poverty, Equality, and Growth: The Politics of Economic Need in Postwar Japan*
175. See Heng Teow, *Japan's Cultural Policy Toward China, 1918–1931: A Comparative Perspective*
176. Michael A. Fuller, *An Introduction to Literary Chinese*
177. Frederick R. Dickinson, *War and National Reinvention: Japan in the Great War, 1914–1919*
178. John Solt, *Shredding the Tapestry of Meaning: The Poetry and Poetics of Kitasono Katue (1902–1978)*
179. Edward Pratt, *Japan's Protoindustrial Elite: The Economic Foundations of the Gōnō*
180. Atsuko Sakaki, *Recontextualizing Texts: Narrative Performance in Modern Japanese Fiction*
181. Soon-Won Park, *Colonial Industrialization and Labor in Korea: The Onoda Cement Factory*
182. JaHyun Kim Haboush and Martina Deuchler, *Culture and the State in Late Chosŏn Korea*
183. John W. Chaffee, *Branches of Heaven: A History of the Imperial Clan of Sung China*
184. Gi-Wook Shin and Michael Robinson, eds., *Colonial Modernity in Korea*
185. Nam-lin Hur, *Prayer and Play in Late Tokugawa Japan: Asakusa Sensōji and Edo Society*
186. Kristin Stapleton, *Civilizing Chengdu: Chinese Urban Reform, 1895–1937*
187. Hyung Il Pai, *Constructing "Korean" Origins: A Critical Review of Archaeology, Historiography, and Racial Myth in Korean State-Formation Theories*
188. Brian D. Ruppert, *Jewel in the Ashes: Buddha Relics and Power in Early Medieval Japan*
189. Susan Daruvala, *Zhou Zuoren and an Alternative Chinese Response to Modernity*
*190. James Z. Lee, *The Political Economy of a Frontier: Southwest China, 1250–1850*
191. Kerry Smith, *A Time of Crisis: Japan, the Great Depression, and Rural Revitalization*
192. Michael Lewis, *Becoming Apart: National Power and Local Politics in Toyama, 1868–1945*
193. William C. Kirby, Man-houng Lin, James Chin Shih, and David A. Pietz, eds., *State and Economy in Republican China: A Handbook for Scholars*
194. Timothy S. George, *Minamata: Pollution and the Struggle for Democracy in Postwar Japan*
195. Billy K. L. So, *Prosperity, Region, and Institutions in Maritime China: The South Fukien Pattern, 946–1368*
196. Yoshihisa Tak Matsusaka, *The Making of Japanese Manchuria, 1904–1932*

Harvard East Asian Monographs

250. Wilt L. Idema, Wai-yee Li, and Ellen Widmer, eds., *Trauma and Transcendence in Early Qing Literature*
251. Barbara Molony and Kathleen Uno, eds., *Gendering Modern Japanese History*
252. Hiroshi Aoyagi, *Islands of Eight Million Smiles: Idol Performance and Symbolic Production in Contemporary Japan*
253. Wai-yee Li, *The Readability of the Past in Early Chinese Historiography*
254. William C. Kirby, Robert S. Ross, and Gong Li, eds., *Normalization of U.S.-China Relations: An International History*
255. Ellen Gardner Nakamura, *Practical Pursuits: Takano Chōei, Takahashi Keisaku, and Western Medicine in Nineteenth-Century Japan*
256. Jonathan W. Best, *A History of the Early Korean Kingdom of Paekche, together with an annotated translation of* The Paekche Annals *of the* Samguk sagi
257. Liang Pan, *The United Nations in Japan's Foreign and Security Policymaking, 1945–1992: National Security, Party Politics, and International Status*
258. Richard Belsky, *Localities at the Center: Native Place, Space, and Power in Late Imperial Beijing*
259. Zwia Lipkin, *"Useless to the State": "Social Problems" and Social Engineering in Nationalist Nanjing, 1927–1937*
260. William O. Gardner, *Advertising Tower: Japanese Modernism and Modernity in the 1920s*
261. Stephen Owen, *The Making of Early Chinese Classical Poetry*
262. Martin J. Powers, *Pattern and Person: Ornament, Society, and Self in Classical China*
263. Anna M. Shields, *Crafting a Collection: The Cultural Contexts and Poetic Practice of the* Huajian ji 花間集 *(Collection from Among the Flowers)*
264. Stephen Owen, *The Late Tang: Chinese Poetry of the Mid-Ninth Century (827–860)*
265. Sara L. Friedman, *Intimate Politics: Marriage, the Market, and State Power in Southeastern China*
266. Patricia Buckley Ebrey and Maggie Bickford, *Emperor Huizong and Late Northern Song China: The Politics of Culture and the Culture of Politics*
267. Sophie Volpp, *Worldly Stage: Theatricality in Seventeenth-Century China*
268. Ellen Widmer, *The Beauty and the Book: Women and Fiction in Nineteenth-Century China*
269. Steven B. Miles, *The Sea of Learning: Mobility and Identity in Nineteenth-Century Guangzhou*
270. Lin Man-houng, *China Upside Down: Currency, Society, and Ideologies, 1808–1856*
271. Ronald Egan, *The Problem of Beauty: Aesthetic Thought and Pursuits in Northern Song Dynasty China*
272. Mark Halperin, *Out of the Cloister: Literati Perspectives on Buddhism in Sung China, 960–1279*
273. Helen Dunstan, *State or Merchant? Political Economy and Political Process in 1740s China*
274. Sabina Knight, *The Heart of Time: Moral Agency in Twentieth-Century Chinese Fiction*
275. Timothy J. Van Compernolle, *The Uses of Memory: The Critique of Modernity in the Fiction of Higuchi Ichiyō*

300. Linda Isako Angst, *In a Dark Time: Memory, Community, and Gendered Nationalism in Postwar Okinawa*
301. David M. Robinson, ed., *Culture, Courtiers, and Competition: The Ming Court (1368–1644)*
302. Calvin Chen, *Some Assembly Required: Work, Community, and Politics in China's Rural Enterprises*
303. Sem Vermeersch, *The Power of the Buddhas: The Politics of Buddhism During the Koryŏ Dynasty* (918–1392)
304. Tina Lu, *Accidental Incest, Filial Cannibalism, and Other Peculiar Encounters in Late Imperial Chinese Literature*
305. Chang Woei Ong, *Men of Letters Within the Passes: Guanzhong Literati in Chinese History, 907–1911*
306. Wendy Swartz, *Reading Tao Yuanming: Shifting Paradigms of Historical Reception (427–1900)*
307. Peter K. Bol, *Neo-Confucianism in History*
308. Carlos Rojas, *The Naked Gaze: Reflections on Chinese Modernity*
309. Kelly H. Chong, *Deliverance and Submission: Evangelical Women and the Negotiation of Patriarchy in South Korea*
310. Rachel DiNitto, *Uchida Hyakken: A Critique of Modernity and Militarism in Prewar Japan*
311. Jeffrey Snyder-Reinke, *Dry Spells: State Rainmaking and Local Governance in Late Imperial China*
312. Jay Dautcher, *Down a Narrow Road: Identity and Masculinity in a Uyghur Community in Xinjiang China*
313. Xun Liu, *Daoist Modern: Innovation, Lay Practice, and the Community of Inner Alchemy in Republican Shanghai*
314. Jacob Eyferth, *Eating Rice from Bamboo Roots: The Social History of a Community of Handicraft Papermakers in Rural Sichuan, 1920–2000*
315. David Johnson, *Spectacle and Sacrifice: The Ritual Foundations of Village Life in North China*
316. James Robson, *Power of Place: The Religious Landscape of the Southern Sacred Peak (Nanyue 南嶽) in Medieval China*
317. Lori Watt, *When Empire Comes Home: Repatriation and Reintegration in Postwar Japan*
318. James Dorsey, *Critical Aesthetics: Kobayashi Hideo, Modernity, and Wartime Japan*
319. Christopher Bolton, *Sublime Voices: The Fictional Science and Scientific Fiction of Abe Kōbō*
320. Si-yen Fei, *Negotiating Urban Space: Urbanization and Late Ming Nanjing*
321. Christopher Gerteis, *Gender Struggles: Wage-Earning Women and Male-Dominated Unions in Postwar Japan*
322. Rebecca Nedostup, *Superstitious Regimes: Religion and the Politics of Chinese Modernity*
323. Lucien Bianco, *Wretched Rebels: Rural Disturbances on the Eve of the Chinese Revolution*
324. Cathryn H. Clayton, *Sovereignty at the Edge: Macau and the Question of Chineseness*
325. Micah S. Muscolino, *Fishing Wars and Environmental Change in Late Imperial and Modern China*

Harvard East Asian Monographs